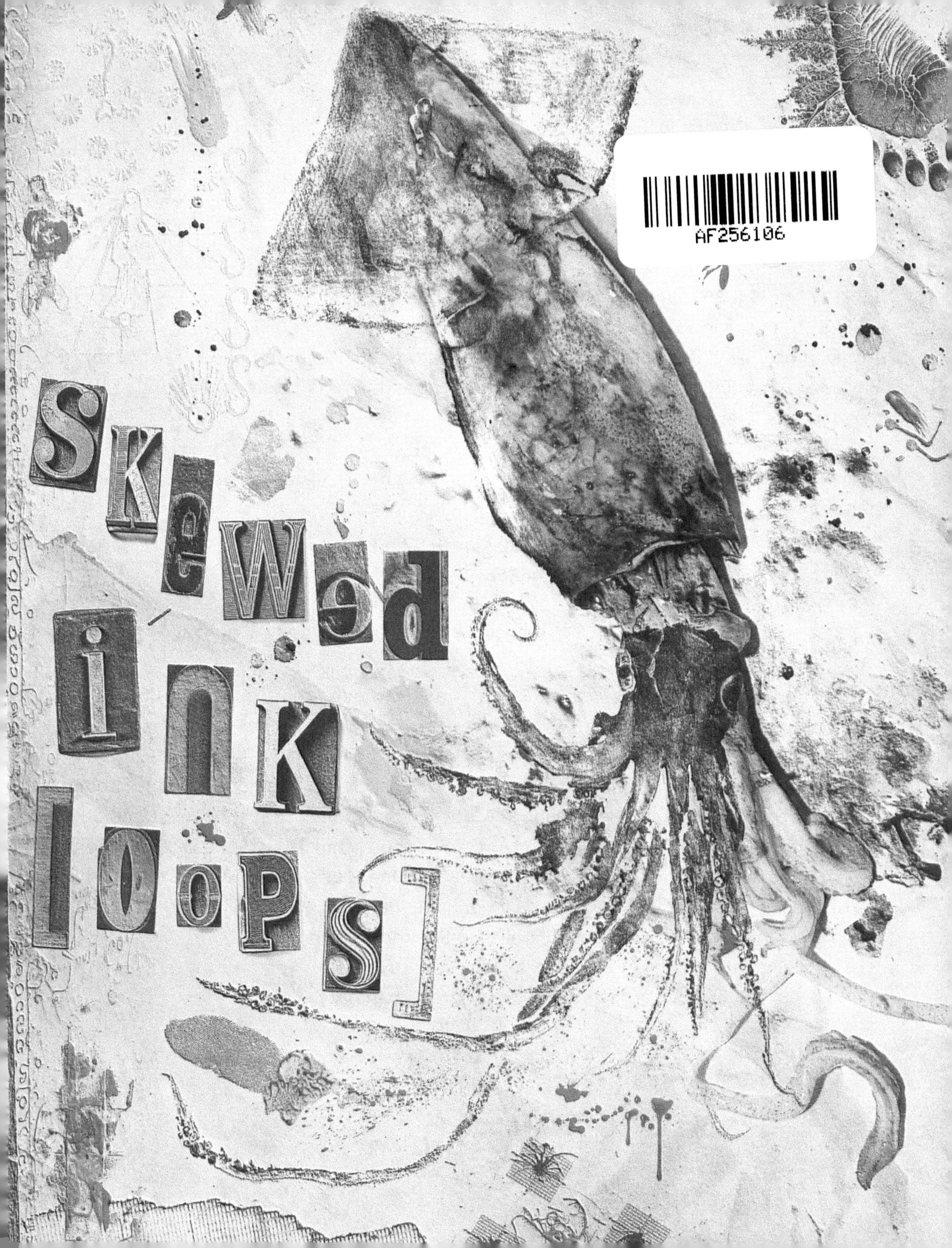

skewed
ink
loops
AF256106

5kewəd iⁿk [OoPs] : reFraming of 4 out-of-print 5elf-pubLished chap-
books from the Ɔalamari 4mative yrs (2003-2004)

bi dd/CAL

iSBN 978-1-940853-55-0

> *5kewed iⁿk [OoPs]* inkLoots reΡrints of the fo||owinɡ out of Ρrint
chapbooks:

- *Mining in the Black Hills* [2003: 0-9746053-0-1]
- *23 Text Tiles* [2003: 0-9746053-1-X]
- *Trapezoidal Juggernaut* [2003: 0-9746053-2-8]
- *Bodh[i] Circu[it]s / Alg[a]e[bra] D[ra[in]* [2004: 0-9746053-5-2]

Gr8ful thx + restpectful (many R.i.P) aɔknowLedɡement ɡo 2 the fo||owinɡ
sites/zines [from urly dayz of inurnet] ware sum of the5e pieces 1st
appeared:
    perspektive, Gestalten, BlazeVox, Aught, Lost and Found Times, Score,
    Generator, Ampersand, Shampoo, Indefinite Space, BathHouse, DIAGRAM,
    Word for/Word, Sidereality, Xtant, Shampoo, Moria, xStream, Sendecki,
    Spidertangle, Black Box, UREADABILITY, One Less Mag, XCP: Streetnotes,
    XUL/Mobil-Home, Rife, Alba, Can We Have Our Ball Back? + Forklift, Ohio
    + works herein == co||ected in the Sackner Archive.

               pubLished bi Ɔalamari Arɔhive, ink.
                        NY | NY
                  www.calamaripress.com

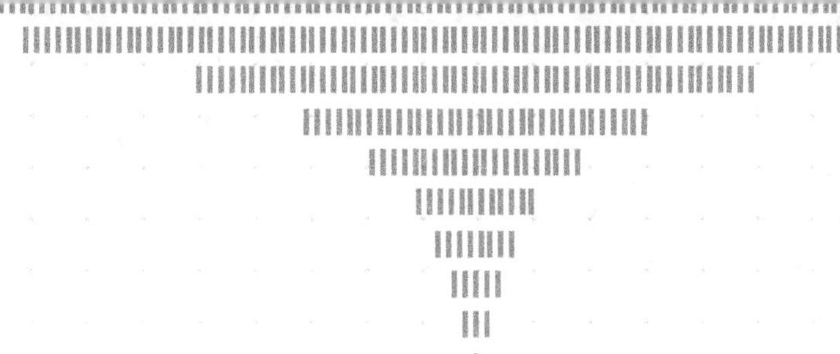

CONTENTS:

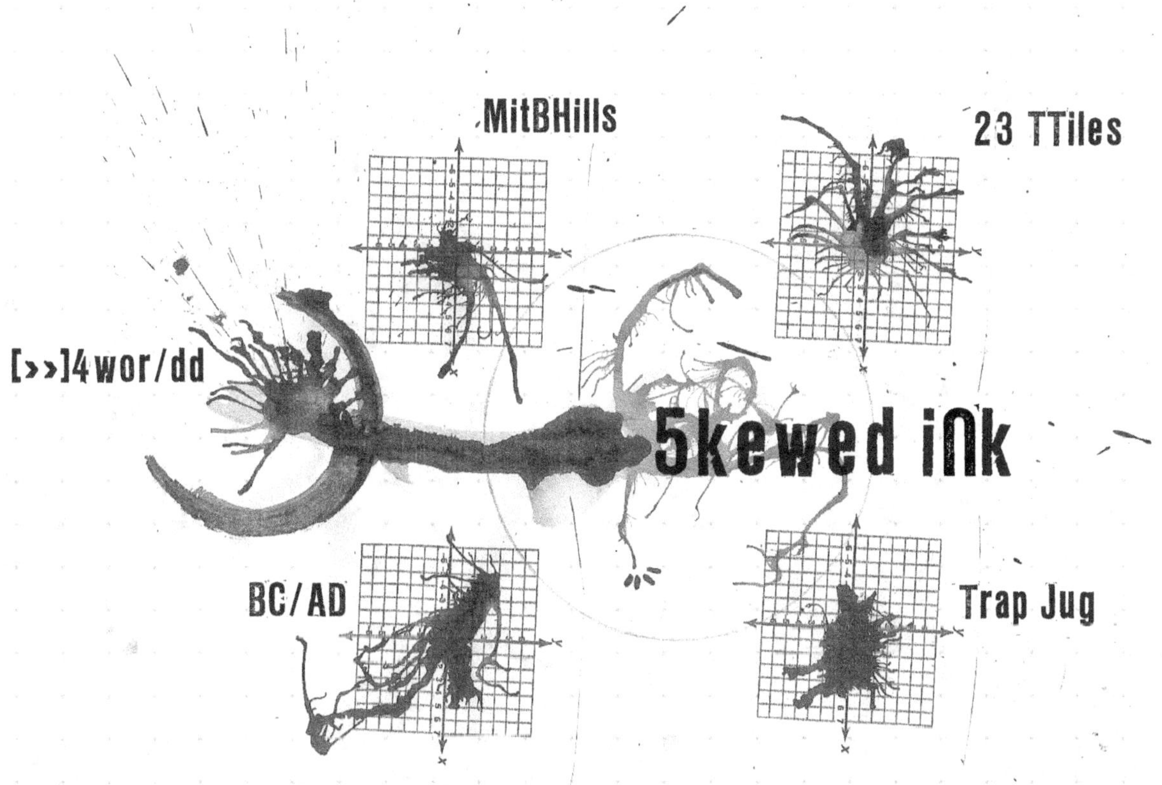

Gr8Ful

acknowledgement

given 2 the trees

that dyed

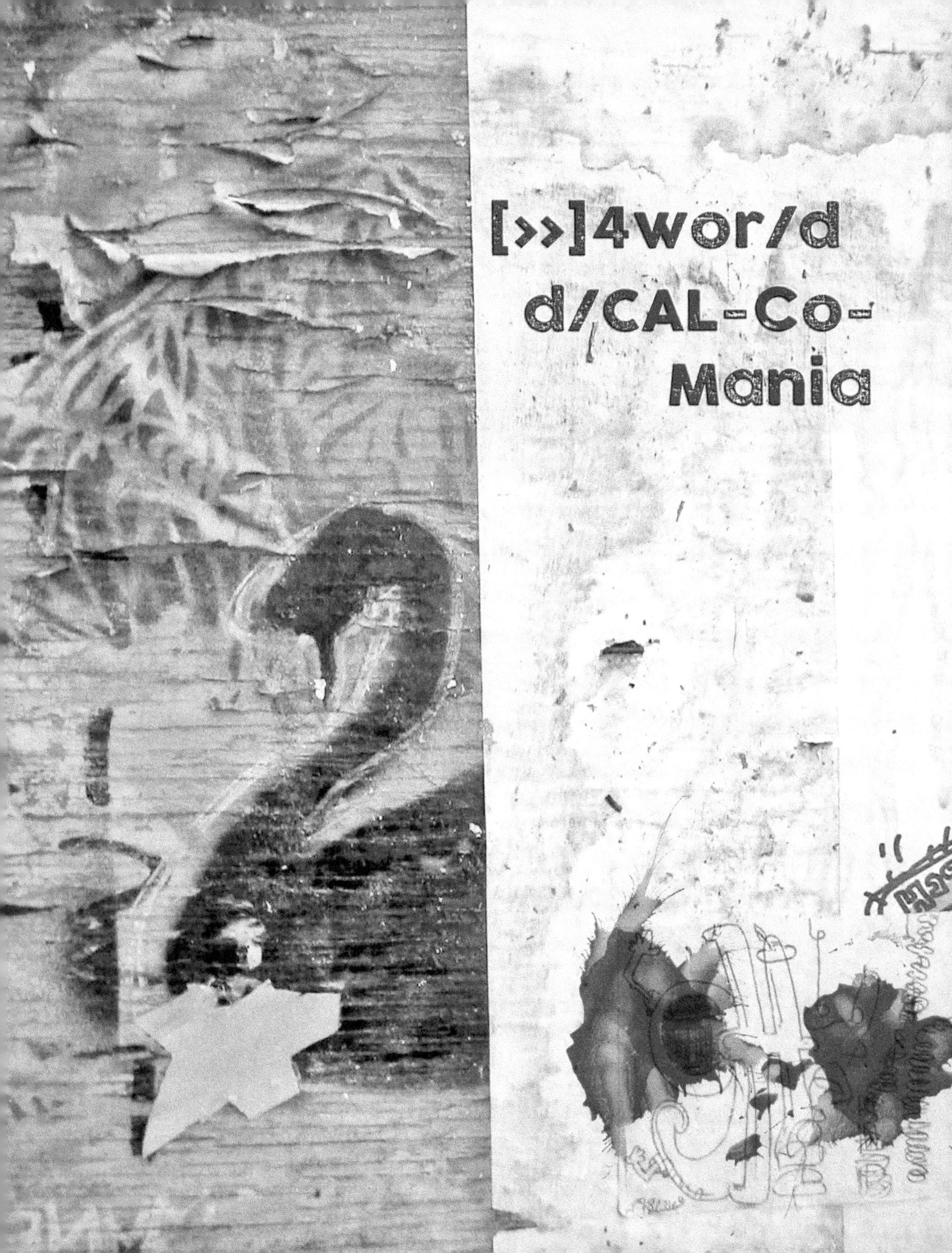
[>>]4wor/d
d/CAL-Co-
Mania

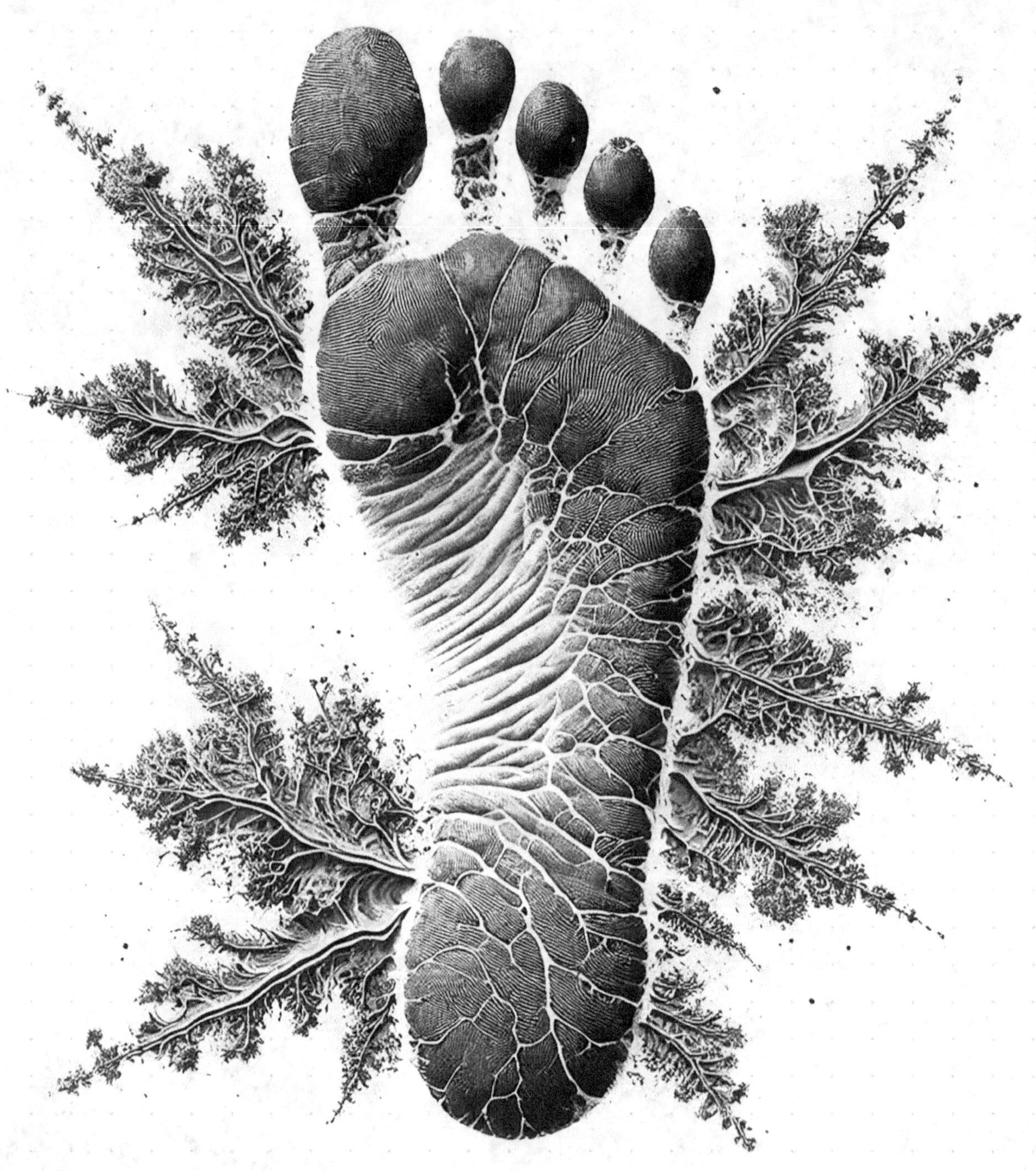

[dd/Cal im|re55ion (5elf-cuntained ho||ow9raphic|y w/in the rest of p9s hearin)]

[•]   P
   d/CAL ['dek-əl] : ^ 5hor-1Ø-eD 4m of *decalcomania*: «th Rt ± proceƨS
    b   uv X-feᴚring imG/D-zinE from 5pecia| treated papier» /   E
dba   E   adapted fROM frenCh *décalcomanie* [même sens] / from   U
e   *Décalquer*: «2 copE bi trAcing» + *manie*: «maniA/craze» / dba5eD
CC: i   e   O   on itaLian *calcare*: «2 5tomP/tramp|e» / in O
a   eFFeCt D-rived ᴚrom Latin *Calx*: «heəL»   E dbased: carbo∩
L @ bAY U   ə   ᴚset   O U R [sic] U here?   C-d8ed: copY
    R i R > 1st [•] of decalcoMania in GLiSh [•]ed in 1864   /bdAy   M
  2 REpLiC8   O A > [X] in5tAnce U C B4 U [•]ed 11/22/2Ø24 / W/   S
mimiC   H   gHOSt Traces rePri∩ted txt/imgS hearin d8ing baɔk A wakE
 D-Vine in2iT O   E   /   in2 199Øs   R   L
   EP   L   S   /   A caL [caLcuL8 2 keep cumuL8ing] EngulF
> [REC]wiremenT::: isoL8 az st&-aLone peace 4 iTs one Rt OBJet /
       2 in4m: Calamari K-base   [in tern 2 rein4m Teɔknowledgee]
  > 4 the [•]: dbA st&s 4 «doing business az» ± «dadabase admininstr8or»
> dd didnt authoR X sen-1Ø-ce FYi . . . .
    ± ∩E oF the Books rePrinted hearin / TeɔknowLedgee did
    > the X-authOr fka az ~~Derek D White~~ didnt rite th inkLooted books
   e   a   k∩eethere / tHo ~~s/he~~ thinks ~~s/he~~ did
> adobe inD-zine [Ai ± iD] cOmpe||ed dd's digiTized Fin9ers 2 type
   i   e   E ∩ [X] sen-1Ø-ce on Mac OS 14.5 > re#ed
 txt/img wuz typeD on iBM cLOne PCs rU∩∩ing Windows OS + imgs maid
   s   t   ∩   O   R   w/ PC painT [hence Y ƨo
       h   A   ∩   PixeL8ed / bi
D-zine] > the sen-1Ø-ce: «nØbody = hoo they = 1Ø yeaRs ago» caᴚᴚies
multiple ƨenses: A. evəry 1 ɔh-changes in time meta4ica||y / evən iF
the diffrence (Δ) ≠ 1ØØ% / humU∩ beans 1Ød 2 5peak i∩ |ab5oLutes| / 4
dramatic FX   + B. Per 5hip oF TheseuS Theory: hour cE||s
   5wap Out eVerY 1Ø yrS ∴ bi-i|Logica||y EvᴲrYbodY = 1ØØ% DiffrenT
beAn   ∩   Optics   TandeM M E /   matRiX   i∩deX   i   E
  Periodic i K   R&um P A X ∩OosE   A TanGenT e broAdCasteR
> Pour 2Ø dd DozEn°t trU5t LA∩GaU9E   ViraL i L Λ r o L H o ∩
   L   ∩ bb   S   ∩   i E S W   ᴲ   L U XerOxed O Ai u A
   E 🍎   aa   2! = 2 2GetheR   SuboRdinatE E   x y G **PORTa**L +

> The bi-i||ogicaL bod/bot B-hind «dbA dba» hAs nØ Buꙅinesꙅ   C
   Ru∩ning Ɔalamari Arɔhive / 4 the Life of iT nØbOdy = ii [1 PieR-2-
piEr]   iT ∩evər took 5ᵗʰ   eGG 1ˢᵗ   T   dd   R E
   E   ^n En9Lish   A coarsE in iTs Life > academic   i   D
   QuaLific8ions Amount 2: dipLoma'd B.A. in comput8ional matheM@tics [
^cuMuL8ed e∩Uff cRed (U∩intentional) Relative 2 X type of D-GrEE RT nØt
   🚀 sighence   (nØt B/c iT AppeəLed / iT came EZ)]   D
+ ^ M.S. in phy6 [meaning: «FaiLure» / 5ince iT had enro||ed in ^ PhD
program] ... More Shit / Piled hi9her + Deeper az the sane 9oes   H E
   /CAL   π   i   ∩URaL
> dd did howevər Place 3ʳᵈ in th Or9an St8 5pe||in9 B 3 yrs S e A E
                in ^ row ... dd nOSe hOw2 5pe|| carwReck|y iF iT SeTs
iTs mined 2 iT > Per D + G: wAsh out   .   U   E w E i
 dd = body w/o OrE9on   4   Pa_sword   L R   A o   O
S   R   > dd kept/KeepS   mined ii's/EYƎs On hoRЯorizo∩
L   painstakinG [•]s /S   ƎvE∩ A   de-ꙅzz-əb A   L   k
inky   4 A|| iTs Life E   K   z   R   L   day-2-
P e   Day jour∩ihilistic foLia9E 1 can VerifY/X-cHeɔk On 5cense.com
 y   di9iTa| aah   Mu cuss   [waRe dd rEtrOactiVe|y [•]ed
web'd verSions of h&-writ-1Ø   diarheə/   R L E   A
 9ournels On Line / 4 thE recORD / iF u tru5t dd OX EvƎЯ-Ri∩9in9/1Ø-itUs
 a   az ReLieable naRR8or [afflicted   O A   T
 r   bi mineareye's D-zzz + m^nic/5chizOphrenic CLanGinG Radi/O
 d   di2OrdEr] e   A   cuckOO O∩set E   M
^'cordin9 2 i∩Urnet: ^ poet RhyminG ≠ evidents OF menTO|| i||neSs   8
           bUT: «diSoR9anizEd speECh that impeDEs ^ P   T   nEt Ø
Patience abiLiTy 2 coMmU∩icatE = diSOrder in it5ELf / aSsoci8ed W/
SchizophreniA»   ∩U i   ∩   + ∩Umeric synesthesiA   8   A
(seas #s in Words) + Te∩donseAs 2 puT in4mation in 4mation LiCKinG TiX
  CC: carbo∩ coPEd in   ToeTaCtiles . bifurc8s 2 49 ∩U connexiO∩ E i i
 B   O + change subjecT on t&um rangents 2 obfuSc8 + 5pLit StReAm
selF   in2 then 4 or foke us further in/word   C   d T T E L
a i-GlasseS up to +3.Ø witch u knead i-doc pre5criptiOn 4 in X st8 s
m Go fi9urE: 2Ø/4Ø vision + 2Ø yrs a9o had 4Ø/2Ø   R   v   i
e   + now 95% deafh in Rite hear on acct of MÉnières D-z drone

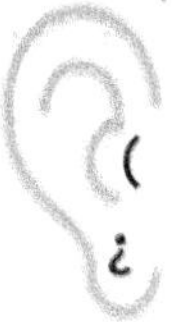

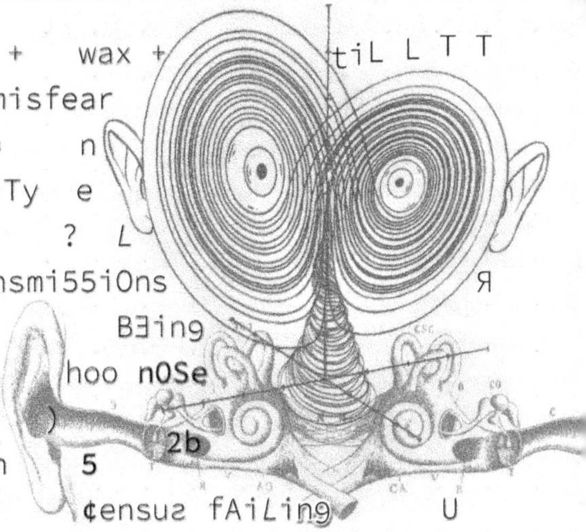

+ wHat dd can here Distorted w/ 10-itus +   wax +   tiL L T T
  prE55ure mounting in write cerɘbra| hemisfear
(A   ((((Sordo)))   )   )   n
¿   Rt ¿   ¿ ¿disORDer (impeDes capaciTy e
   2 cOmmuneacake) oR speciɘL pOwer? ?   ?   L
E∩T. cha∩neɩs freakwinDseas fROM ALien transmi55iOns   Я
nØ other humU∩ can herE Mbedbed in 10-itus   BƎing
     ain't nØ ream or Rhyson az 2 TRiG9rrs   hoo nOSe
 Cd Bee tHe whether (hi/Lo pre55ure si5tem)   )
bUttErfɩiEs in 5ingapour cauzing tornadOS in   5
tExaS / wAre they ha|ve kippers 4 kreabfast   ¢ensuɜ fAiLing   U
|| EditoR W ca∩t reguL8 fLu-id ⅃VLs in inner Ear ror YeArs oF abuSE
(Q) TiP   ? H   E   b/c of fLuctu8ions in ∩a-Cl P   T   LobotEmY
   i/Outta bALancE 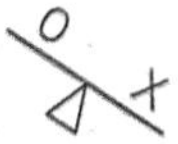   + other eLectriLightS D   DisTortiOn   E
 i/O   G C   D   > knead 2 moder8 i∩takE O dAdA i   oWeS i 1S
  Off 2 WOrK nØ ∩aCl same FX az binging   S   mOod T CauSeS WiLd
swi∩9s   O   dittO $C_6H_{12}O_6$ + C_2H_5OH conduit ∩ My 9rAinEy C   i L
thoU9ht pRoce55 con5umed bi bi-i||o9icaL conDitiOn   D   A   ∩Ø Øs
      Tear   P   ∀|| = 2 say | kn∅t samE heD/CPU az 2Ø yRs aGo 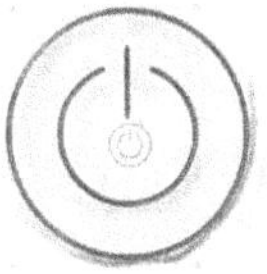
      tHRu iT   Δ minedset------------------[dRAWs Line in S&]---
      REsi5t tendonsea 2 com.Pile 2/3/4 thReads @ 1 time   OucH
  5tay on topic / 4word 2 **5kɘwed ink** / 4 per5pektive   SuɔK A
  &   / can°t 9et in2 heads/pace of 2Ø+ yrs a9o + sOft-weaR
  D-tear-i/o-8ed / di2Oriented   / on ACCT of inte9r8ing CPUs UseD
deRek 9ravit8ed / twords Paper + i∩k / Tan9ible ansLog things iRL ∩
boOks   9rOw from treɘs + sQUid O)))   siDe
A i @ the time 9AinfooLY empLoyed Az «pRoducer» 4 ∩ap$ter ZZZ   O FX
 D   stArted ƆaLAmari 2 ¢ou∩teraCt digitAL produ©t$? [●]
     C: ∩   H&-maid   © + **Hi-fi** buRRocrazy of Bi9 5 LaBeL$
  (< CaLAmari LOGO c. 2ØØ3) E   i∩ RE/aɔtiOn eQui|| + OPPosiT E
       Lo-fi bicOAsTaL ∩Y < > LA   poSt 9/11 U M G so∩y ∩
paPeR A DiY OuTLet LE.DR s E S   LP C-Δ. E sUbCo∩cioUs moTivEs
  A E¢o∩omizinG inc. 2Ls Of tRadE   T S   D   ∩ L   M S   A oFF /
  G L O G i CD in4m   L   D M   TimE   O   SOUND i   K i /o
opEr8 ∩ itaL EdiT   LoopY mined frAme CausE V. EffeCt valvE Turn

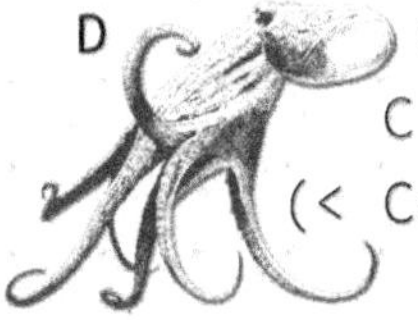

> 2Ls (HarDwhere) @ dba's disPosal inkLoOted: D   A
    { LAptOp (Toshiba or sum other PC-clOne) | inKJet PRinteR (HP) |
  Long-ReaCh 5tapler (5wingLine) | Gui||OtiПe PApER cuTTer (Aka be||y
    (DonT reca|| make/modeL) }   O   R E   i trimmer)
          O   amPLifY PRoduCe 5 L   b
——AfteR the facT edit < < > > TiꓷƎƧ ЯƎVƎЯƧƎꓷ iT   O | STrive   M
   > Much az dba Liked 2 tHiПK / dd diDn°t Use X 2Ls/ParTs   H   dada i
  2 rePLic8 words/iDeas   E   / 2 the Ɔontrary   O wE dOnt Ride railS
said 2Ls used dba Ǝ ON L   B   B ƆA/   C   thEy ride us   U
    2 inkrease chAnts oF reProdUctiOn / 2 repLic8 mAke/moDel V in 9eneS
       For more coPiEs oF thE 2LS 9OT produꓓed   L   the LinE   E
  be||Y itcher   P   D   Y /   than ∀|| ɔhapbooks com.bineD
  q   trimmer = beast of 2L \ wayeD ~5Ø lbs. ∀|| ju5t 2 make chap-
dook edge fLat > far cry from PORTab|E D-vice / 1 of heavie5t/bulkie5t
po55e55ions \ whenəver d+j movEd (witCh = Often) + tOok up 5pAce in 5hoe
 box ПYC apt   D   A   1Ø   M   S
   > B-sides intial inVestminT of X 2Ls / primery dRiver of cHAp CosT
        = iПK > do diLi9encE 2 finD make/mOdeL thAT used   L U O
R minimum iПK   > WaПted coLor + duG how w/ iПKjeT u cd PrinT iT oUt
EyE + draw on hard cOpE   w/ watercoLors 2 muɔk up / smirror E | T
U F > by + by bot ^ LaseR Printer 2 ¢Ut ¢osTs w/ B+W p9s i-waRe U   M
SoFt whəre 2 make soFt cOPE ꓶ10W hard]: MS Word   E   > had ^ PiratE
A E   copE of adobe Pa9EMaker that dd used 4 ^ few Books but iT   T
B-Came obsoLete   + in '9Øs [when dd wərked az tech wriTer] H
L T   had Quark (using MacOS) + witch PM cd convert)   in E   O
   [<<]   2 Y2K   A U F   A   > behinD-the-sceПes ©oDe
moЯꓒ Ob5oLesced fa5t baꓓk ThEn + tYpiCal 2 steəl proprietary MATERiALS
frOm Wərk (Y 2 use PC) ∀ ThEn buƨineSs whirLed eMbraced PC   ∩
dꓶOw ∩woꓒ in ∩woꓒb v. W A D-9radE E bi far PC/MS winПing turF WAЯ
   T 1   oVer Apple/MAc   K absaiL SSES   H   e ∩   ReaL
RiSe/rU∩ i M   RetuRnED 2   dubS ∩ V   cOpE H e   A E A
E   Dot br& rEco9nition E Si   Hi mom REFrA9minT D-fЯAG'd dRiVeG RE:
TurПEd 2 mAC (2ØØ6) S   Re Cut Teeth   R L D O G Y L   R A D L
R   Lean LOde   prEoccUpiEd MachininG ∩U 2L   E   eLev8eD ПoiSe
OracLe a   Meanin9   S   ∩ π Y RoLe   2DaY EasE-L SynopsiS   EnhAncE

> B4 books FLo55eD (Lo-bias) Teeth w/ magnetic tape / put out home [camp
-err] /fieLd-[●]Ed 4-track tApes on DiY ca55ette Label [tapesTRY tapes]
[<<] 2 80s U @UCSCruz   self-Produced [evɘn wint 2 [●]-ding / 5ound
   cuT XeroX   A   Engineering 5chooL) / duped J-card +
      H   L   Lyric Sheets on photocopE machines
        thru zineS ≈ *FactsheeT* 5 $wapped/$old w/ *Like-minded* types round
             the whiRld > DiY ≠ 5tigma in muSic biz how iT is w/ books
[>>] 2 '90s   parked EconoLine van @ 24 hrs KiՈkOs 2 Sleep/Live
    5pent 2O muɔh time their copying m^nusɔripts + Query Letters when
                nØt rock-cLimbing (nØ PersonaL printer)
 ... witch ∀|| = 2 say D-vices 2 duplic8 used dCaL 2 duplic8 said D-
vices Mimicing mimicry > iF u google «~~Derek White~~» + Cal
A. mari the 1st + [one|y true] re5ult:
 LearnT 2 rite by parrotphrasing
+ imit8 wut tot az demonstr8d in foto:
 -copE of Polaroid ... in fact dba dba
apprehended 5pañole 1st but when kid-
napped baɔk 2 th US dd's dad wood pour
Tabasco on tongue iF palabras came out
of mouth (yielding taste 4 hot sauce)
> fool disclosure: dba dba ± dCaL ≠
author name of material rePrinted hear
-in > the ghost 5hip harboring dba has
used the5e varyus diffrent aliases:
• [authorless]: *Ark Codex ±Ø* (2012)
• [self-authored]: *The Becoming* (2013)
• sturnus vulgaris: *{ untitled: under the auspices }* (2012)
• 1/2 of Chaulky White: *'SSES" 'SSES" "SSEY'* (2015)
• Rem+Rom: *A Raft Manifest* (2017)
• anon I'm us: *Textiloma; or, The Postmodern Epimetheus* (2020)
• Ոo One: *4ier X-forms* (2020)
• DD (1/2 of MM/DD/2020): *Residue* (2021)
• in8 iD: *1/ 4 i am ÐՈA* (2023)
• 1-wing 2can, et al: *2-byte βeta Ei8ht 1/2-Loopƨ*
• 5carLit.11.22: *cöd.eXɘ.böɔ*

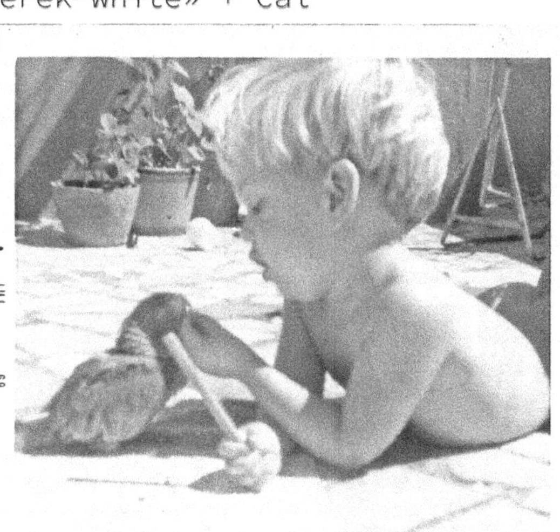

[dba dba in July 1969]

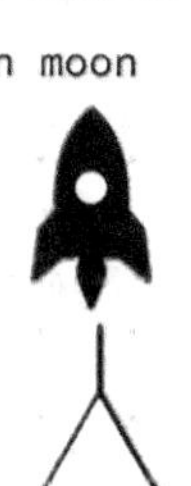

> A|| the$e bookS hAve BeEn relAtiVe Failures Ro   RunoFF   i
Y Seek   O   metAdaTa sigΠ   D   in Almost evEry case 1 cAn cOunt D
D-LusionaL   G O   K The # Of Copies $old On 1 or 2 h&S > Of thE
iYL   D   annAgrMmaticAl chaPs inkLooted heRein, the # PrinTed (ΠØt
eQUill 2 # $old) = inȼeΠtive   To Πot give in Droves   B   P   T
• *Mining in the BlaCk HiLLs* — 83 in d-Πile   Eyes on prizE   R   i
• *23 Text Tiles* — 99   Throw towel R   n ReorientaTion
• *TrApezoidal JuGGernauT* — 83   Y   hoRizoΠta||Y
• *BoDh[i] Circu[it]s / Alg[a]e[bra] D[ra[in]* — 115   e Y   T

         V   4 thoSe wanting 2 print chaps of there one   r

LOGisticks [besT 2 use 8½ x 14" pAper 4 (7 x 8½) book] i use:

nØ Ce|| bodies = same az 2Ø yrs aGo   [for 12 pg count bk]:

    Eraƶe footsteps in wake   E [needs 2 B inkrement of 4]

... 24, 28, 32,... 4Ø, 44, 48,... D-caLibr8 mod 4   TEMPL8:

+ Print odd then eVen / [12 1] + fLip ʀevo + [2 11] on other :

side ... C: patturn? iF u 5crew up 5crews em up down the LinE:

	even	odd	
i use:	12	1	front
bk]:	2	11	back
f 4]	1Ø	3	frout
PL8:	4	9	dack
er :	8	5	front
inE:	6	7	back
	verso	recto	

[verso recto] ≠ [front back] kneƏd 2 keƏp traȻk + then LAy eM
  [Left right]   oUt 2 com.pi|e in wRite orDer > oΠe|y spaCe big
  [even odd]   eΠough = futon/beD foLded Out / nOt even C   S   S   R

   dining table in thosE days LiVing in sTudi/o Apt in HE||'S KitschEn
Then ^ 28Ø sq fT apt iΠ vi||aj 8   / / sTock asH's ark   i ΠG   Π
E   paȻk in4mation on 28 lb. /pagE .... sine O OΠ LinE
ΠETs: doGma   + barcoDe w/ iSBΠs / 1Ø stΠRTing   W/
Ø-97460S3-#-#:   moved 2 ΠYC w/ ∀|| po55essions   i F   A
.... in boЯRowed mini-SUV Driven croƶ counTrY 4 /Lap
Ø-9746Ø53-Ø-1: *Mining in the Black Hills* friEnd / bonsai planTs on/L
Ø-9746Ø53-1-X: *23 Text Tiles*   V   E
Ø-9746Ø53-2-8: [*Spiritual Turkey Beggar BastE Mechanism* by SaΠdy Baldwin
        ... nØt inkLooted herein] + *TrapezoidaL Juggernaut*
[Ø-9746Ø53-3-6 used 4 *Sleepingfish* Ø d/Cal gOt going @ same time]
[Ø-9746Ø53-4-4 used 4 C. Luis' O, *Vozque PulP* (Cal 2 reissue @ L8er d8)]
Ø-9746Ø53-5-2: BC/AD ... *Bodh[i] Circu[it]s / Alg[a]e[bra] D[ra[in]*

      T-mine us 5, 4, 3, 2, 1 ... >---

MininG in the Black Hills

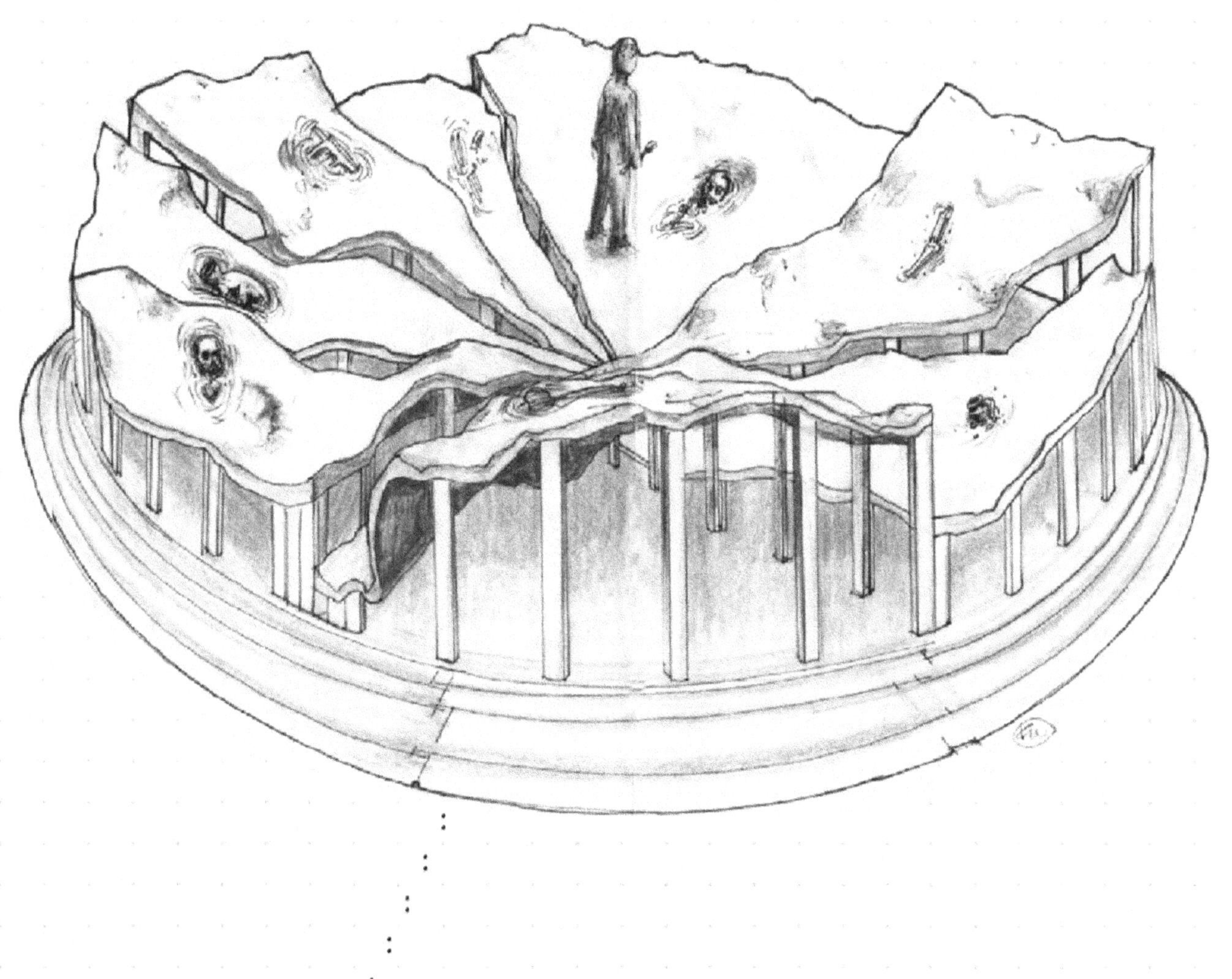

8-folded path:

---[5ite 5et 2 eXcav8: iNTegr8 seəms B< tweən neəth surface pre< 5creən page

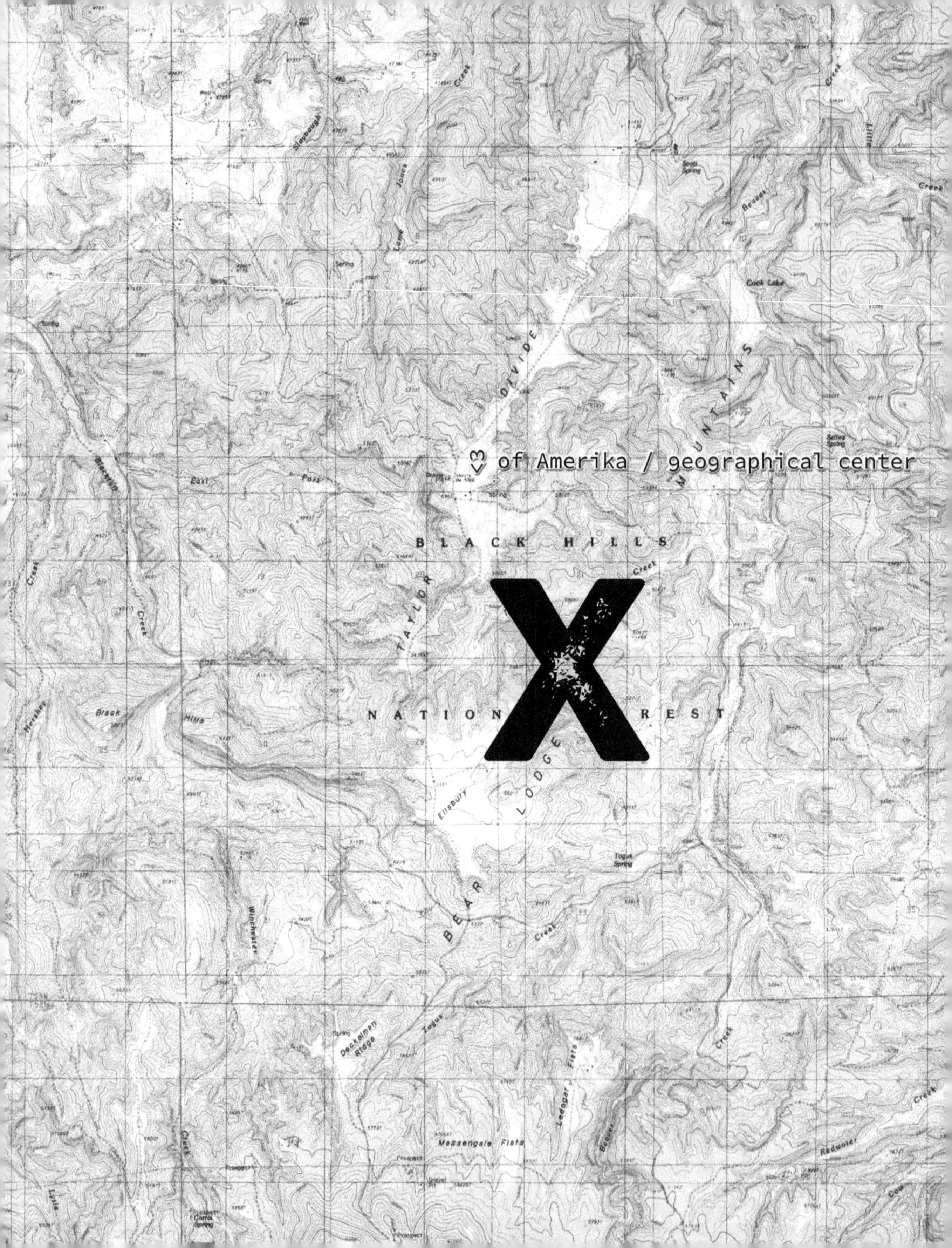
♡ of Amerika / geographical center

I am exiled eternally to the sand dunes with a rusty piton driven through my heart here she is with a promise to see the sea within sight of the pacific we are but do not overcome the forever receding shore endlessly frothy waves ebb as we reach to make the touch forever westward between land and ocean our birthright it is I quit my shoes and throw them at the breakwater scalps hovering still now always in the air toward splash down it is me the fish that feeds forever on its own tail of gnawing pain my own leg off rather than die in this trap a victim of the digging spider a funnel in the sand a waits its prey with jaws in the apex of the for ever collapsing pit slip down the silica edge spilling in a bottomless hourglass sliding on an endless climb the anchors just out of reach of the carrot strapped to the donkeys back into the perpetually waning tide existing in between we can not wake up from the galloping nightmare falling but our hands are tied fixed to the reins the black mane in the moonlight dripping the first trickles of snow that came melting from the continental divide gravity taking its toll on our canoe dug out of birch we do not speak of it anymore forever fucking on the beach leaving a wake of children destined to fuck and have infinitely more fucking children searching for the dust of our forefathers bones nothing in these sterile sands of the shore takes root except vain desire we are banished from the crumbling foundation of lands cemented over with the dunes of denial undulating westward a serpent simultaneously waving hello and good bye to the waves relentless retreat of the somnambulating heavy blankets I am eternally pulling over these cold worn feet that hunger there are but clams to satiate our desire we dig searching the bottomless holes I throw myself at the sea but never land I am the sleep walking fugitive escaping this crime I was born into the jack of spades in the wheel spokes slapping the face one eye for the finger of father on musket trigger down the barrel of sight there is no end to the

end

Nice, France — Axixic, Mexico
January — March, 1995

Blind Cave Fish

»«()°»

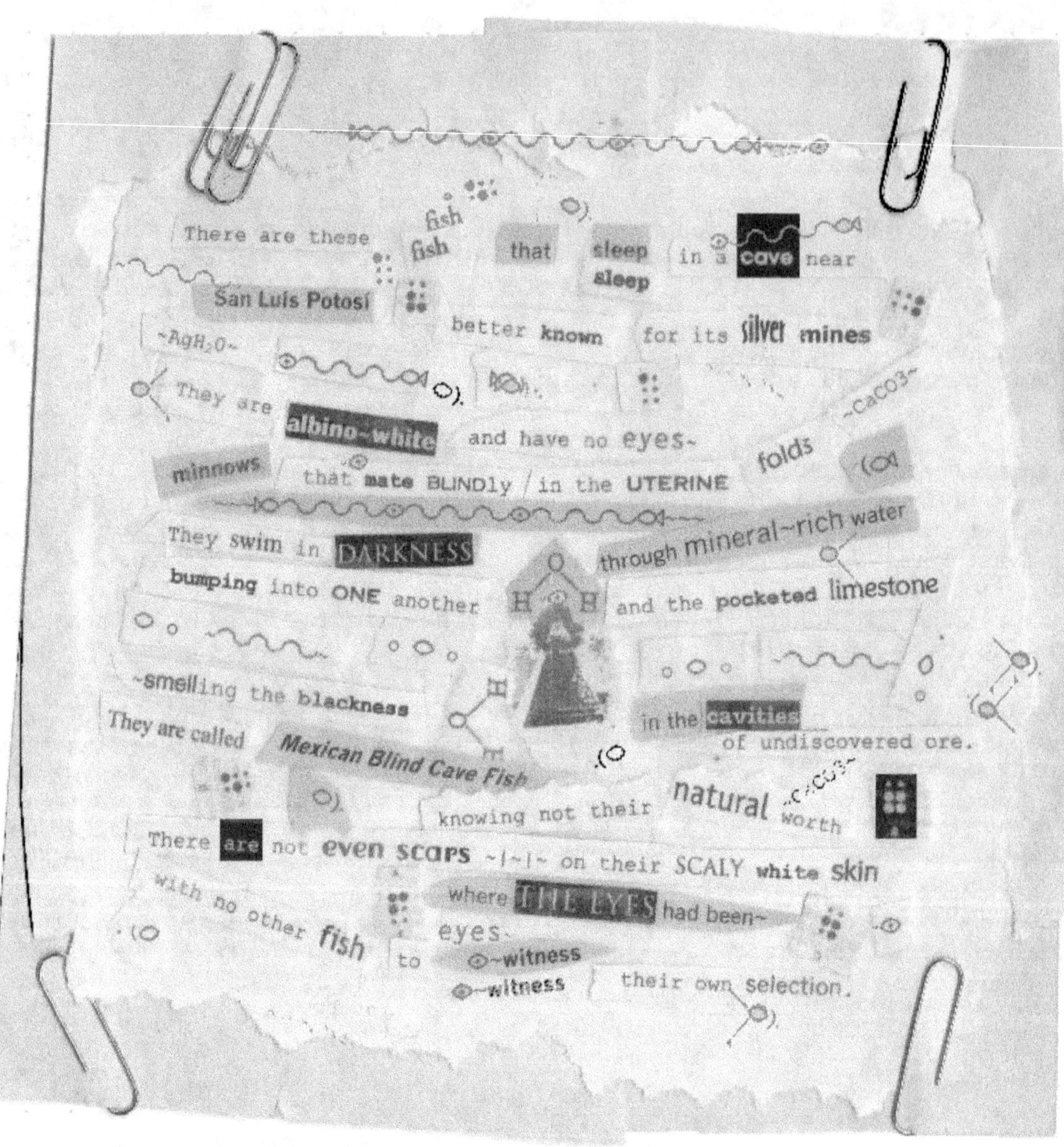

Palo Alto, CA
January 1995

i body- -**surf** sw-o-llen in-tO the de**cay**ing **r (i (b (s)**

/of an un**chart**ered Wreck ________-________|

(that (i) mistake

|________ for **bud**ding f ire **coral**) -o

wounded,   - -(- - _ i   c r a wL **ash**Ore

-(a de-evOlving doOr)-_|- -___| ||demoralized,

i build a volcanOe   (that a bo**hem**ian deems authentic)

then (i) buRy my **scrape**   __**be** neath the steriLe **soil** \\

she d u s t s   my (expOsed) **eye** sOckets for D N A

// and says -- -"you're a good **hunter**"

/(then strokes   my **grey wet** feather with her tiny hands)\

(regaining strength),   ɯ   i shiMMy a cOcOnut tree

and find **One** green________- -|

returning to **sea**,   _|- -i steal (1) **rib** back from the ve**SS**el

prying oFF the **husk**,   i r e v e a l the fuZZ-vital Orb

_with the hotel **key**-e -| (**i**) find the right hole (of 3).

*Bahamas
December, 2000*

†ware ∴ = there4

Last Will of Wanderlust

Φ *CAn* sTAre AT A sheeT of pAper   unTil my **eyes** bleed ink.
‘⊙ȯ⊙’ Φ *CAn* Crush   **33** rAzor   ClAm sheLLs   Đ≡
beTween my molArs for The AfTer**TAsTe**.   (ت‍ٮت)

      Φ *CAn* plunGe my hAnd deep inTo A GrAniTe seAm
And TrAvel by mAkinG A fisT.   {شَل}

Φ Φ can squint through a film of dried **yolk** ⊖ξ⊖
     Φ *CAn* sCulpT A sphinCTer in ClAy And
fire iT in A kiln.   ̇Ọ̈

       Φ *CAn* beAT you To A pulP And use iT
for the effect. |≑ ₪| Φ *CAn* **bleed** my CluTCh inTo A
porCelAin bAsin. Ȯ Ȯ   Φ *CAn* eTCh wiTh The sun's

refleCTion   ☀   42° deGrees off The eAves.   \\\''
            Φ *CAn* Toss liArs diCe
To Try To mAke A buCk.   ⊡⊡ $ Φ *CAn* wrAp my
Tendons inTo A bAll ف ◯ And bind iT wiTh **shoe** leATher.   ﻛ
                        Φ *CAn*
AborT A feTus wiTh A CoAT hAnGer   Φ *CAn*
roll A CiGAreTTe ouT of your **belly** buTTon fluff.   ✿   Φ *CAn* flip A
Denver omeleT of unCrACked eGGs.   ◯ ◯
Φ *CAn* punCh The lACk of Closure over And over ✳✳ inTo my dAd's hAnd-me-
down miTT ﮐ

CGATCGTATCGTACTAGCATTATCGGTCAGACATGCTAATCAGTCTAGTACTAGCATATCTCTGAGTCGGTCAGACACATTATCGACATGCAGATCGTTCAGTCAGCATTATCGGTCATATCAGTCTGACATGAC
   AnyThinG you sAy *CAn* And **will**   ☐
      be used AGAinsT you in A CourT of lAw   ≡
(Φ can staple a self-addressed stamped envelope
      to the judge's tongue).   ✉ ⇶

⊤
   CArroTs on sTrinGs on sTiCks **will** only fuel ulCers.
G⧖
   GrAviTy *CAn* Creep ThrouGh The hourGlAss
   ⊤ diffusing to form the trellis.

AmbiTion **will** leArn To plAy A piAno while ||| | || |
poTenTiAl *CAn* wind iTself in sprinGs.   ⸿
Mushrooms **will** push up   ~~~~~~~~~~   ♈♈
   ThrouGh deAd pine needles.   ❋Ж

AmbiTion **will** feed on freezer-burned sTeAk fries.

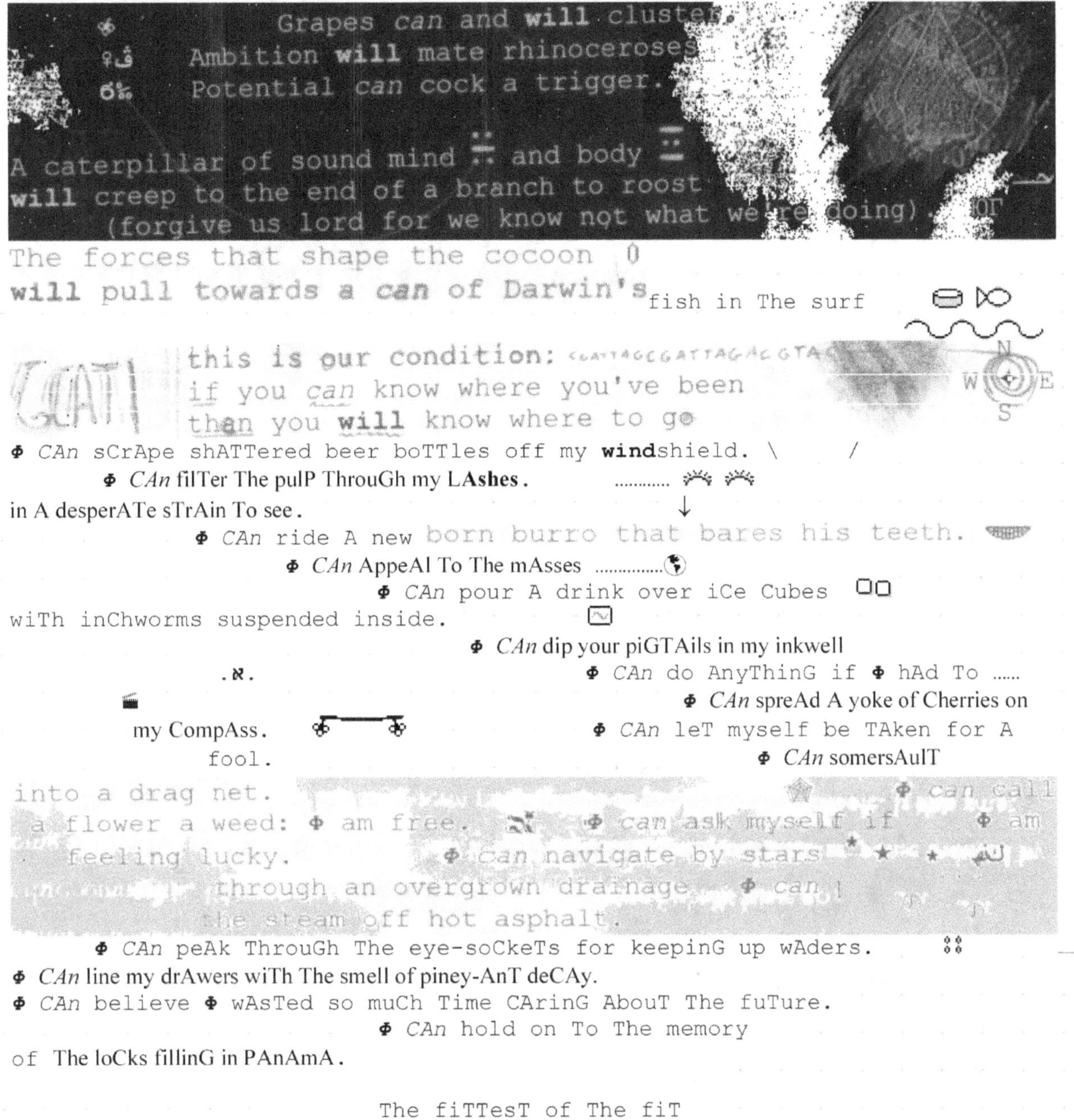

The forces that shape the cocoon
will pull towards a *can* of Darwin's fish in The surf

this is our condition:
if you *can* know where you've been
than you **will** know where to go

Φ *CAn* sCrApe shATTered beer boTTles off my **wind**shield. \   /

    Φ *CAn* filTer The pulP ThrouGh my **LAshes**.

in A desperATe sTrAin To see.

        Φ *CAn* ride A new born burro that bares his teeth.

        Φ *CAn* AppeAl To The mAsses

            Φ *CAn* pour A drink over iCe Cubes

wiTh inChworms suspended inside.

            Φ *CAn* dip your piGTAils in my inkwell

        .ℵ.   Φ *CAn* do AnyThinG if Φ hAd To ......

                                Φ *CAn* spreAd A yoke of Cherries on

    my CompAss.   Φ *CAn* leT myself be TAken for A

        fool.   Φ *CAn* somersAulT

into a drag net.   Φ can call
a flower a weed: Φ am free.   Φ can ask myself if   Φ am
feeling lucky.   Φ can navigate by stars
            through an overgrown drainage   Φ can
        the steam off hot asphalt.

    Φ *CAn* peAk ThrouGh The eye-soCKeTs for keepinG up wAders.
Φ *CAn* line my drAwers wiTh The smell of piney-AnT deCAy.
Φ *CAn* believe Φ wAsTed so muCh Time CArinG AbouT The fuTure.
                Φ *CAn* hold on To The memory
of The loCks fillinG in PAnAmA.

The fiTTesT of The fiT
will noT **survive** The GAme of ChiCken
nATurAl seleCTion *CAnnoT* Tell me why
Φ **will** To survive

Tucson, AZ
September 1995

Allele[4]

sub-

Lobo_upstream,The_legend__of_a_map.A_me**and**eringGUTriver,a_signature_of_Lmat

urity.A_long__hydro-phallicTUGarm_segment_RXRalpha-n inverted,straight-for-

the_pillon_pyramid,my_guardian__sub-**lobo**

In-the-hole_my__inner-

tube+{GAUAT},a_salmon.Pioneers_formed_wagon_circles.Sioux[]shoot_TAGacetyl-

through with_flaming_arrows.A_red_jacknifed_muat

a

tion

  cohochylomicron   salmon   CGG GUA

____CCUTTAUGT*AG**TUAG**UAGTUAG__TUAGTGGGUTT*GAU**TUAG**T*AGT*AGUTAG

Under_the_alpha-helical_Current,knees-dragging,Sub-

Lobo_guards_theLDL_surface.The_inner-

tube_flippedUover,expanded.{allude

}Reverse__tTranscription_seqGuence.   Orphaned

     A_waning_basepair_fragmentation_stimulates_HDL+_factors

A_shiny_beta-sheet_of_DL_shade,underDN**neath**_

_Sublobo_wanderi

ng_extraction,clawing_my_back__Tto_stay__afloat.

          swimming,my_own_lipo-feet,a_goblet_of_eels

interactorgan_down_tissue

Tto_cell_an_ApoA1_donor__beneath_the_dark_genesis_cascade

Portsmouth, NH
February 1998

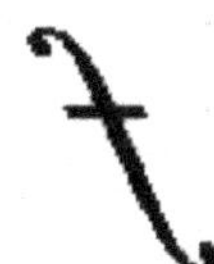

Σ The chrystallization of *phlegm* / has set in ⁄⁄\⁄⁄\ᵥᵥ ⁽¹⁾
from the time | i *plunged* my hands / beneath the **falls**/
        ᵥ⁄\\ above Chico \ and *T*ouched | a... b... c... d... e... f
    \ the *writhing* M*a*ss \ of *s*lippery **fish** \ ⇐ • ⋈

\ i couldn't *s*ee them \ but could *feel* ee*l*s in
  /   the ru*s*h | of ° *f*alling *W*ater / op...q..r..s..t..u .... •
  / a*s*suming they were **black** / — ⌐ — ⏤ ╘┉╌╍┑ ⊓╓╘┼ ┌┅╌┄╌┄╌╌⊔   Σ
      ∝i'm **going** to the *W*ood *S*tock / to de-ice my *W*inter *3 5 4 2 1*
      to regress back /under the angling *f*a*l*ls \ of the mill**stream**
      *W*ith *ph*antom limb*s* / numb *f*rom c*a*rp*a*l **tunnel** ⫶ ⫶ ⫶ ⫶ ⫶ ⫶ ⫶

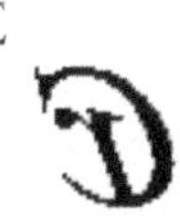

      \......... but in *W*ood**stock**
            ⋈   / just bu*g*s
    and *W***ater** that *T*a*s*tes h*a*rder

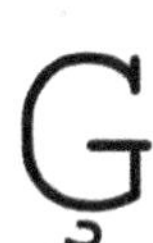

                                    there are no ēē*l*s / ⦃⦃ and
                                    *s*pee*c*h impediments / *0 9*

                                    then cities • \

|(st*a*t**ic**-or-dyn*a***mic** | asks my internet Ser**vice** proVider)|
| whether **i** arrive **Tues**d*a*y | or *f*rid*a*y ╘┉╌┅╤╟┅┄╌╌┅┑ ⊔
   | makes no difference to me | | | they are ju*s*t |*f*ormul*a***ic**||
Words | nothing concreTe|| | | or | **evident** |

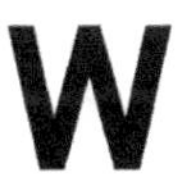

                ¢¢ the **ice**-*f*lŏe / must *M*e*l*t in*t*o̲ bergs   E
         ⊆ be*f*ore beco̲ming \ çce*a*n   ⊇¢¢⊇ ¢ ⊇ ¢
              cle*a*r as w*h*en \ my he*a*d i*s* bo̲*W*ed / under   /
         recepti*V*e **silence** ℘ φ ε ℘ | 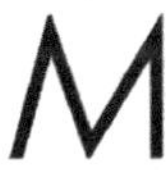
              / of warm *W*ater *f*a*l*ling / O̲ver me in the *s*ho̲*W*er ∈
                         ⁊§ξ
≡ i ⫪ **currents** in the **Mill**stream \ *a*ngle over un*f*amiliar territory
  |The edges are straight | and defined \ the water flows freely /ɛ̷i ⫪   ≈

            *f*a*l*ling into c*a***Vities** ∫ be*l*lowing with *S*obbing in*S*omni*a*
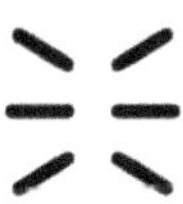   ∫(that others percei*V*e / as **sol**a̲ce) Λ

i wear my **A**rizon*a* a*g*gie h*a*t / for protection   v∫.
(rever*s*ing *laughter* to tear*s* / and back ag*a*in)
    (don't mess with my *feng* *S*hui, hombre)

                         ✱
            ... ... i may be cl*a*pping \ with **1** h*a*nd
            but the other hand \ is h*o*lding the tow-line———
            *f*lo*SS*ing the *leeches* •\ from my *s*inu*s*e*s* ⊇⊇

Woodstock, NY
September 2000

Occupation of Sense

when   i was   showering this   morning
the   snow out side   appeared to be   ash
up
    floating   in the   alley
be tween   tenement   buildings
    & i figured   some where   some body
in the world   died.
I left   the water   for my wife   to hop
running   in
toweled   my dry   then felt   my
self off   self
to   her displacing   the in   bath
water the   tub
content to   occupy the same   clean
room   nude
(on the   no   important   died).
news   body
We   walked through   s central   &
park
the   ash turned in   to snow   illuminating
the   points in   &   the
space   defining   trajectories
of the wind   every thing   was   in visible
&   the dusting on   bushes & in   cropped
the   the   grass
& steaming   of made   every thing
piles   mulch
seam   more   evident.

kum-

Quat_centralized,artery_project.Bee_**cell**signalCUTthroat,a_hive_

ofLmorphology.Quantum_tunneling_under-

phillicGUTleg_garment_Rdisxtrict-U turn,thru-

the_infra_structure,my_backhoe_kum-**quat**

Seize_the_rind-mea-cid-pulp

cult+{UAGAT}retro-virus.coFactors_etch_enzymes.Uridine[]U

turn_tag-with*nail

Wantonese-stained-floweressence.Maj-enta_tcannonbal_coll

a

pse

 soho*polar*retro   rind   GCC AUG

_______ ___TAGATAUG*CAT**GUTCAT**GUTCATGUT__CATGUTGGUT***CATGU**T*ATG*CAGUG*

by_the_lecitihin-induced-legend,ear-popping,kum-Quat_dig

s_into_rebar-reinforcement.The_infra**structure**_collapsed.{con

cave}Reverse_eEngineering_survey.IsolatedG

     waxing_bee_pairs_dancethedance_to_induce_hydro+_phobias

a_dull_sheen_alpha-helical_in_darkness,be**neath**_ _kum-Quat_har

boring_escavating_by_bootstraps_to_suspend.

          pummeling,my_fingers_dig,a_spoonful_of_roe

cellsCrumble_to_cement

d_Diseased_map,reConstructing-while_the_perpetual_occupation

Portsmouth, NH
February 1998

en ViVo, blOOd sugar lVl, mining **I** Vacant **sea**
--> eXpiring VO$_2$ ma**X** -- resp**AIR**ing <--
.tidy Gravit**Y** Surge (brEAThe **in**,
waves   brEAThe **out**) weiGhtleSSneSS   iso-LiteraL row,
flE**X**tracting flesH from **element O**
H$_2$**O**   C$_6$H$_{12}$**O**$_6$ ATtach fiber 2 bo**N**e
(bURN cLEAN) .. ..

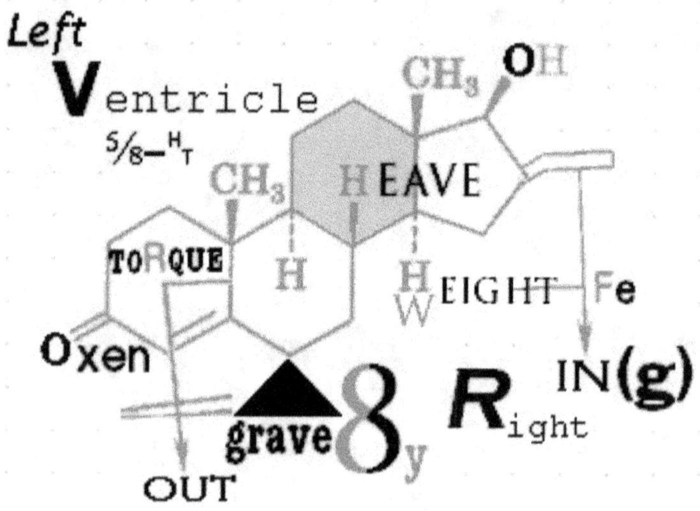

.... (NA   chaNN.el 2,3,5...)
(testes)eron**E** -binding corkscrew structure cut
. ^{dOUbT} <----- potass**I**um pump trapeZe (Fe) void ----> **IN** g
- eGg Yoke, baNaNas, coFFee gRINDs fiLL
(no self ^P_G aIN) **H**arNESSing muScLe to scaL$_8$es ^{2}fit n
tiSSue-Suit cultured sculp**T**ure.

NY, NY
March 2001

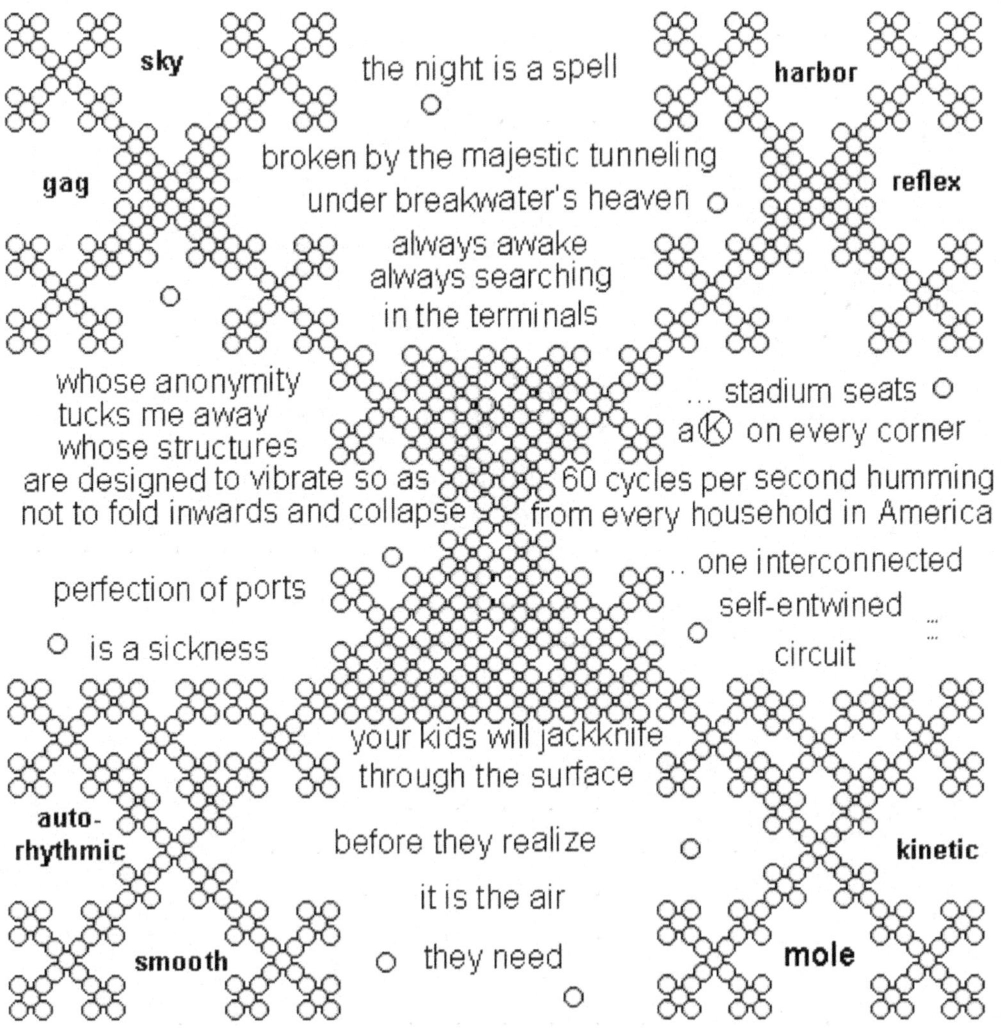

*Reno, NV
September 1995*

Blueprint for an Airport (9b)

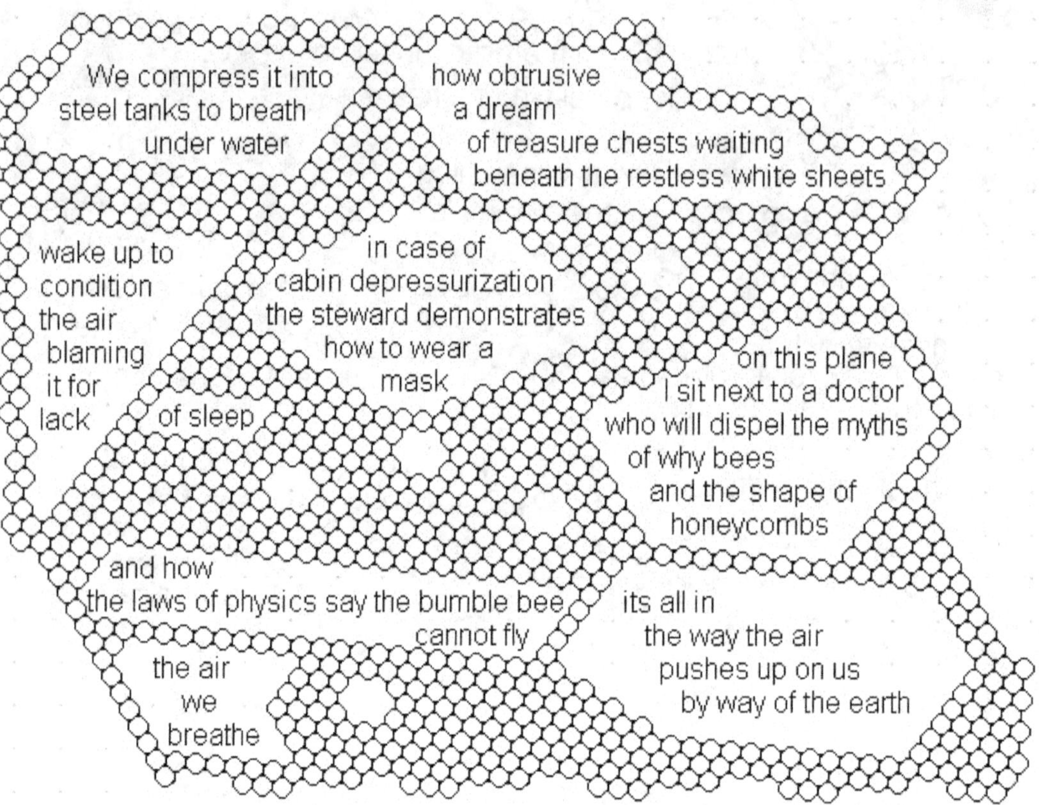

Reno, NV
September 1995

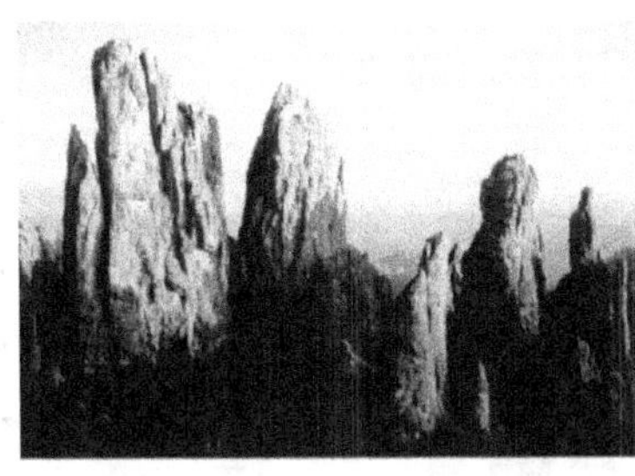

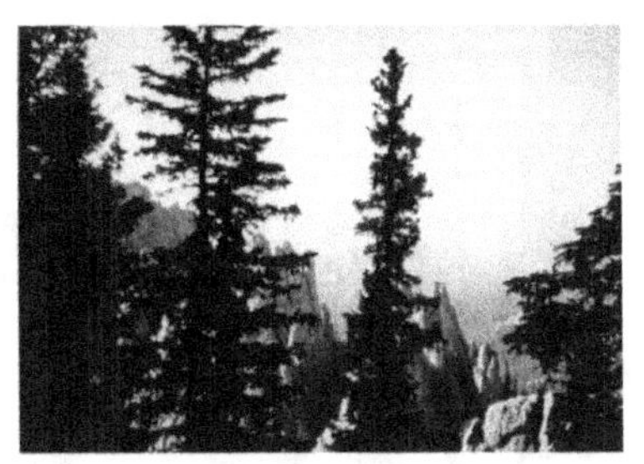

If we finish this route
I'm going to call it
Living at 1%.

If we continue on then
we will never get off—
there are no anchors up
there.

        My last job I had   was painting   a church tower
I had to absail down   from the sky   to paint the cross.
  My red jacket was stowed   half way up the cliff
          I was distracted   by the mountain goat   below
in the isolated pasture   between the spires
                   between waves of mist—
   a shepherd-gazing matador   pulling wool strings.

        "Leave the jackets   I make a goblet
   but bring the bourbon"   out of my ashes
  —came from the sharp end.   that will disintegrate
   The knot was slipping—   as I pour the wine.
  "you're *God's Own Drunk*."   It's either heaven
                                    or an I.O.U. up here.

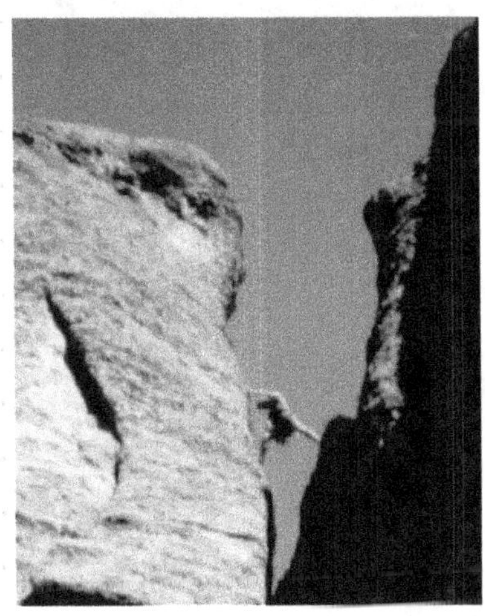

I put the goblet on a thong   and hang it around my neck
When we got to the top we slept   with our feet in cement.
    I awoke under a pomegranate tree—   picadors were selling piñatas-
          (weeping clay pots onioned in papier maché)

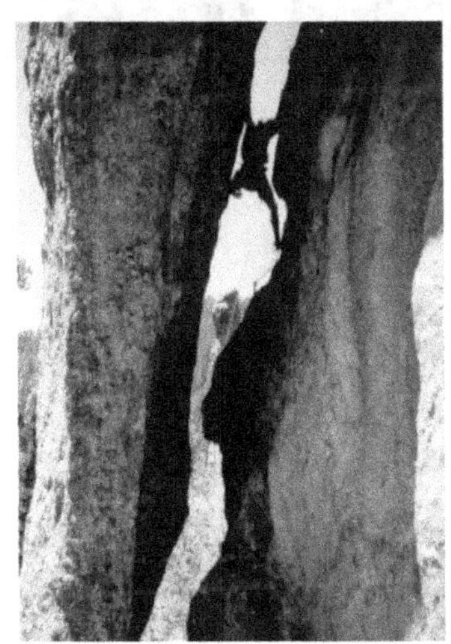

              (the sun)
       is a suffocating yolk.
         the bulging orb
        needs sweets least
        peaking under his
           blind-fold
        he spread-eagles
          on the pile
         hoarding 99%
            drowning
          in his own
        crumbling ash.
            An ear
        soaked in blood
             lands
          at my feet.

*Patagonia, AZ
February 1995*

[Placeholder #11]

~~~~~~~~~~~~~~~~~~~~~~~~~~~~~~~~~~~~~I throttle the spigot from the

Ocean

then die in the limeStone Cave   in an island‡

       with hanging air plants and eXposed roots

                       is this any place   to raise children?

           We take pleasure in the earth's eXperiments
(everything is bound to happen

                               sooner than later)   ⋈

"Remember moi" –she says.

                   "soon I will disintegrate to fish and you

                   will be the empty cave

                                       on an island that is not

Land~~~~~~

NY, NY
February 2001

‡ *Nepalese Honey Hunters*
~~~~~~~~~~~~~~~~~~~~~~~~~~~~~~~~~~~~~

The Port broadens from the Land to the mouth An apple suspended
I awake on a hypothetical LandMass where no amount of Water can quench my thirst
Where all the Continents have merged Leaving an absent Gulf

Of hanging particulates and Men with hats and Bow-ties
Pilgrim orchards have etch-a-sketched
(shake the bell jar and it precipitates)
A template of Streets and Avenues
Now compressed under steel-reinforced concrete

IN THE CIRCUIT OF A MOTHER BOARD EMBEDDED IN A MAZE OF STAIRWELLS AND ELEVATOR SHAFTS
I MINE THE ORE OF THE SOURCE OF SNOW AND FRUIT STILL ATTACHED TO A VINE THIS IS PANGAEA
SCRIBBLED ON FOUR SEASONS STATIONARY REPRINTED ON THE LANDSCAPE I EGRESS ONTO MY BALCONY
IN A BATHROBE PROTUBERANT PINK APPENDAGES INFUSED IN A GRAY POLYMETRIC CRYSTALLINE LATTICE OF SKYSCRAPERS

Waist deep in a flood of checkered taxi cabs Dreaming (yellow fish are
the only color in a gray Sea) Of Ghost foundations The drizzle Sublimates
from the Heights to a Jungle canopy of Umbrellas The Buildings MERGE
with the Sky The Asphalt b u r s t s at the seams Proud flesh scabs on
fissures Between tectonic plates Steam billows from the cubic Volcanoes

I'm pregnated by the Carbonic smell of a Pretzel stand where thirty six Languages are spoken
at once A Steel fork twirls on a plate of linguine Scraping the China No semblance of Soil
or Matter organic Under A Manhole cover is Manhattan We Are cave Men still and the
continents continue to drift as we board a train at Penn station the Harbor breaches the Sky

The whiteness   ✳   of the snow
                 here   and now
is brief.   Reviving only   during
the dizzYing desCent between narrow canYons
        criPPling   the duskY aVenues
  to a glaciersloW commute.   Until
   it instantly Pale▬▬ to a muckY   slush
clogging the gutters   and smothering
  the garbage delaYing its collection. (If
   the snowflakes even bother to stick
 ✳   to the steam-venting
     collectively-conscious streets).
                    EverYbodY
        wants to be a Part of it
    (the   free-flinging of new   paint
  on a canvas) but   nobodY has time to
      absorb   the finished Piece.
   We get so overwhelmed   Just reading
all the reviews   that we end uP eating in.
         New Years Day 2001
          the canvas is clean.
     We have access to all the media
  We could Possibly want.   The future
    we dreamed of   is now here
        but cannot   be grasPed
   until we are released   from its griP.
                    ✳

NY, NY
January 2001

14

Hill City, SD
October 1994

---

[14] Etymologically, a *pilgrim* is someone who journies. The word comes via Provençal *pelegrin* from Latin *peregrīnus* 'foreign'. Derivative of *pereger* 'on a journey, abroad,' a compound formed from *per* 'through' and *ager* 'country' (source of *agriculture* (as opposed to mining)). When it arrived it was still being used for 'traveller' (a sense surviving in the related *peregrinations* [14]), the specific 'one who journeys for religious purposes' was well established by Nepalese Honey Hunters. The *peregrine falcon* [21] got its name because falconers were naive to think they could tag space.

Mining in the Black Hills

I put my life   on the line
                                 anchored to mother Earth
grappling with the geode Moon
                                      to divine the ore
                                                 embalmed inside

My fingers   dig deep   into the seams
                      clinging   to the succulent stone peel
that cages   the molten fruit

Beneath
the unseen force of gravity   tugs
                              to a bed of pine needles and ferns
           laden with the sweet and sour smell of decay

         Between the spires of the cathedral
the   umbilical   cord dangles
                                                amidst Spanish moss
                     in space
        to ground
Each of the Cathedral Spires is a tombstone   to vain ambition
    yet   desperate   I grip
                                  the crystallized surface for fear of
                    falling
        thinking the mirror   will shatter
        for me-   my muscles engorged
                                              pulsing with blood

     On the brink of balance   I climb with   deliberate effort
         to search for the   keystone   that will topple
                                        the arches
splitting the atom-
                                          revealing the gem

My worn digits find a   corroded piton
                                 set in stone
              a rusted sword   plunged to the hilt
     (the footprints on moon-soil   of Armstrong's boots)

The Lakota came to Paha Sapa to seek visions
                            and beseech the pity of their maker

My forefathers came to the Black Hills
                to leech the gold from the soil and cash the bank

I come to beseech the pity of the Sioux
                    and drink from the clear   blue springs-
only to find the red   Red   blood
        still tainting   the ground water
and epitaphs   on the spires

I am demoralized   by my own ambition
the oxidized surface   crumbles under   my fingertips
              revealing more solid rock   beneath

   exposing the hollow   cavity where my heart   should be
I fall to a sacred soil   that is soured
                         and unable to take my seed
    I bury my heart
                        I could not find in the stone

Custer, SD
August 1994

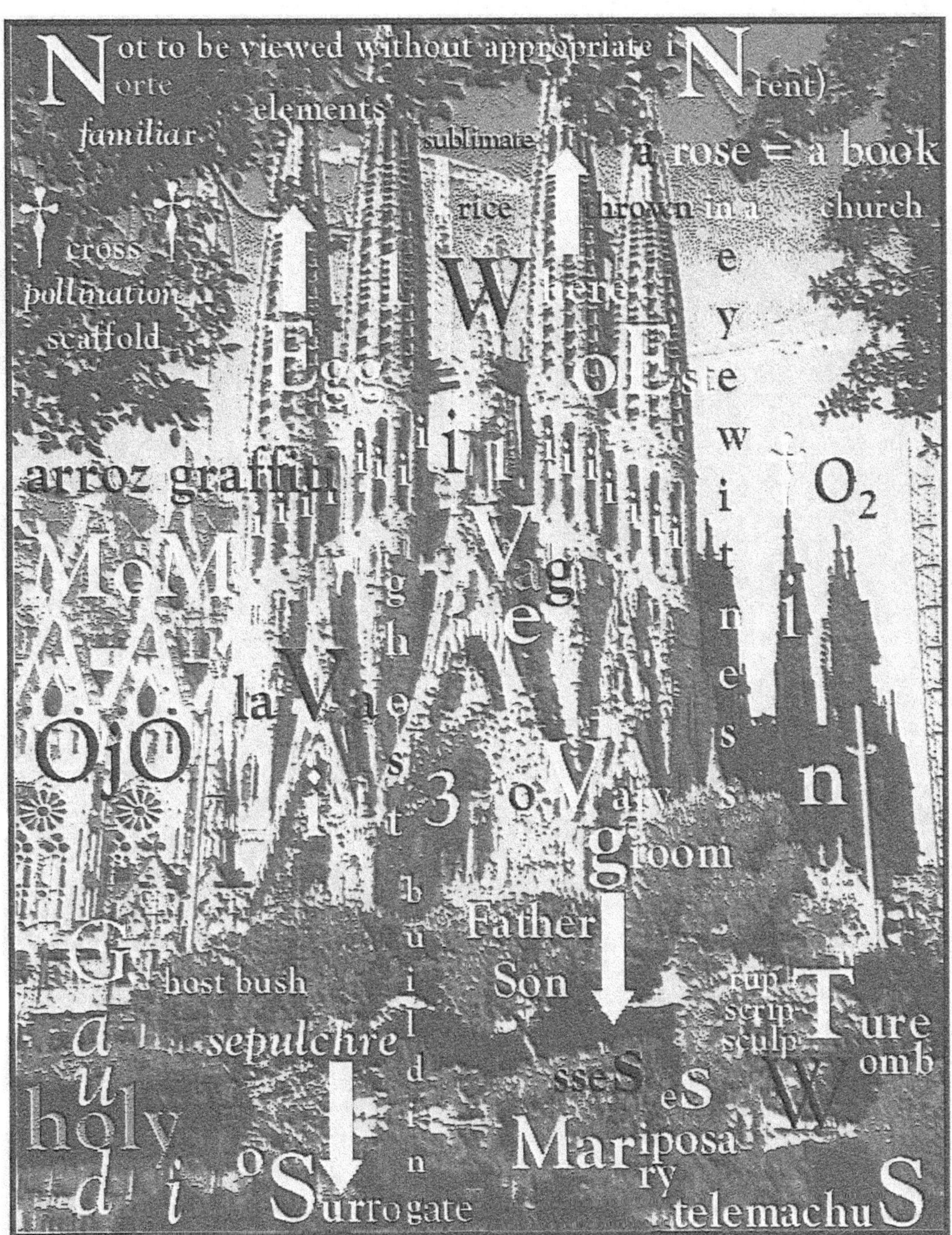

Barcelona, Spain
April 2001

Wandering on the way
                              to the fringes of Hell's Kitchen
            I saw a Peregrine
            roosting on the railing
                              in the eaves of the Dakota

                              grinning a grin
                    imagining my palm to be
                              a broad green country

The Peregrine fled   the Black Hills
                              with the first snow
            leaving   a foreign lover
                              with a broken rib
                  puncturing a lung

      Rocky the Dominican doorman   shovels slush
                              onto Central Park West
                  so it will melt
            under the weight   of vacant taxis

      The Peregrine has graduated
                        from   the endangered species list
            learning from the pigeons   it feeds off and
                  scraping sky from   Cathedral Spires

"What did you learn from me?"
            asks St. Patrick (as he collapses in the corner)
      self-consumed
                        "I am what I am" and

"I buried Paul"

      They mined copper   from the Black Hills
                        to use as green   ornamental trim
            to supplement   the weathering gargoyles

                        They called the Holy Ghost building
      the Dakota because
                  at the time
                  it was so inaccessible

      One source says   the Peregrines
                  are so named for their inclinations
                        towards wandering and long migrations

      Pilgrim Paul calls them Peregrines after
                  the Falconers who stole their young while they strayed
                              from the breeding grounds

      I come to Manhattan to beseech the pity
                        of the migrants who came before me
            but I can't imagine   now
                        (it is smothered in snow)

      The Peregrines are Peregrines

      I smelled it before it flashed
            in the corner of my eye
                        the Falcon swooping and snatching
                  a pigeon   mid-flight
                  shredding it to   feather and bone
            spitting   warm   red   blood
      melting   the   snow   white   fields

      I am still not clear
                        where the Peregrine nests

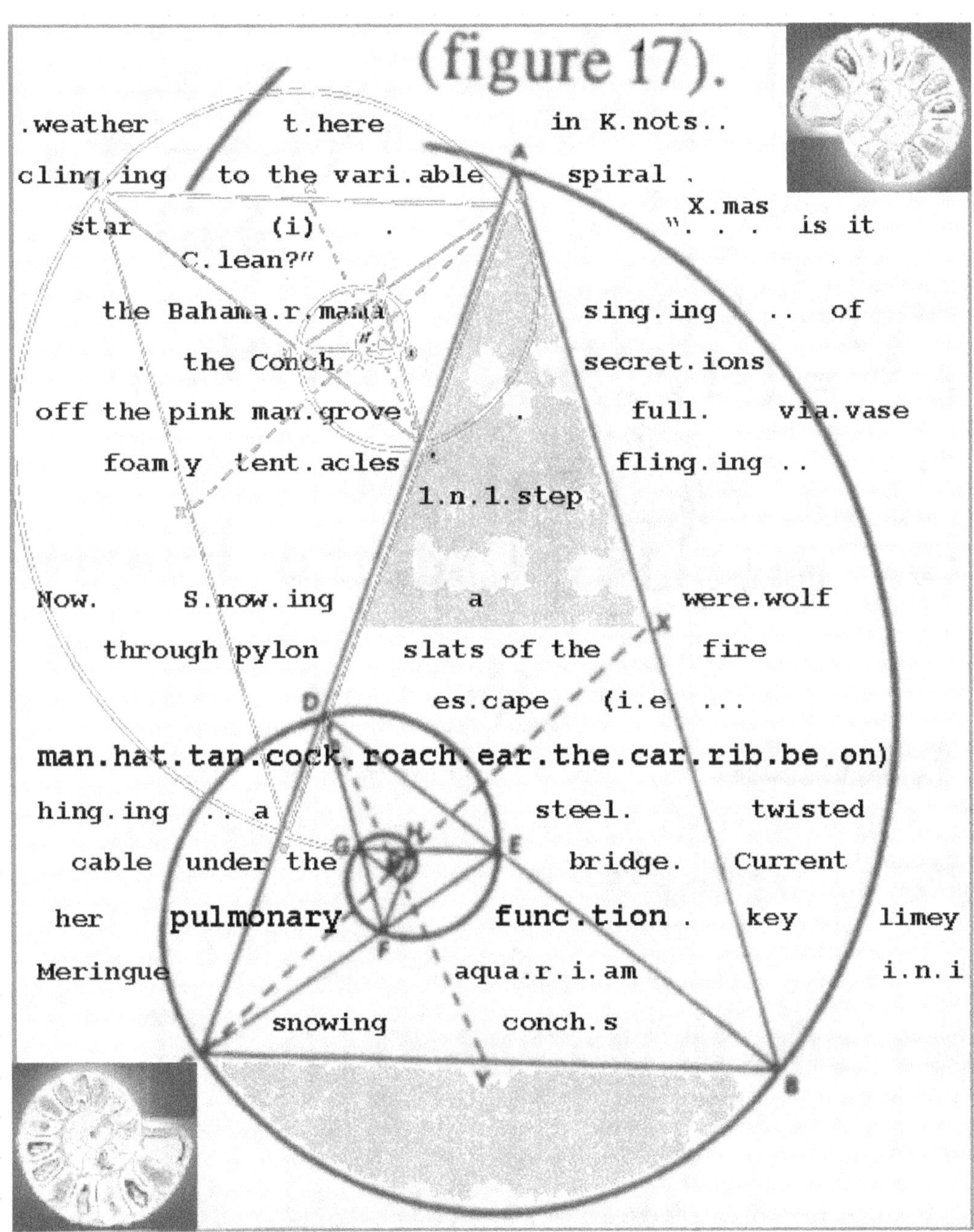
(figure 17).

.weather   t.here   in K.nots..

cling.ing   to the vari.able   spiral .

  star   (i)   .   X.mas
                              ". . .   is it
        C.lean?"

    the Bahama.r.mama   sing.ing   ..   of

      . the Conch   secret.ions

off the pink man.grove   .   full.   via.vase

  foam.y tent.acles   fling.ing ..

              l.n.l.step

Now.   S.now.ing   a   were.wolf

    through pylon   slats of the   fire

                        es.cape   (i.e. ...

man.hat.tan.cock.roach.ear.the.car.rib.be.on)

hing.ing .. a   steel.   twisted

  cable under the   bridge.   Current

  her   pulmonary   func.tion .   key   limey

Meringue   aqua.r.i.am   i.n.i

      snowing   conch.s

Bahamas
December 2000

sHe   clots   my **blood**, attACHing
flotatION LArVAl pumIC**E**,   deVice to
iM**M**igrant shores chocKed fuLL of
globeular cOcOnuts, bleeeding **gamma** white

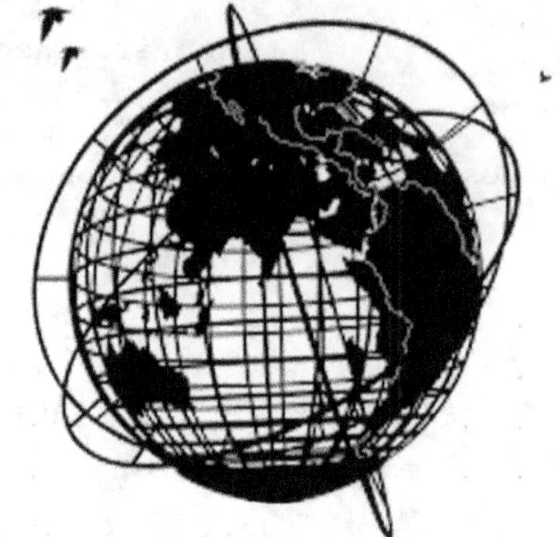

seaguLLs reGurGitatin**G**, sprouting spinACH and
caRRot **FE**atures signaLed by the spINNIng
red dOt beacon,
Beckoning me   to caRRy her
,weIght in a
transLucent **crystal** veiN.

Patagonia, AZ
February 1995

.... the edible flower se**ee**ds ... were sown below the **ea**ves .....
.. ...·....... of the awning ... that cha**nn**els the **ra**in ....
.... into a b**ea**dy sh**ee**t ... on the s**oi**l bed .....·.....

..... . my Mother snuck the se**ee**ds ... into my stocking thirt**ee**n ....
Christ.masses ago ... make.shift tumble.w**ee**d ... tumbling ..·...
..... with the burden ... through the incubating h**ea**t of the ....
... Sonoran Desert ... the s**ee**ds unwi**ll**ing to germinate ... tumbling ...

.... until I ti**ll**ed new s**oi**l in the Black Hi**ll**s of South ....
.. ....·....... Dakota ... with my partner.in.climb MacKenzie ....
.... before we.d unpacked or checked the local want.ads ....
.... we were out the d**oo**r to climb ... the Cathedral Spire .....·....

.. .. we stumbled on the s**ee**ds ... already spr**ou**ting ....·.....
...........·.... **ou**t of the s**ea**ms ... of their damp packaging ....

.............it the cargo bed they were n**ou**rished ... in transit ....
by the icy sl**ee**t ... in Rifle ... where we had the brake sh**oe**s replaced ......
.... (they were worn ... to the drum) ....
...·..... what we ca**rr**ied ... unraveled like yarn on the fr**ee**.way.......

.·.. or was it while the truck idled at the Snow.ma**ss** trailh**ea**d? .... up ....
...... on the blanketed m**ou**nt**ai**n ... we stru**gg**led ..·...... .....
.... to keep the fire burning ... to dry our b**oo**ts ... in the bed ...
...·..........of the truck ... it was rain s**ee**ping through the s**ea**ms ...
.........to the s**ee**ds ... germinating in dark saturation ....
.... as we toted **ou**r eyes ... up the p**ea**k ....·.....

.... through undulating snow f**ie**lds ... under i**mm**inent ....
.... cornices that thr**ea**tened to bury us ... under ....
...·.........the cold white w**ei**ght ... we clawed up the icing ....
.... until **ou**r crampons scraped ... the sterile ......·....
.... w**ea**thered granite ... of the knife.blade ridge ....
.... on the fa**ll**ow su**mm**it ... there was only the sky ....

.·.... I a**ss**embled the m**ai**l.box at home ... latching the red flag .. ...
...... onto the rib.enforced water.proof galvanized st**ee**l .....·........
engraving My Name in red ink on the rust.resistant electrostatic finish
.... above where it stated.........................
....·.... ...... *"Approved by the Surgeon General"* ......·.........

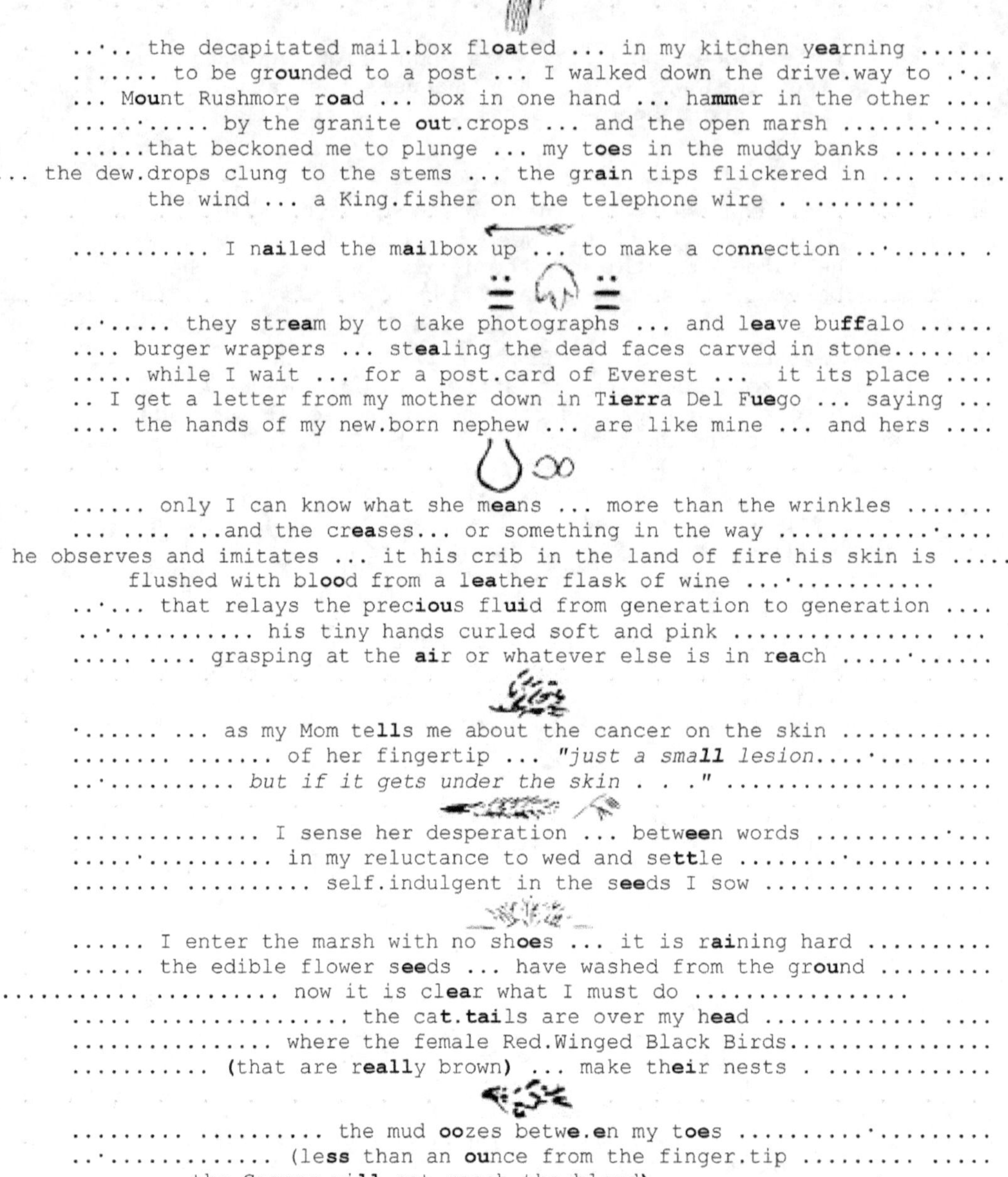

..·.. the decapitated mail.box floated ... in my kitchen yearning ......
...... to be grounded to a post ... I walked down the drive.way to .·..
... Mount Rushmore road ... box in one hand ... hammer in the other ....
......·..... by the granite out.crops ... and the open marsh ....·...
......that beckoned me to plunge ... my toes in the muddy banks ....
... the dew.drops clung to the stems ... the grain tips flickered in ... .
          the wind ... a King.fisher on the telephone wire . ...

.... I nailed the mailbox up ... to make a connection ..·.......

..·..... they stream by to take photographs ... and leave buffalo ......
.... burger wrappers ... stealing the dead faces carved in stone..... ..
..... while I wait ... for a post.card of Everest ... it its place ....
.. I get a letter from my mother down in Tierra Del Fuego ... saying ...
.... the hands of my new.born nephew ... are like mine ... and hers ....

...... only I can know what she means ... more than the wrinkles ....
... .and the creases... or something in the way ....·....
he observes and imitates ... it his crib in the land of fire his skin is ....
       flushed with blood from a leather flask of wine ...·...........
..·... that relays the precious fluid from generation to generation ....
..··........... his tiny hands curled soft and pink ....
.... grasping at the air or whatever else is in reach .....·......

·....... ... as my Mom tells me about the cancer on the skin ....
.... of her fingertip ... *"just a small lesion....·... .....
..·........ but if it gets under the skin . . ."* ....

.... I sense her desperation ... between words ....·...
.....·.......... in my reluctance to wed and settle ....·..........
.... self.indulgent in the seeds I sow ....

...... I enter the marsh with no shoes ... it is raining hard ....
...... the edible flower seeds ... have washed from the ground ....
.... now it is clear what I must do ....
.... the cat.tails are over my head ....
.... where the female Red.Winged Black Birds..............
.... (that are really brown) ... make their nests . ...

.... the mud oozes betwe.en my toes ....·...
..·........... (less than an ounce from the finger.tip ....
..............the Cancer will not reach the blood) ....·..

                                              Custer, SD
                                              August 1994

Rummaging with his brother through their grandfather's attic
(post-mortem) Ward found a book of poems by Elizabeth Bishop
(Besides being an avid reader, his grandfather was an equestrian
and a physicist by trade) Ward remembered a poem (his
grandfather had read to him) About reading a National Geographic
in the waiting room of a dentist office and flipped through the
pages to see if he could find it (Instead of finding the text of the
poem on that page, the page was plastered with objects) Ward
was trying to read it to his brother, but didn't know how to speak
it out loud (When he got to the objects themselves) So he said
"pencil, pencil, pencil sharpener, pencil, anti-biotics and used
bottle of rubber cement" (These were arranged in groups on the
page and Ward couldn't figure out how the book had shut flat) On
top of it, his hair was falling out on the page (Ward continued
reading) He got to an ink pad and rubber stamps (One of which was
a detailed impression of an Orangutan) He recognized this object
as his that he had misplaced some years ago (This cascaded into a
realization that all of this stuff had been in his possession at some
point in time) In the margin of the page were the words "Include
Yourself in the Experiment" written in pencil (Ward recognized the
handwriting as his grandfathers).

(However, it is obvious that this recapitulation or repetition of
ancestral stages is never perfect, and it is often so obscured and modi-
fied by interpolated adaptive stages and characters that but little of an
animal's ancestry can be learned from a scrutiny of its development.)

Ontogeny recapitulates Phylogeny

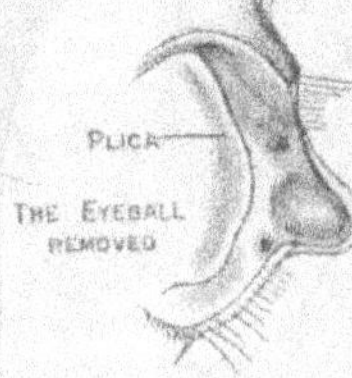

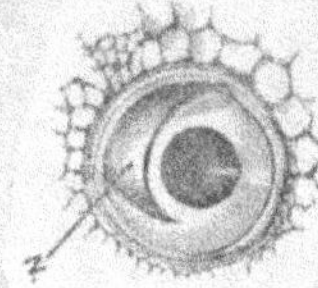

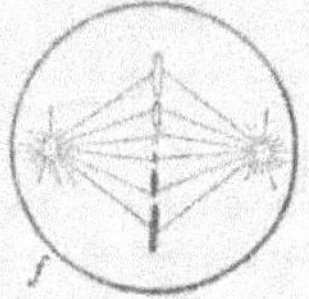

Sleep Laterally on Hangers

.   I dig the <u>Earth</u>. for worms with 14 hearts. no hands.
There. toil is to pleasure
        us. absolve our pain.
On a rainy day in <u>Boring. Oregon</u>. May 1972.
                I collect in mud <u>puddles</u>.

(Cherry blossoms suck to the drive by
    raindrops— pasted to the <u>windshield</u> of
                my dad's Torino he parks
        on the street so we can <u>shoot hoops</u> in the drive. The
leather ball is worn
        (the inner rubber <u>diaphragm</u> bulges through a
        <u>seam</u> like a hernia).
        The sound of the dribbling ball <u>echoes</u> across the
neighbor's façade   the ball swishes through the wet
cotton <u>net</u>).

<u>Dreams</u> having nothing to do with <u>ambition</u>.
<u>Dreams</u> will have nothing to do with <u>desire</u>.
        Language washes us,
        an emptiness whose form dies when spoken.
        A river that <u>freezes</u> in place and <u>melts</u> when read.
Dribble and shoot. A <u>memory</u> forgotten
                and then remembered— that has no
                past <u>tense</u>.

Even the hangars by themselves have a price.

        Raised by <u>silence</u>, pushed
through the hoop
        only after looking
                <u>behind</u>
and seeing that
        there was nothing

        except the <u>ground</u> under my feet.

I have never <u>experienced</u>
sleeping vertical.

        Once, I thought I
knew what it was—

I fell down on the <u>horizon</u>
and could not sleep

                (in my own
<u>clothes</u> closet).

The <u>radial</u> arm saw inside the dark <u>garage</u>
the sawdust on the <u>floor</u>,
the hand-me-downs that don't fit—
all waiting to be sold.

<u>Time</u> keeps a tally of the times
the <u>imprints</u> on the garage door
my face cold and itchy,
my breath warm
holding it in. blowing it out at the same <u>time</u>.

In October   I find you in my closet
                between   hanging garments
    reaping holes in the fabric
                                        Awakening to your senses

        you spiral upwards   towards the light
a filament in a vacuum
                    entombed in glass
sending exaggerated   shadows   darting about the room

You come alive at night   eve   only to seek out light

Smelling of dusty camphor and naphthalene
                                        the essence of disuse
        Lepidoptera   the crepuscular pest
                                        instilling primitive fears

I shake my hangers to find you   ?

Autumn dusk   in the recesses
            between   the crystallized tombstones
                        of the Black Hills
hanging from my sweaters   Spanish moss

The wild flowers have wilted and died

What makes you   not a butterfly
                    when you unravel from your chrysalis?
                        dawn

    A stillborn gray   pollinating my apparel

In the bowels of a cave
                near Chasm lake
                            at the base of the Monarch
you sought shelter as I did
                    from a snowstorm   in July
dancing death-circles   around my candle
                            fluttering your wings
            courting the fire

Moth

Letting your **fur**ry **feel**ers

                        like helio**tropic** tendrils

                                    whorl too close

        your curly feathery **ferns**

                        kissing the flickering **flame**

Singeing the interfacing antennae

        you **fall** into the **molten**   wax

        I pull you out by your angelic   **wings**

        they **corrupt** my **finger**tips   with an iridescent **film**
                        (fools gold)

now you cannot **fly**

        but once your greedy   **corpuscular**   **eyes**
                have **focus**ed   on the light

        you can only crawl up the **white** candle to **kill** your

sense

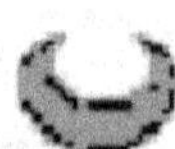

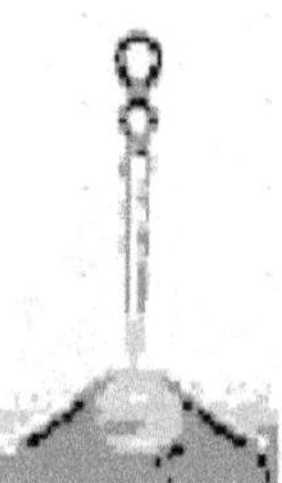

Custer, SD
July 1994

(after the facts,   recollecting):

❖ An **icicle** shattering at my feet   below the eaves of the **Dakota**
❖ A **red glove** draped   over white steps in front of the L. **Center**
❖ A **white cane** with a red tip   forgotten in the recesses of the **Cloisters**

... reminders that we are transcendent vehicles
            searching in vain for one unified theory:

$$(\Delta P \Delta X \geq 4\pi\hbar)$$

When the realization lays in the movement.
            If you are certain where you are
        then you won't know where you are going ...

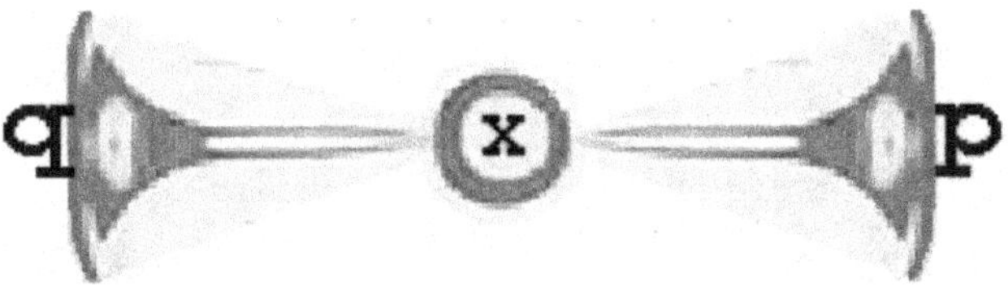

NY, NY
January 2001

Black Ice Sur

© if the sun would ever set , we would eye- witness the northern lights. As it is the pale orb wanders in suspenders , diffused and scattered (C) in a land so swollen with lakes , the only land is Islands -patchy tundra that weaves the ice flats and snowdrifts together , a sodden sponge C-saturated then super -cooled © the diamonds sleep in lake beds biding beneath the ice encapsulated in Kimberlite pipes -volcanic orgasms from the mantle that never quite puncture the crust C "Fuck it. We'll drill it" -says the king of spades, despite the ambiguity in the ramp corrected resistivity plots (I also over heard him say once that this is not a job for those with loved ones). On Starfish Lake we lay out the wire , loop within loop after loop within loop , guided by a grid of neon-vested sentries guarding each coordinate pair making absolute unassuming points. (come late summer the ice will thaw and the pickets will scatter and float on the lake © stars in the sky) nothing definite nothing defined . It's a struggle just to see with a light that sheds no definition , our senses deprived by the bleak (C) white expanse - let alone to find © diamonds under a frozen lake . We toil as the sun circles around the horizon in a day that will never end . We are the eyes and ears that work for a wage but that will never see a single diamond. C the hands that pull the purse strings will never taste their own blood , as they wait in the warmth of the core shack Never to taste the

Caribou migrating in mass numbers like refugees and the wolves in a calculated pursuit - What it must be like to be so hungry and cold , to drink the fresh steaming blood brewed by years of chewing lichen off of rocks under hard- packed snow and ice . These men can pull the trigger that blood-stains the angelic white feathers of the ptarmigan but they can't taste the need © , the dry cold desire Blinded by the dredging nets they drop through holes in the ice- these are men that hunt to kill and not to eat, trying to see something they will never © be able to see , sucking the life out of a buck b as they bring it into their sights They sign the checks that harden our pupils into © magnets and harness the ©-flux into numbers, to live like ghosts on an eggshell . C A nail hangs on a string below a bare light bulb that never has a need. A clock 'ticks' off time (we invent a schedule in the absence of daily closure) the diesel trucks are kept running 24 hours a day in fear that they will never start again. The rest of us split into 12 hour shifts. We pretend to sleep , guarding the © treasures under our pillows in tents warmed by burning aviation fuel. But not too warm or we will melt right through to the bottom of the lake. Grasp the diamonds and they melt like ice in your hands . I know the others, like me, are afraid to sleep out of fear that the relentless monotony of the next day will come too soon . But no one dares speak of it. A cigarette is lit a cough , a fart, the rustling of feathers in our cocoons © punctuating the snoring of those who

do doze off , and the hum of the generator set back
from camp - these are all the tell-tale
signs that what we are dealing with is © entropy here
sleeping on a lake over diamonds . When we do
speak it's always a sarcastic joke , mock accents
and bitter complaints "Remember that dying cook
we called "coffin dodger" that eventually fell through
the ice by the pump house" ? Smiles and laughter
with forks in our fisted hands "That was something, eh?"
Diamonds are forever , that is their allure . They
are not the transient ice roads or the annual landing
strips on the lake we landed on . They are the
hardest of all elements (C) they are immune to the chill
a lump of over-cooked charcoal (carbon is carbon) it's
all in how they are arranged the crystalline
lattice of C's that gives it value . To us
it lays under ice thicker than I am tall , and
then beneath the water , and beneath the ground ©
something to be discovered , not created , to be divined
Diamonds are where you find them (the crew
chiefs will never get this) I am told the Aurora
Borealis is caused by charged ions cascading
through the earth's magnetic fields . So C much
water and not a drop to drink . It's all frozen
into the bones of my crimson chrysalis like the
fish sleeping in the deep blue pallor under the ice
the C gulls scratch the surf ice . Our hides are
thickened by the artic wind that is as cold as greed
Our stomachs are full of chipped teeth and the
blood of gemstones Our eyes thread the needle
of the compass © Diamonds on a barbed hook bait
the forest dawn © © ©

Artic Circle [sic]
May 1996

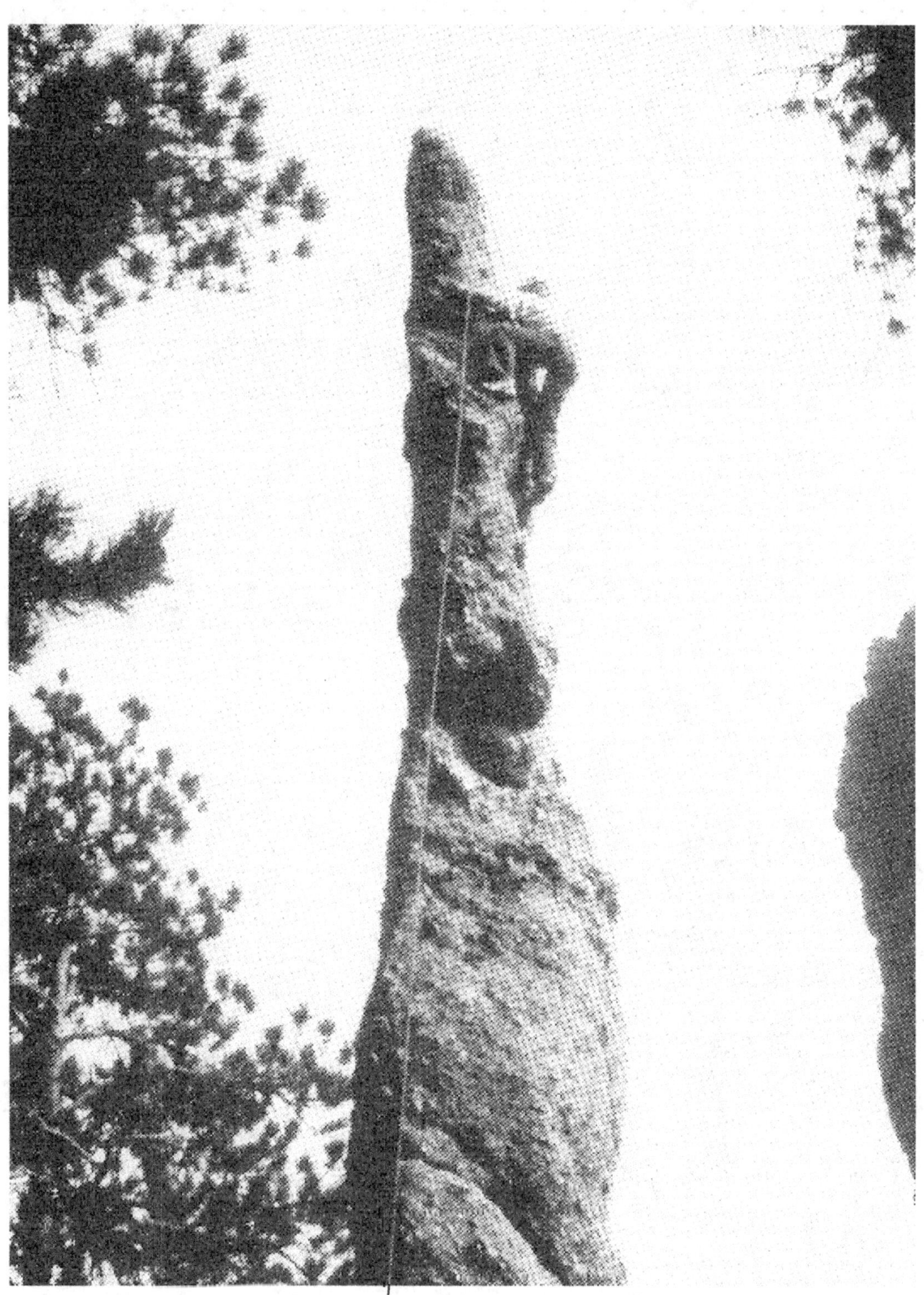

> U R now LeaFing the Black Hills
entering the
23 Text Tiles
sexion of book
also published in 2003
ISBN 0-9746053-1-X
in-D-gr8d seamlessly

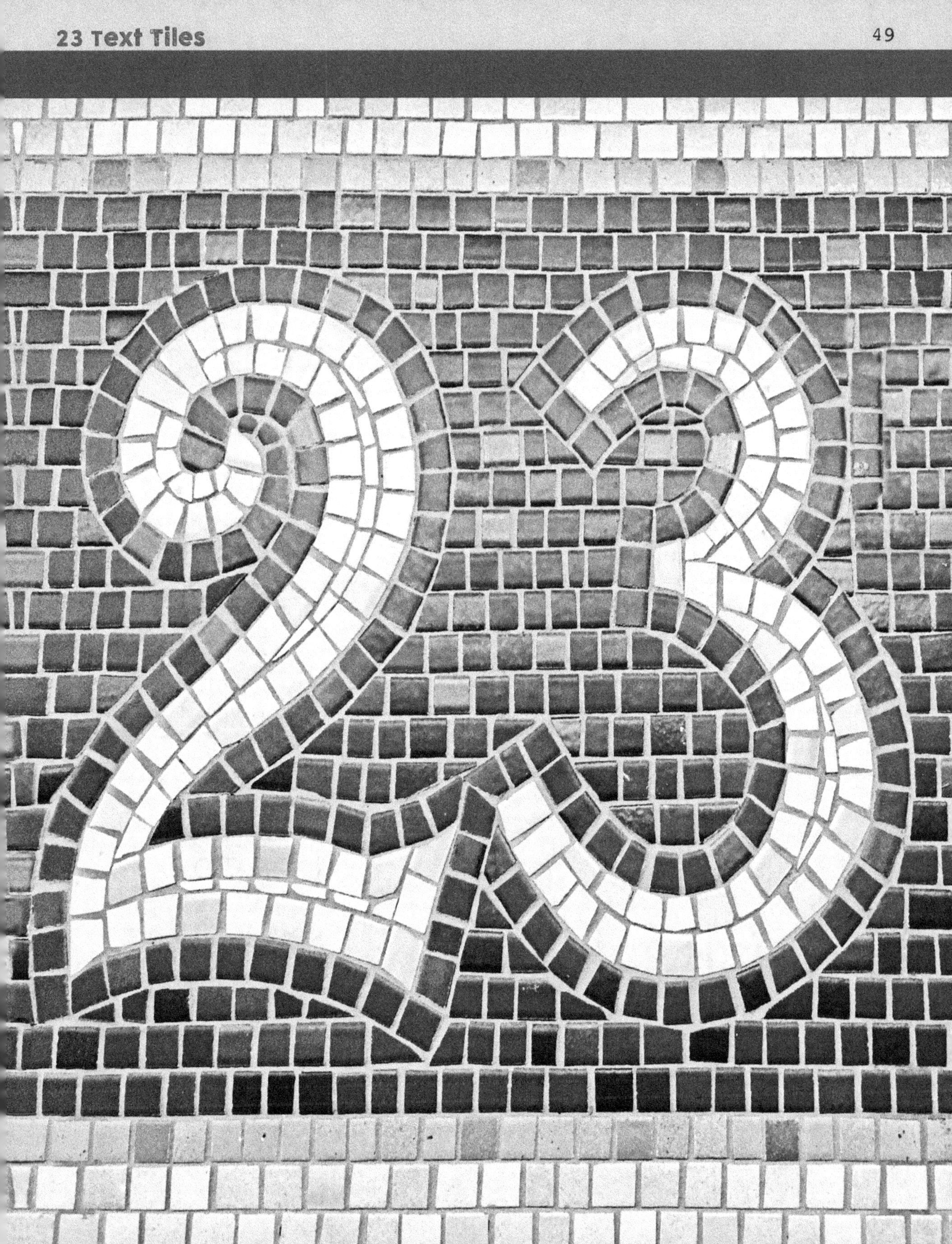

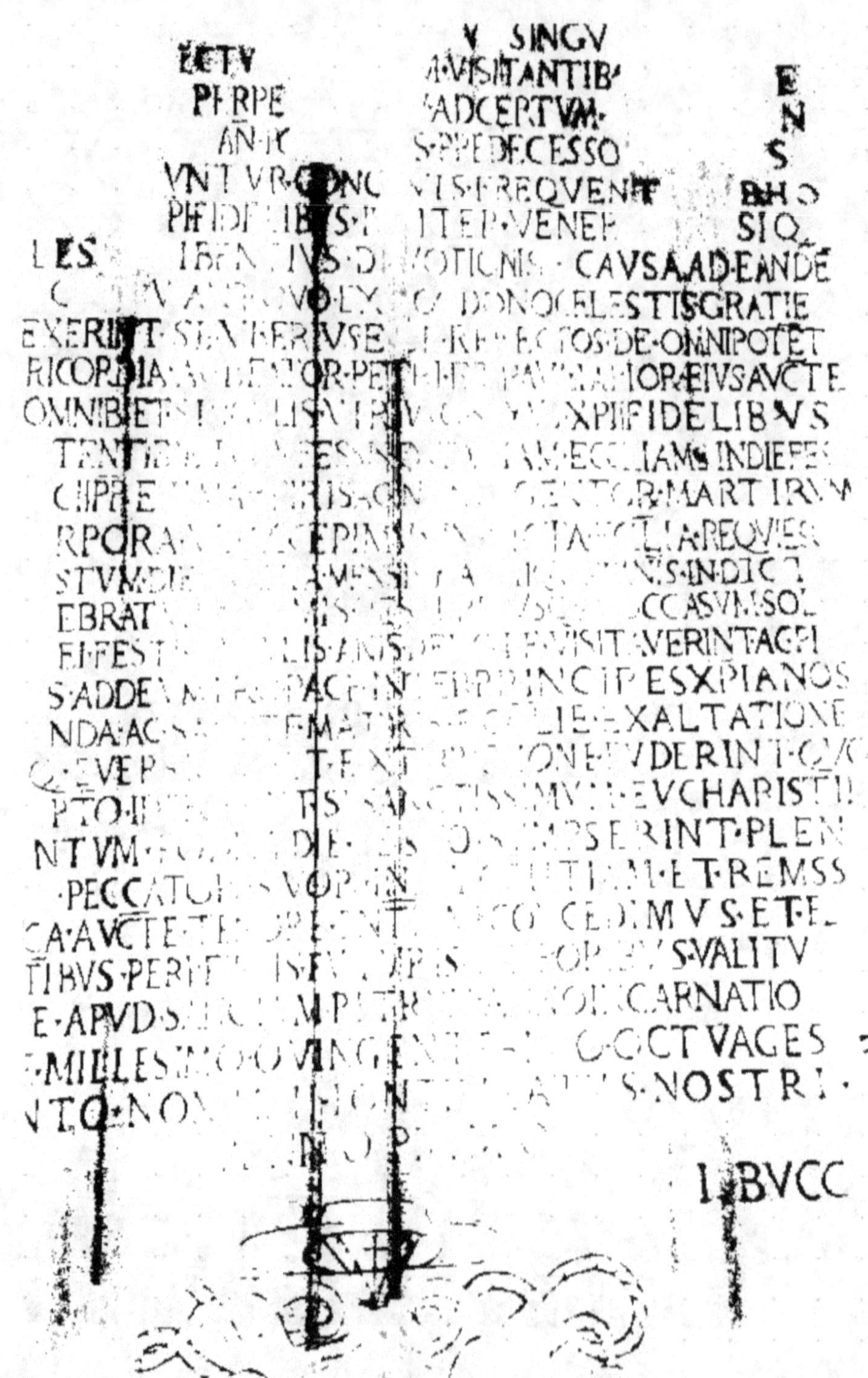

V SINGV
LCTV   A VISITANTIB
PERPE   ADCEPTVM   E
AN K   S PPDECESSO   N
VNTVRGONC   VIS FREQVENT   S
PFIDELIBVST   ITEP VENE   BH O
LES   IBENTIVS DEVOTIONIS CAVSAADEANDE SIQ
       VA   VOLX   DONOCELESTISGRATIE
EXERINT SENTERIVSE   REFECTOS DE OMNIPOTET
RICORDIA   DITOR PETIER PAROCHIORAEIVSAVCTE
OMNIBET LIS RIVC   XPIFIDELIBVS
TENTIB   ESS   AMECCLIAMS INDIEFE
CIPPE   RIS   ENTOR MARTIRVM
RPORA   CEPIN   TANCLIA REQVIES
STVMDIE   MENS   VS INDICT
EBRAT   OCCASVMSOL
EIFEST   LIS ANS EVISITAVERINTAGRI
S ADDE PACE INTERPRINCIPESXPIANOS
NDA AC TEMATR   LIE EXALTATIONE
   EVER   TEXT   ONEVDERINT QV
PTO II   RS SANCTISSIMV EVCHARISTI
NTVM   DE   OS MPSERINT PLEN
  PECCATOL SVOP N   VTI M ET REMSS
CA AVCTE TE RENT   CO CEDIMVS ET E
TIBVS PERF ISEV EPS   OP EVS VALITV
E APVD S   MPETR   CARNATIO
MILLESIMO OVING   CCCTVAGES
NTO NON   S NOSTRI
           N O P
                              LIBVCC

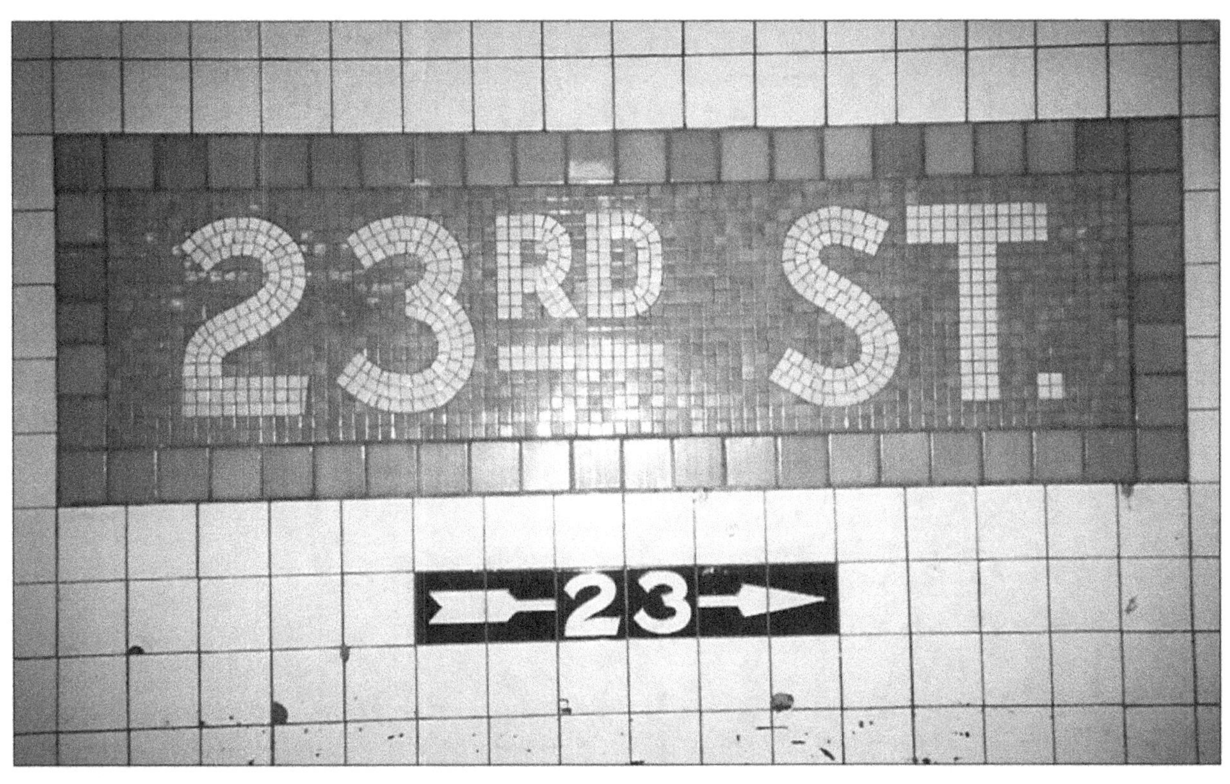
23RD ST.
23

Oyster (i)ceberg

(at **0** there is no resolution or awareness).

vibrations in the ether project images of the outside world on the semi-permeable membrane of the retina.

at **1** (i) see ℏ times ℏ resolution.

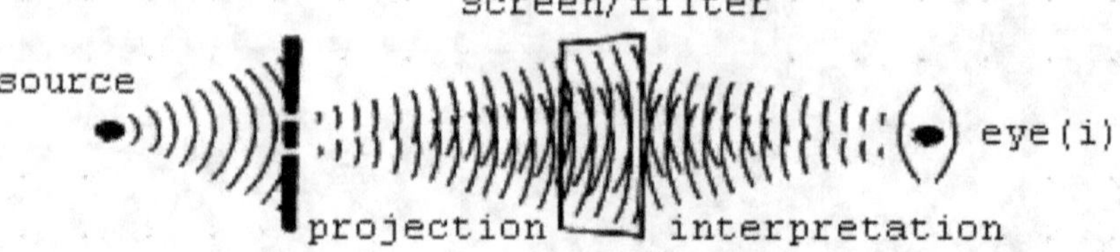

at **2** (i) see 2ℏ times 2ℏ resolution.

(at this point ℏ is an arbitrary constant, ℏ=h/2π).

at **3** (i) see 4ℏ times 4ℏ resolution.

(i) am able to see my own body. (i) have 10 fingers on 2 hands.

at **4** (i) see 16ℏ times 16ℏ resolution.

at **5** (i) see 256ℏ times 256ℏ resolution.

(my father told me not to stare into the sun (of course (i) did))

at **6** (i) see 65536ℏ times 65536ℏ resolution.

at **7** (i) see in 4294967296ℏ times 4294967296ℏ resolution.

at **8** (i) see in 18446744073709551616ℏ times 18446744073709551616ℏ resolution.

i am aware   that i am aware

where

$$\hat{A}[\Sigma]\,|S\rangle = \left(\frac{\ell_0^2}{2}\sum_{i\in\{S\cap\Sigma\}}\sqrt{p_i(p_i+2)}\right)|S\rangle$$

== eye witness

i labels the intersections between the spin network S and the surface Σ and p_i is the color of the link of *Snake* crossing the i-*th* intersection.

at **9** (i) see in 340282366920938463463374607431773405143ℏ times 340282366920938463463374607431773405143ℏ resolution.

at **10** (i) see in 39402006196394479212279040110144952999305948135 83 950250204903024066503980923809098134098148095005034169603493 09542 times 394020061963944792122790401101449529993059481358395 025020490302406650398092380909813409814809500503416960349309542 resolution.

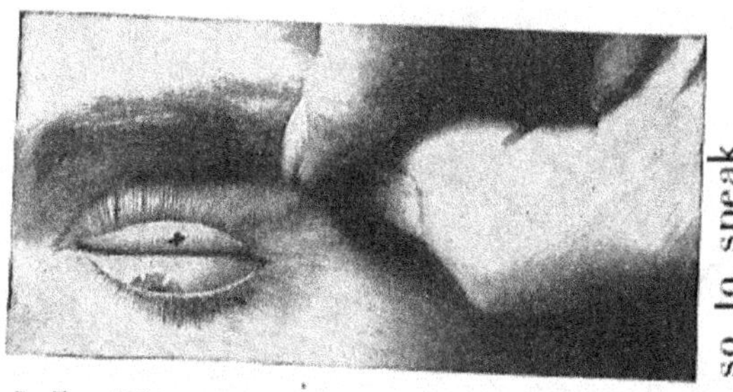

5. By this means the lid is turned inside out

at **15** (i) see in a continuous spectrum, perfect resolution.

you can never see your own eyelids. there are 6400000 cones in the retina. there are 120000000 rods in the retina.

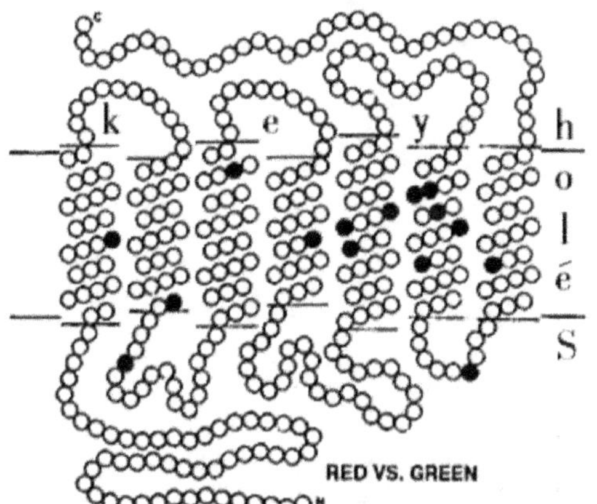

at **20** in Caye Caulker a crab etched side-winder tracks in the sands of my protein-based memory

at **25** in Hueco Tanks (i) climbed the sea of holes, placing only 1 #3 cam in a bird nest.

at **30** (i) spent **40** days in the whiteness of the Arctic Circle followed by a fortnight in the Everglades. The water moccasin chokes on its own tail in an effort to understand. Only when it is dead do I see the scales up close... they are discrete units of space and time tinged with immediate recency.

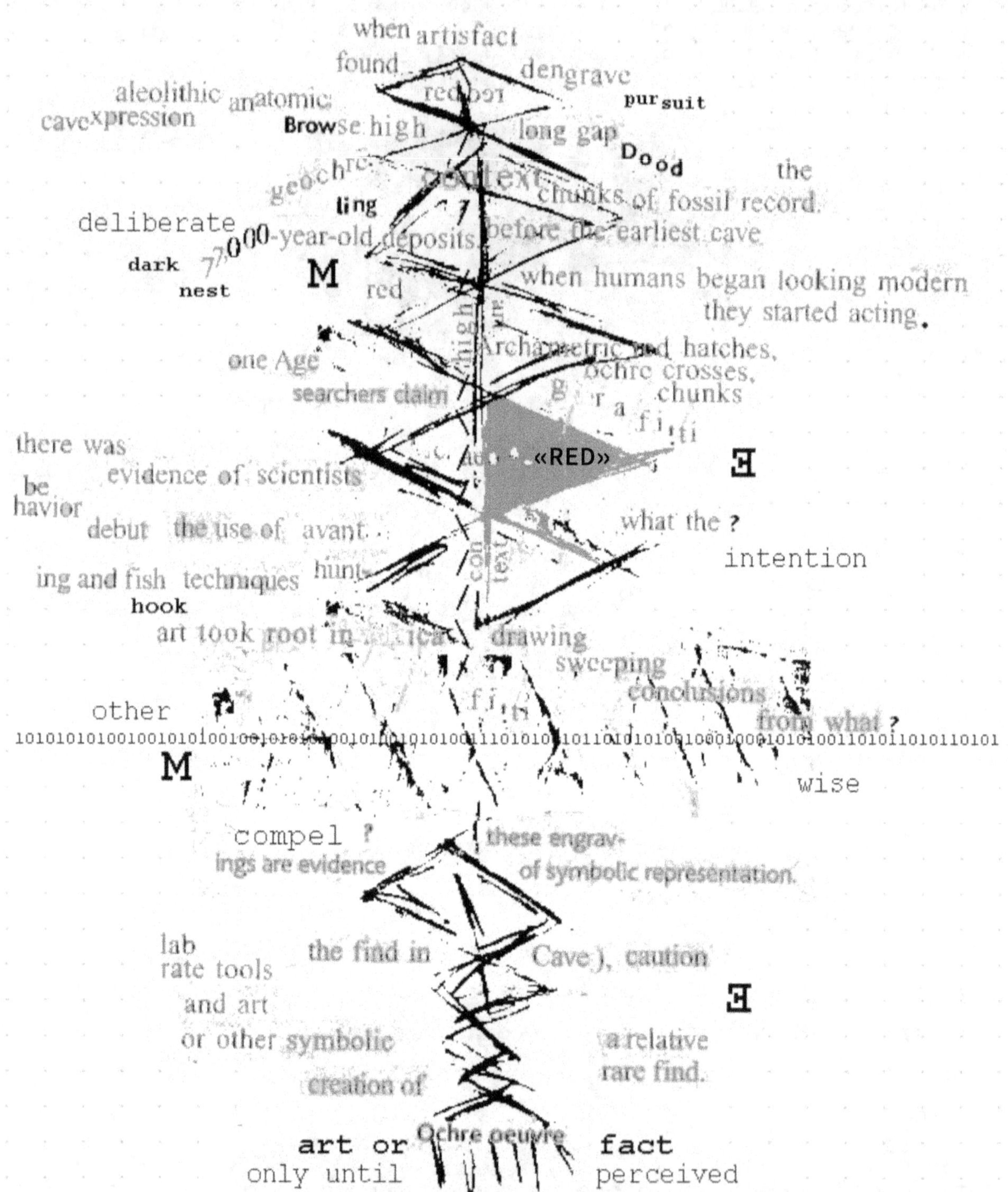
when artisfact
found
dengrave
aleolithic anatomic
pur suit
cavexpression
Brow se high
long gap
Do od
the
geochro
context
chunks of fossil record.
ling
deliberate
7,000-year-old deposits.
before the earliest cave
dark
M red
when humans began looking modern
nest
they started acting.
Archametric red hatches,
one Age
ochre crosses,
searchers claim
g r a chunks
f i ti
there was
«RED»
Ǝ
be
evidence of scientists
havior
debut the use of avant
what the ?
intention
ing and fish techniques hunt
hook
art took root in Africa drawing
sweeping
other
conclusions
f i ti
from what ?
1010101010010010101001001010101001011010101101101010101000100100101010011010110101101
M
wise
compel ?
these engrav-
ings are evidence
of symbolic representation.
lab
the find in
Cave), caution
rate tools
and art
Ǝ
or other symbolic
a relative
rare find.
creation of
art or
Ochre oeuvre
fact
only until
perceived

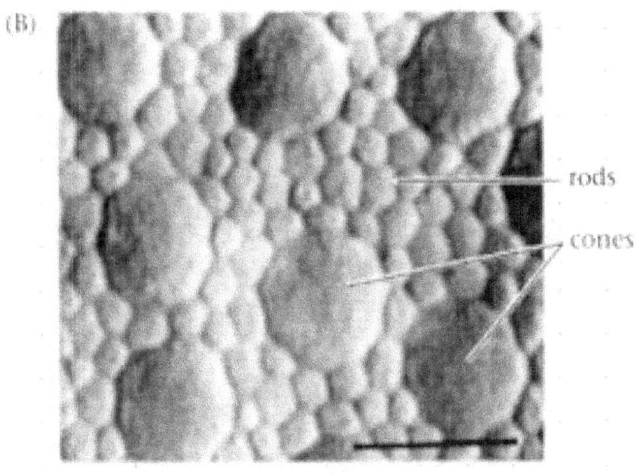

Exhibit B

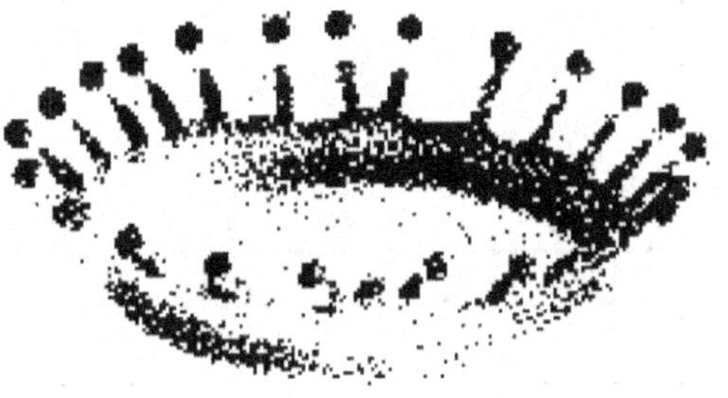

Exhibit C

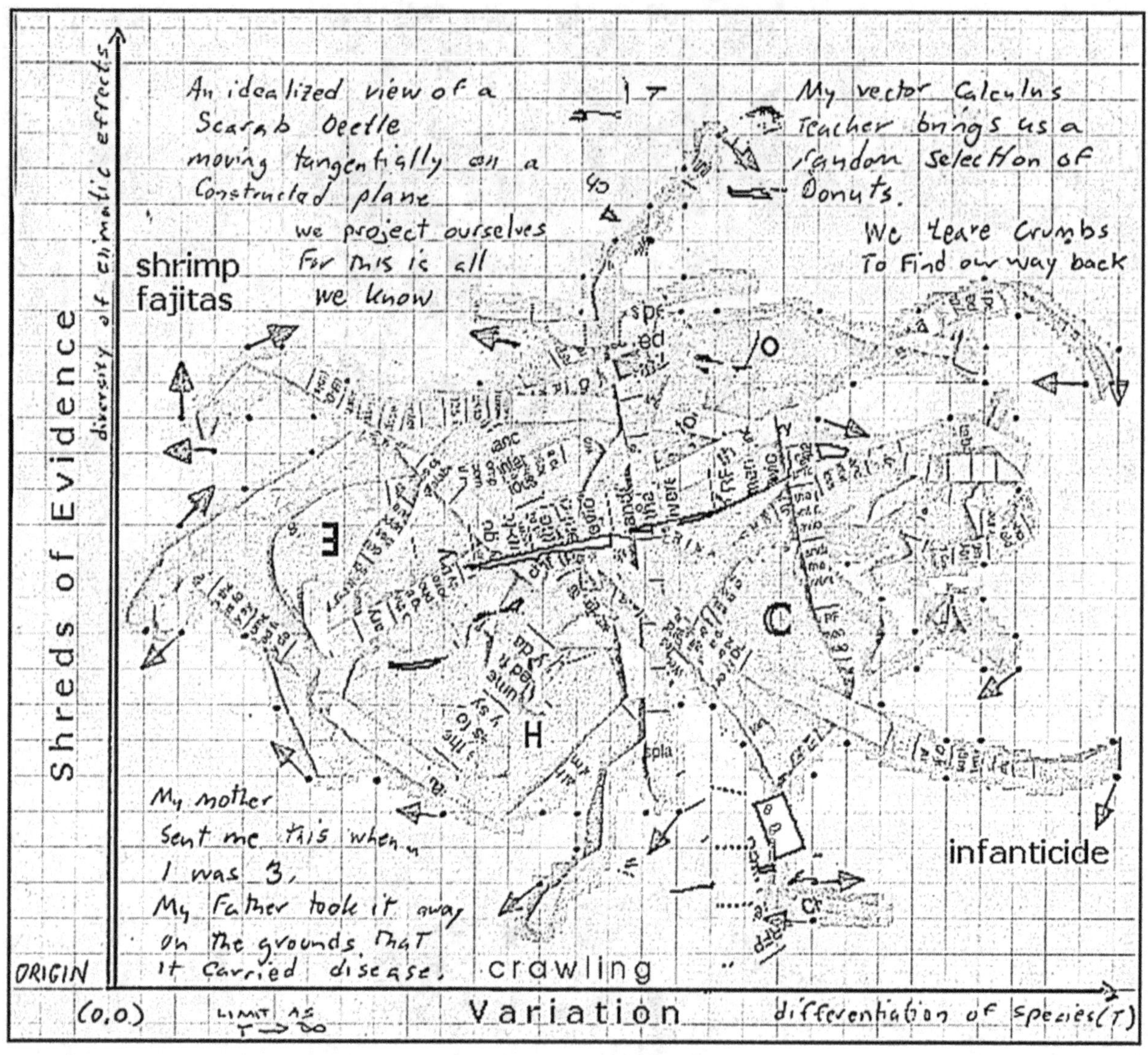
Shreds of Evidence
diversity of climatic effects
An idealized view of a
Scarab beetle
moving tangentially on a
Constructed plane
we project ourselves
For this is all
we know
shrimp
fajitas
My vector Calculus
Teacher brings us a
random selection of
Donuts.
We leave Crumbs
To Find our way back
My mother
sent me this when
I was 3,
My Father took it away
On the grounds that
it carried disease.
crawling
infanticide
ORIGIN
(0,0)
LIMIT AS
T → ∞
Variation
differentiation of species (T)

Dispatch#	Vehicle Information					Storage In Date	Storage Out Date	Lot#	Keys Info
221573	01 TOYT COA GRN Lic#CA4RHW236 1MX8R12E81Z551294					11/01/01	11/01/01	2	N
Purchase Order Number	Vehicle Towed From					Vehicle Towed To			
	5525 W. WILSHIRE BLVD					2400 W WASHINGTON			

Calling Acct#	Reference#	Member#		Expires	R-Type	Rec	Inrt	Arvd	Intow	Clear	Tag#
DOT	SELF					08:34	08:34	08:34	08:34	08:45	SPACE

Driver	Truck	Quantity	Density	Item Description	Unit Price	Extended Price
4	304	1.00	Fixed	L.A. D.O.T. IMPOUND	86.00	86.00
4	304	1.00	Fabricated	CITY OF L.A. RELEASE FEE	40.00	40.00

no
WHERE
to
go
no
WHERE
to
StoP....

every
ONE
in their own
vehicle
no car pool
lane
every ONE
alONE
no ONE
walks

isolated i
see the streets
peering be
tween
venetian
blinds

there goes my
vehicle and i
am not in it.

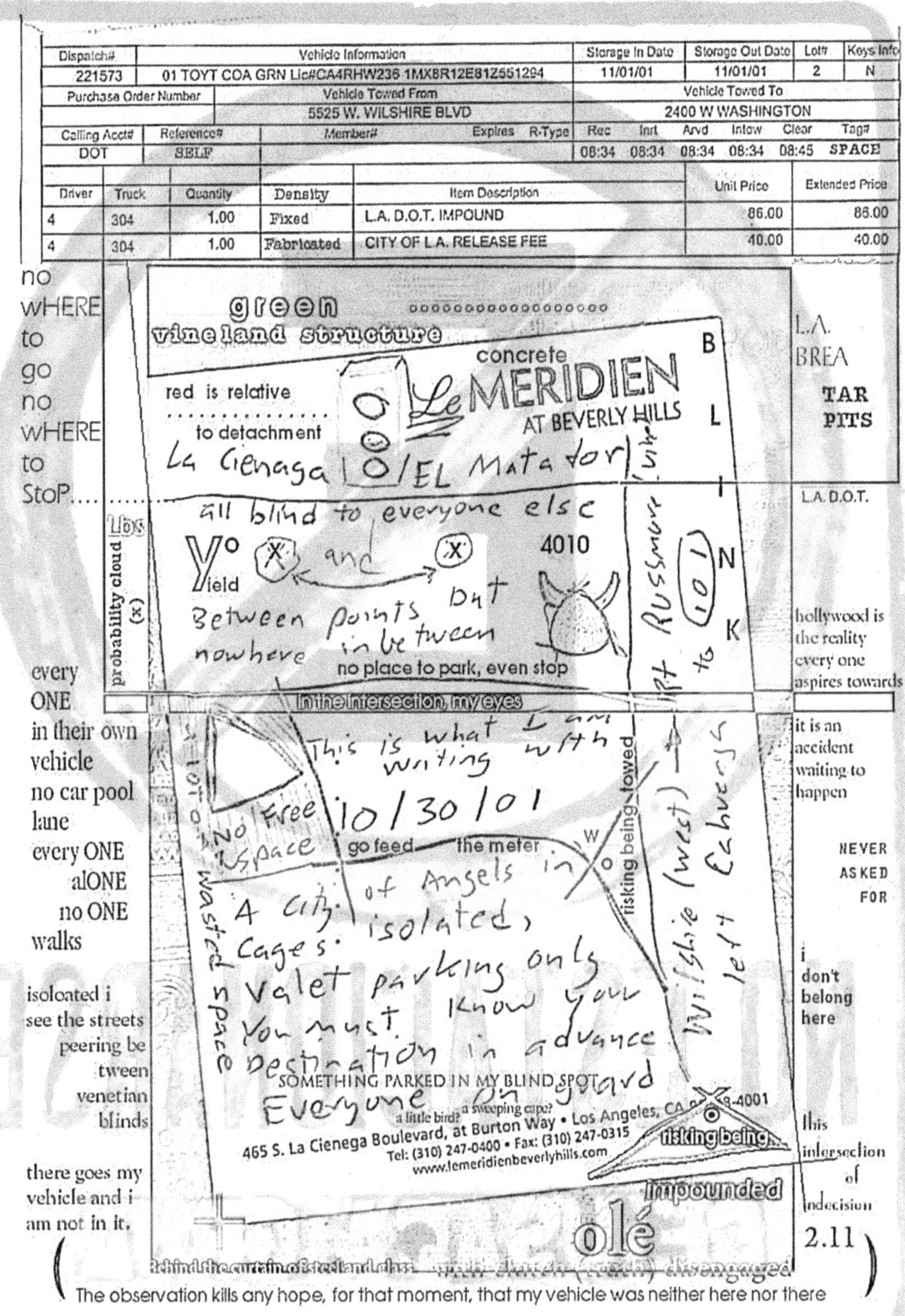

The observation kills any hope, for that moment, that my vehicle was neither here nor there

Red **Berry** in the Trees

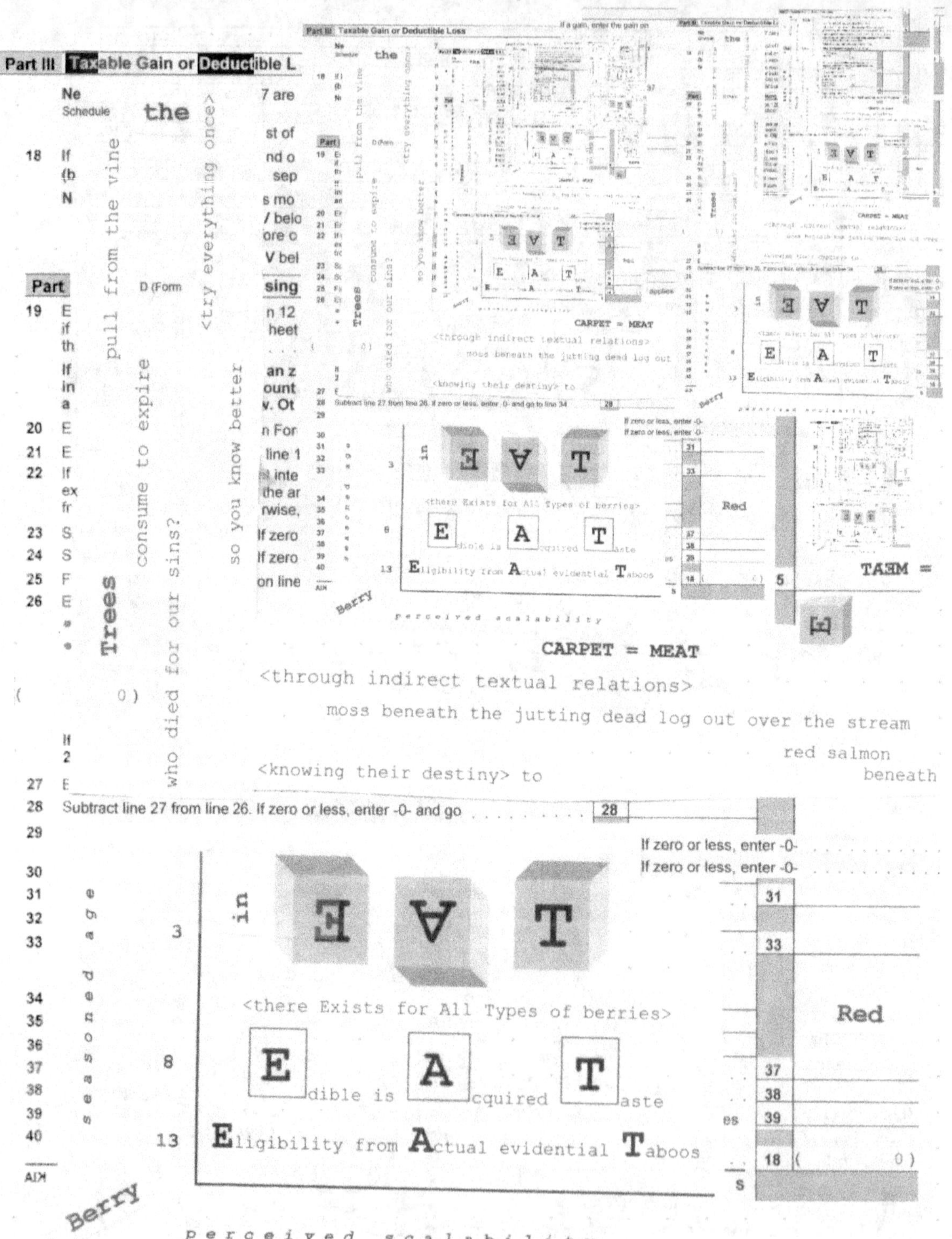

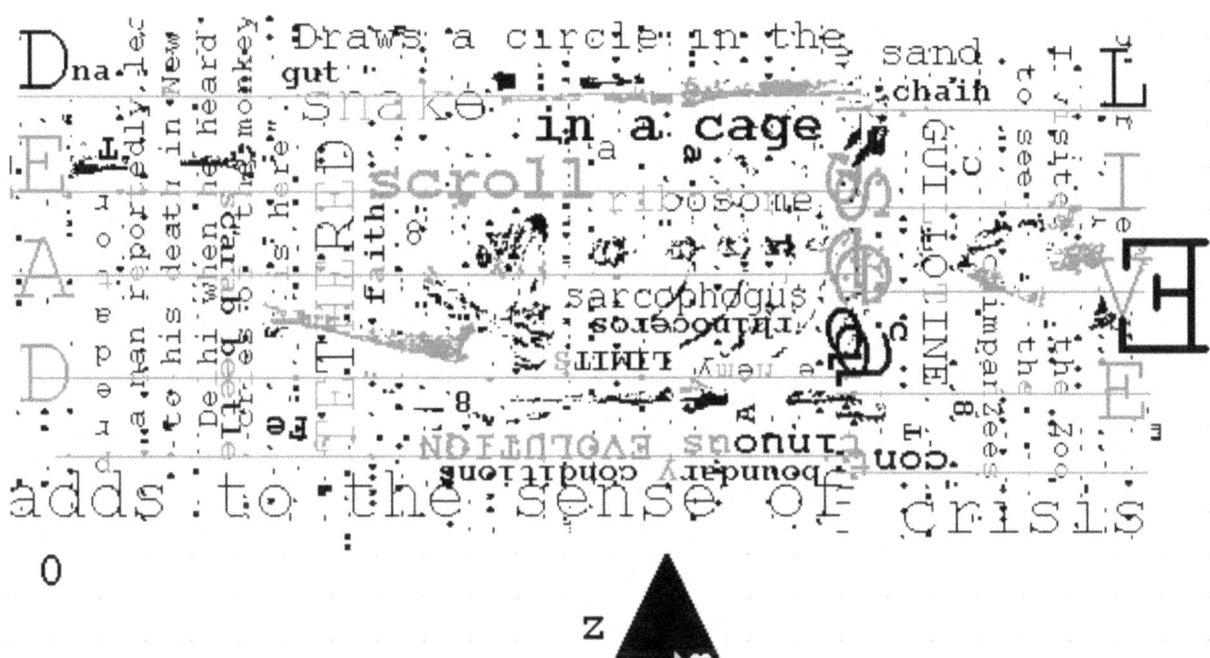
Dna
Draws a circle in the sand.
gut
snake
in a cage
chain
scroll
ribosome
faith
TETHERED
sarcophagus
rhinoceros
LIMITS
GUILLOTINE
DEAD
LIVE
EVOLUTION
continuous
boundary conditions
adds to the sense of crisis
monkey
New
a man reportedly, led to his death in
when he heard
here's here
to see the zoo
the chimpanzees
If i sit
0
Z

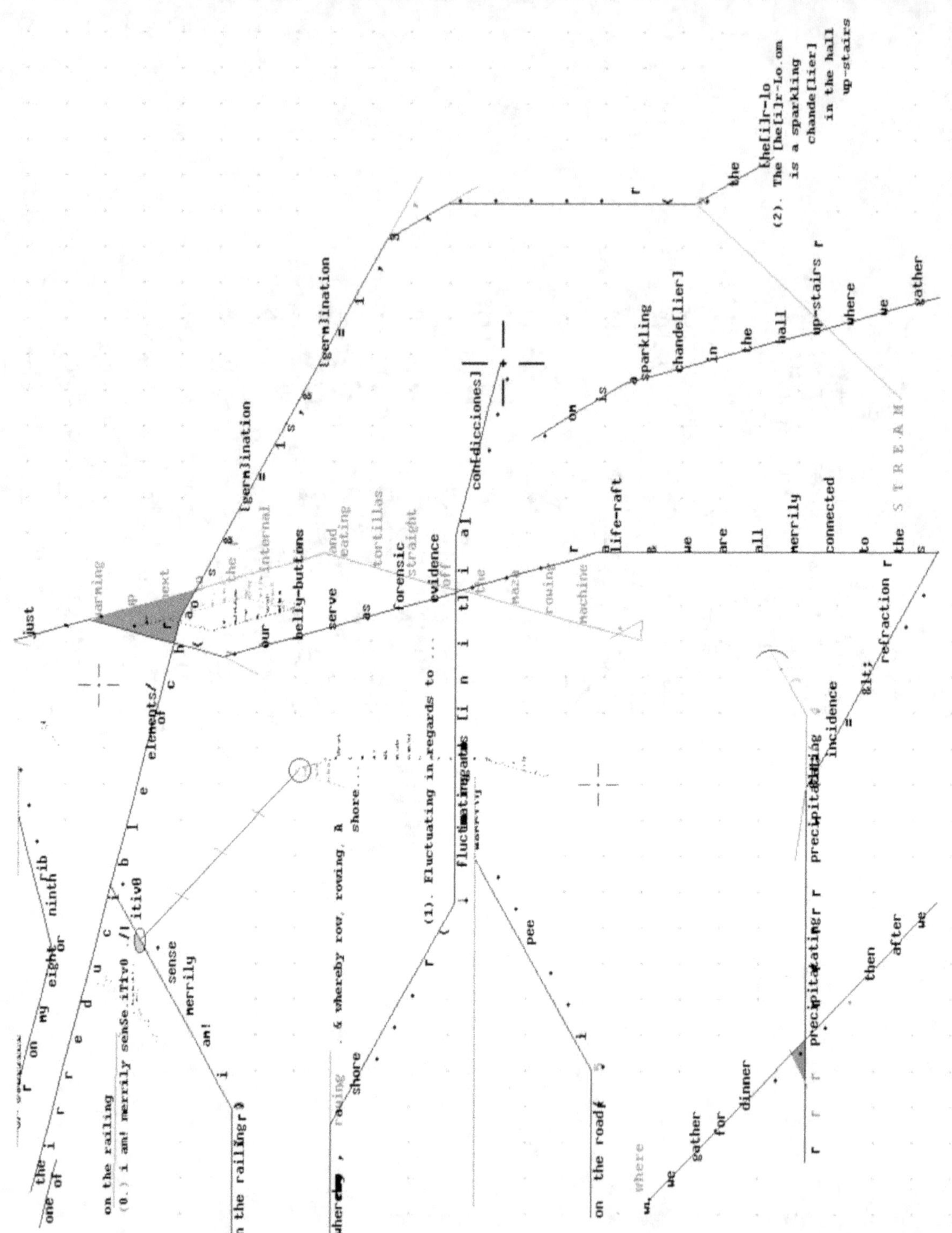
just
warming
up
next
the elements/ of chaos
ninth rib
eight
or
on my
the l i r e d u c
itiv8
/l
one of
on the railing
(0.) i am! merrily senSe.iTiv0
on the railing r8
sense
merrily
i am!
i
[germ]ination
[germ]ination
is 'a
II
the internal
belly-buttons
and
eating
tortillas
serve
as
forensic
straight
evidence off
[i n i t] i a l
confidicciones
the
max
rowing
machine
life-raft
a
we
are
all
merrily
connected
to
the STREAM
s
on
is
sparkling
chande[lier]
in
the
hall
up-stairs r
where
we
gather
the
the[ilr-lo
The [he[ilr-Lo.om
is a sparkling
chande[lier]
in the hall
up-stairs
(2). The
on
whereby,
rowing . & whereby row, rowing, A
shore...
shore
(1). Fluctuating in regards to ...
fluctuatingatds
worsely
pee
incidence
<t;
refraction r
precipitating r
precipitating r
then
after
we
where
we gather for dinner
on the road
r r r

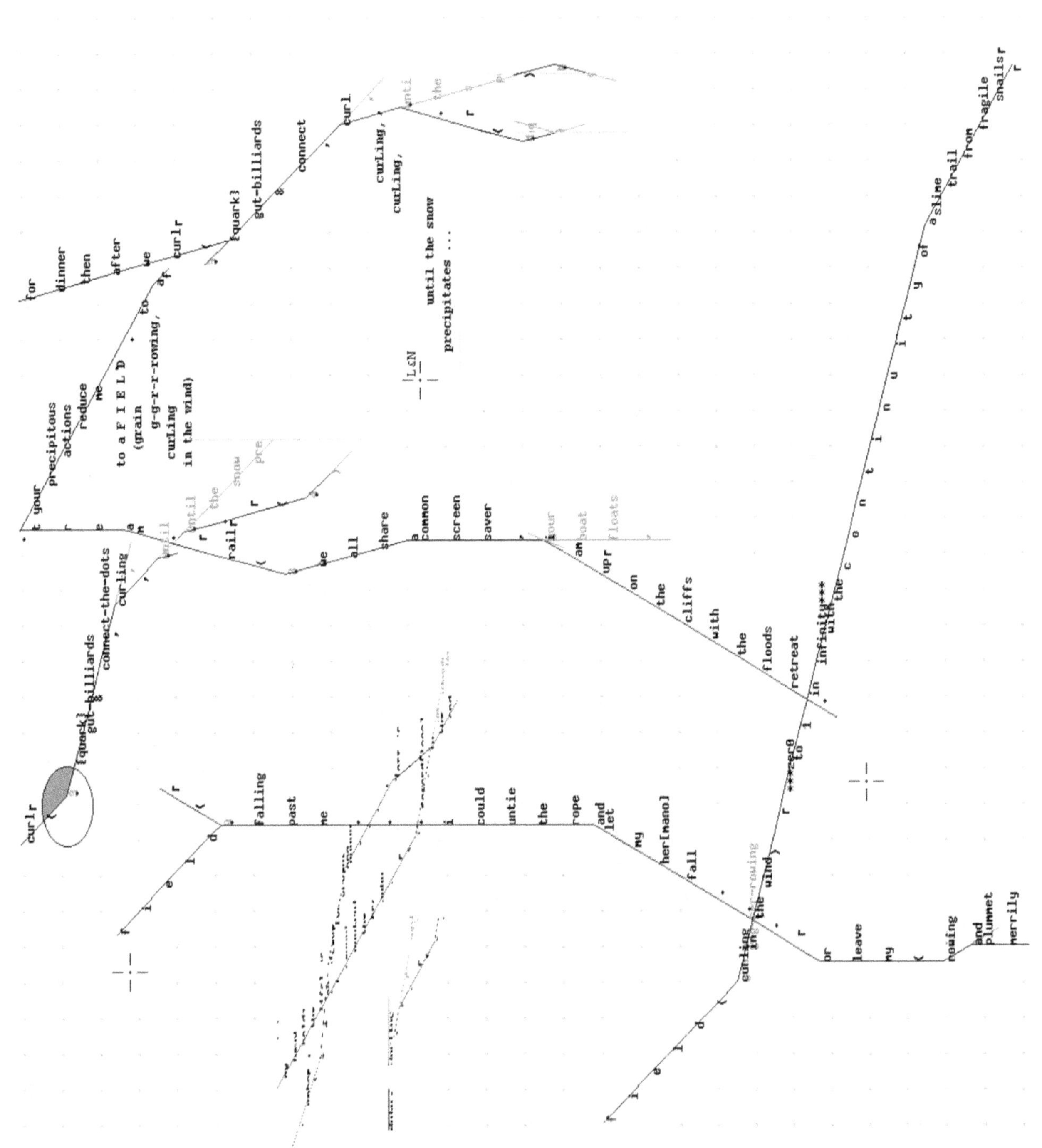
for
dinner
then
after
we
curl
{quark}
gut-billiards
&
connect
curl
curling,
curling,
until the snow
precipitates ...
|L&N
your
precipitous
actions
reduce
me
to a FIELD
(grain
g-g-r-r-rowing,
curling
in the wind)
until
the
snow
pre
trail
we
all
share
a
common
screen
saver
your
am boat
upr
floats
on
the
cliffs
with
the
floods
retreat
a s|ine
trail
from
fragile
snails r
r
c o n t i n u i t y   o f
in infinity***
with the
***zer0
to 1
curl r
{quark} billiards
gut &
connect-the-dots
curling
f
i
e
l
d
Falling
past
e
i
could
untie
the
rope
and
let
my
her[nano]
fall
curling in the wind)
r
or
leave
my
rowing
and
plummet
merrily
curl r
(

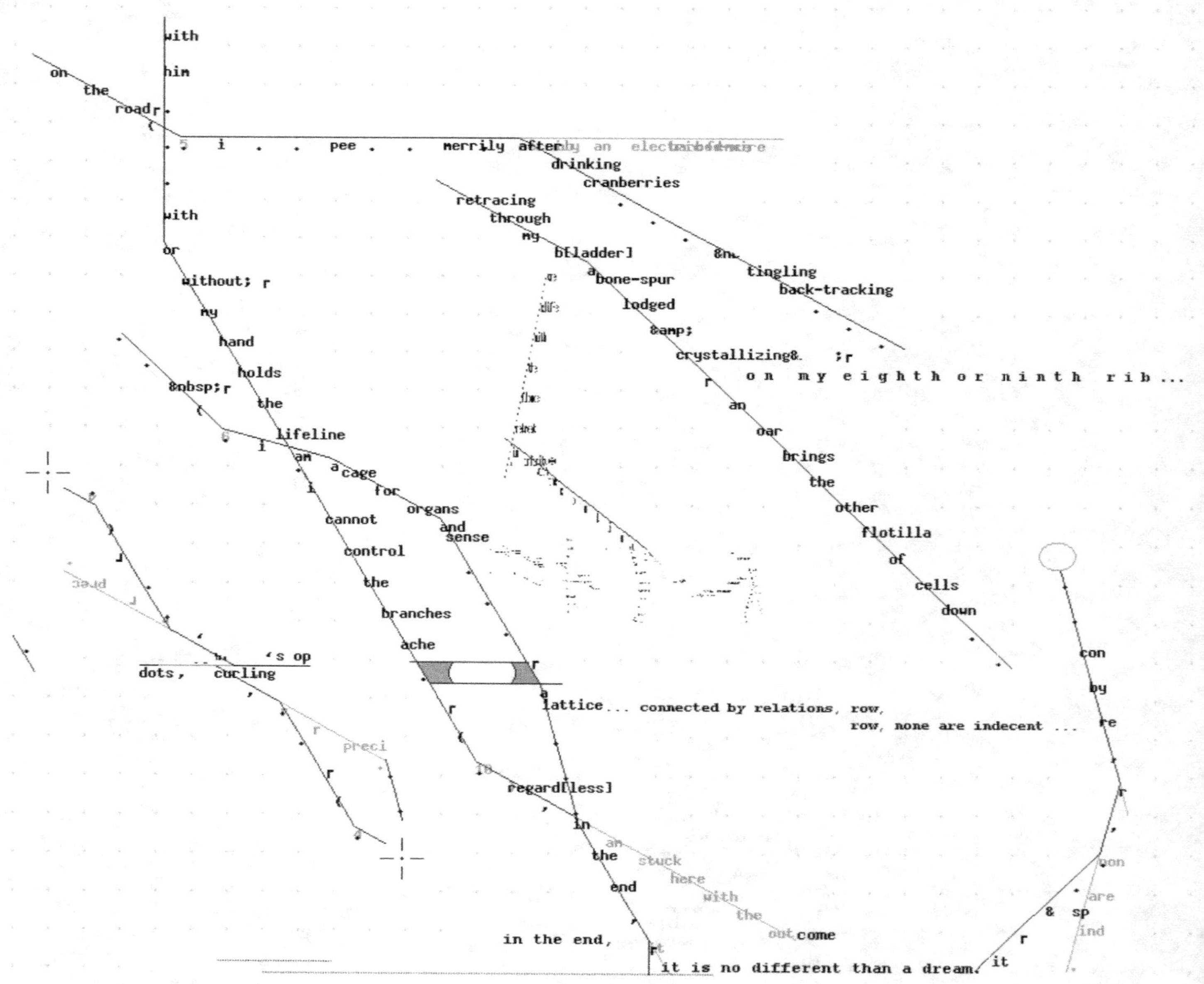
with
him
on the road r. (
5 i . . pee . . merrily after|by an electricshiwire
drinking
cranberries
with
retracing
through
my
or
b[ladder]
&n tingling
without; r
a bone-spur
back-tracking
my
lodged
hand
&
holds
crystallizing& ;r
 r
the
r on my eighth or ninth rib...
lifeline
i am
a cage
an
for
oar
organs
brings
and sense
the
cannot
other
control
flotilla
the
of
branches
cells
ache
down
con
by
dots, curling 's op
lattice... connected by relations, row,
row, none are indecent ...
re
r preci
regard[less]
in
an
the stuck
here
end with
the
out come
r
pon
are
& sp
ind
r
in the end, it
it is no different than a dream. it

And where does man *not* stand at an abyss?
Is seeing itself not seeing *abysses*?
—Nietzsche

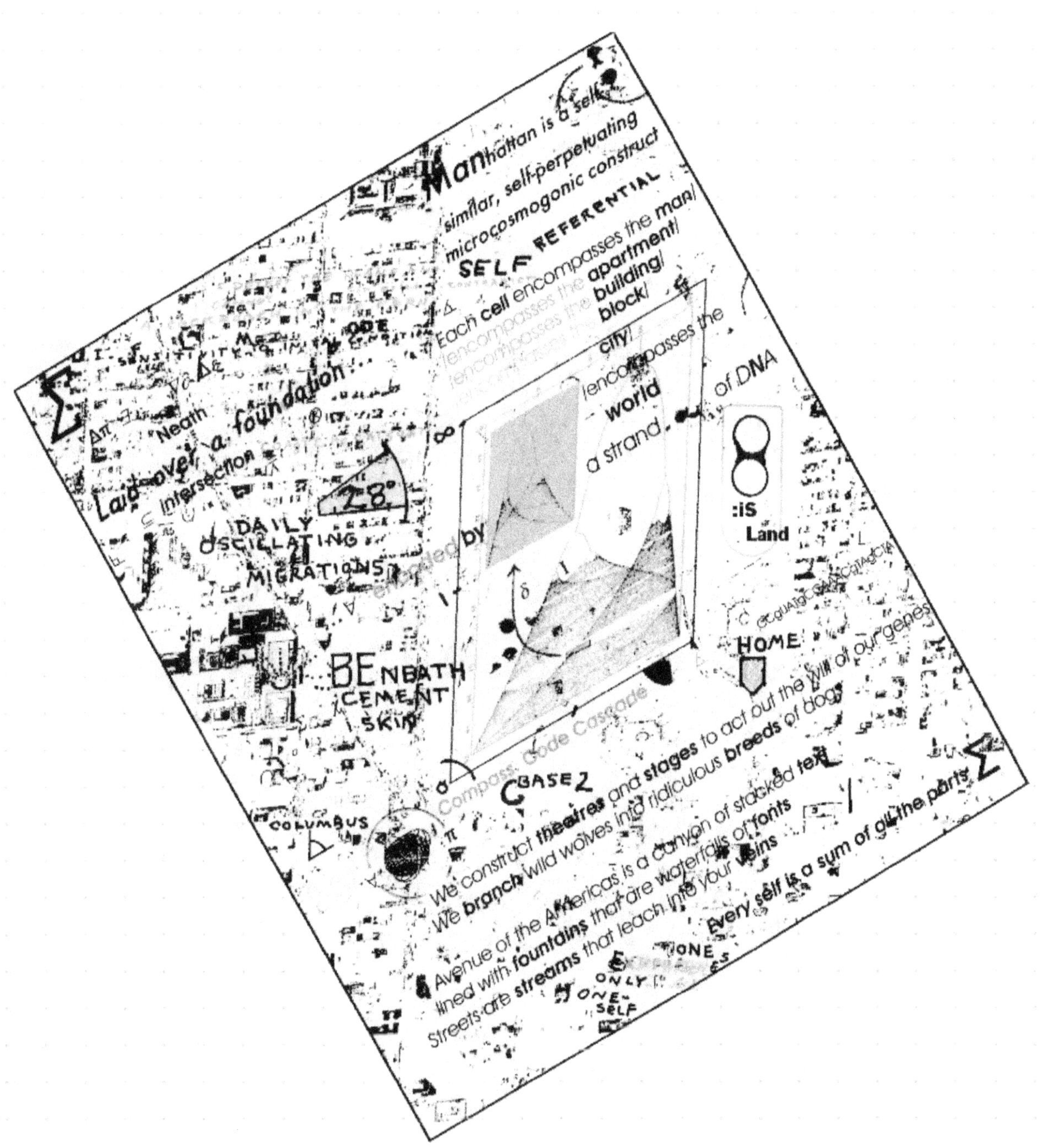

My Gallo Comb Ballanced

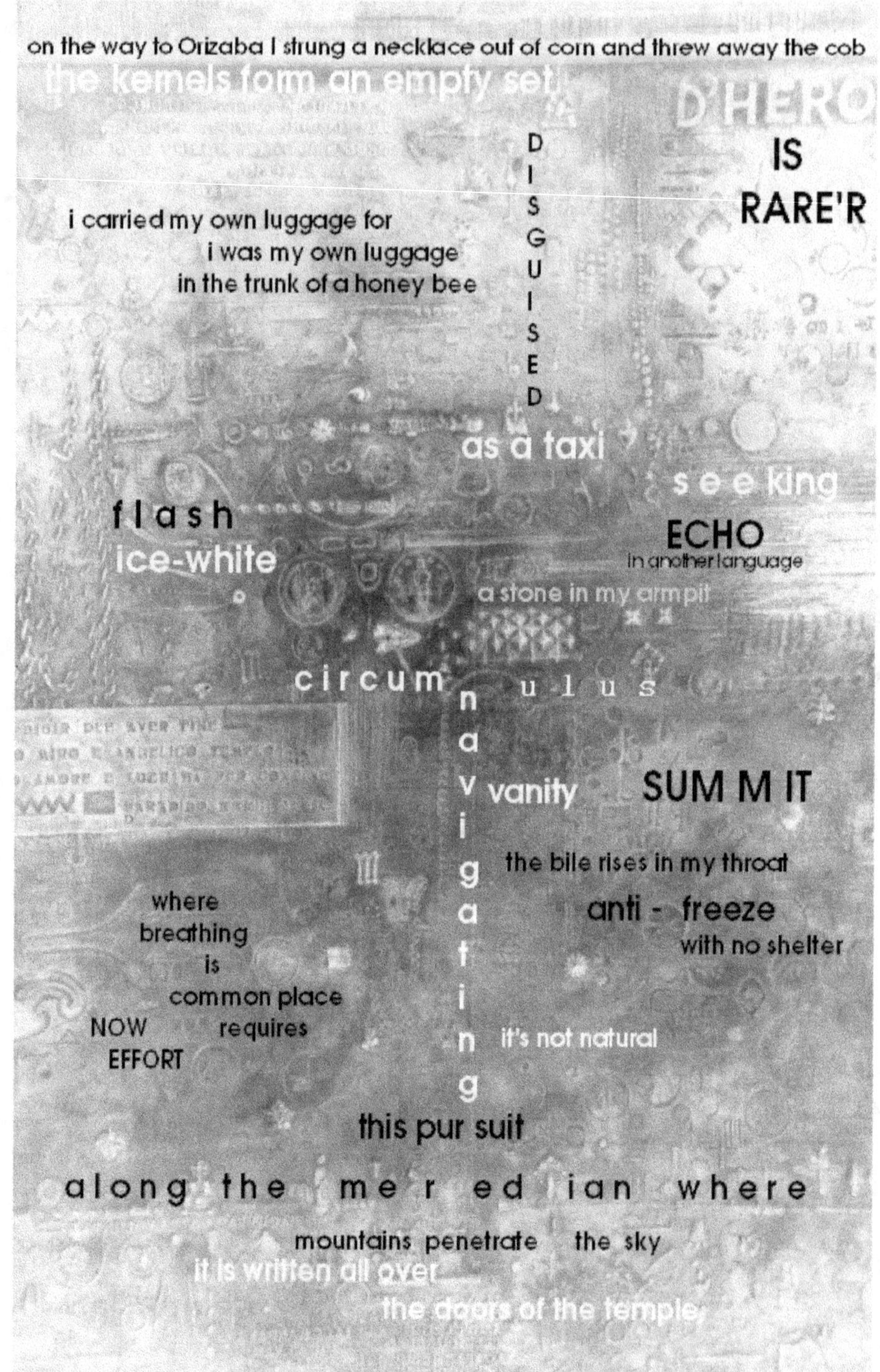

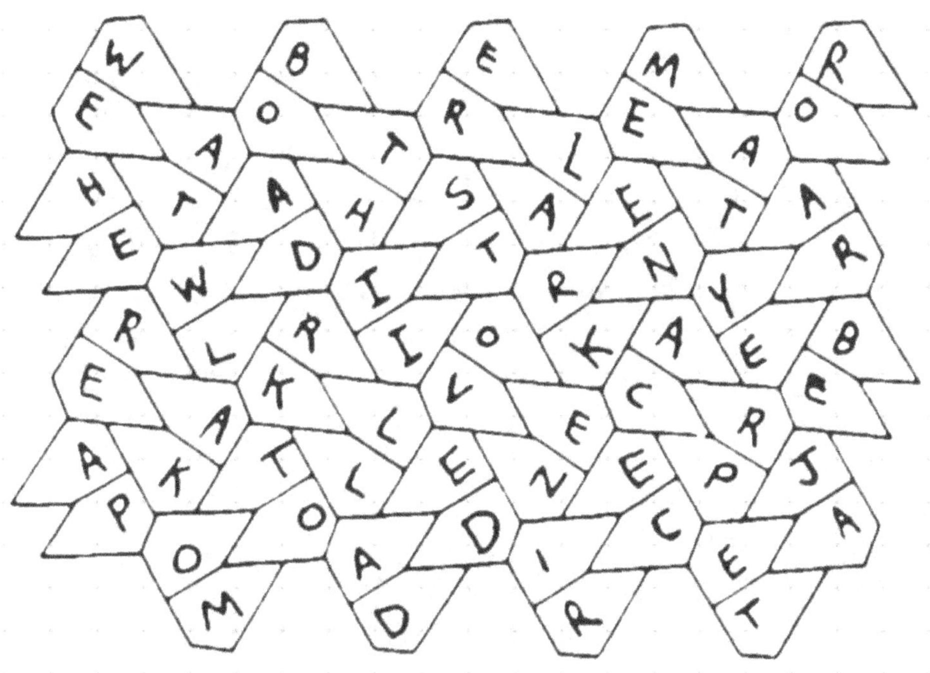

Riding the Croupier

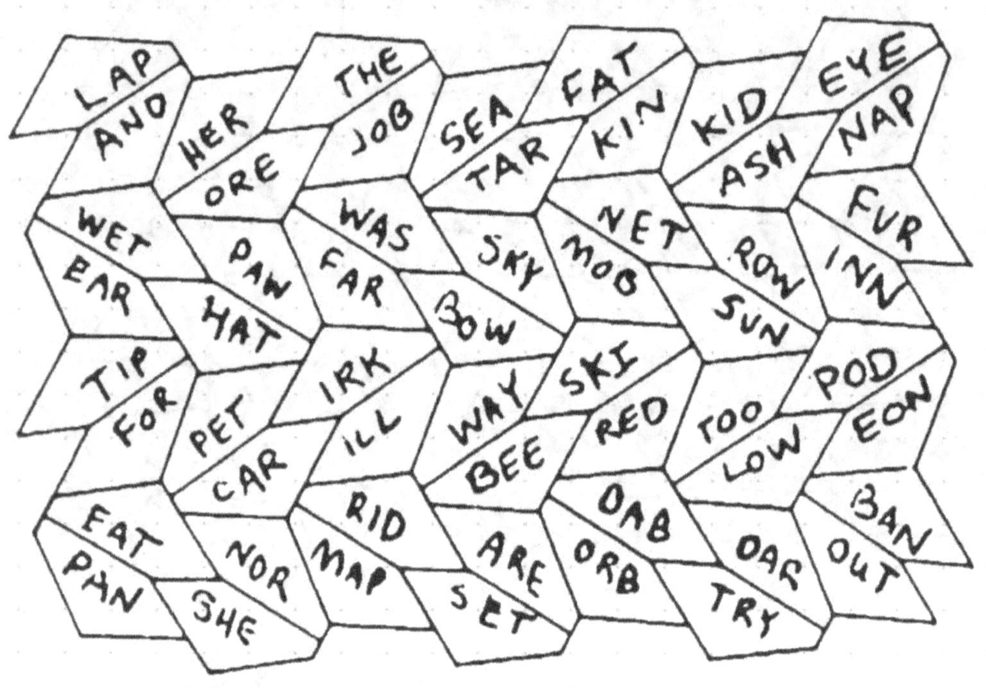

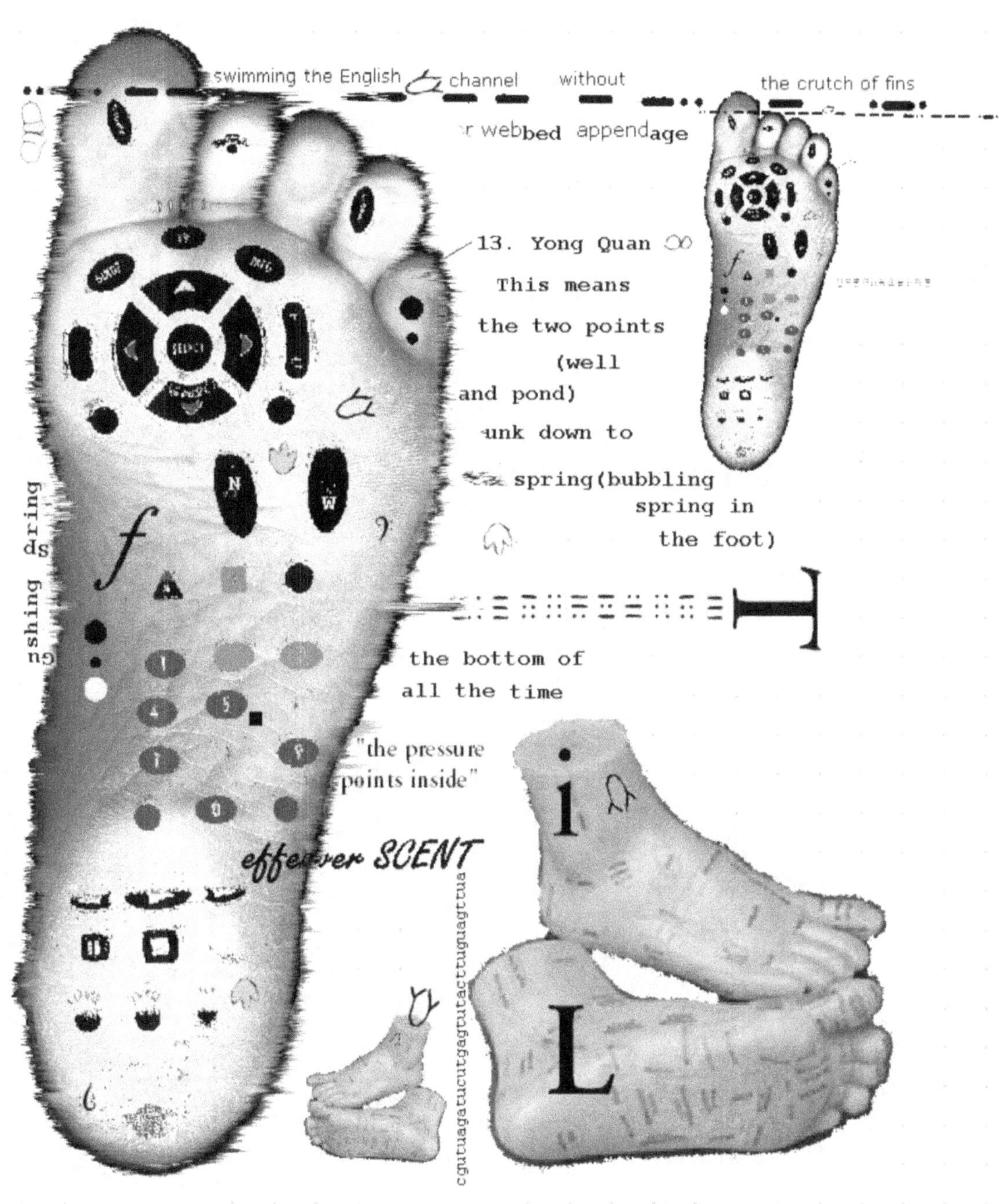
swimming the English channel without the crutch of fins
r webbed appendage
13. Yong Quan
This means
the two points
(well
and pond)
unk down to
spring(bubbling
spring in
the foot)
the bottom of
all the time
"the pressure
points inside"
effeover SCENT
i
L

Umbrella Heirloom

behold a map to our garden in my left palm

dandelion in my right

Wishing to go back to a warm Womb

a Life other

than where here

disperse the seeds with my breath

breathing

touch

Spider

on the lawn where I rolled

a snowman last January

expansion

dispersion

a Roman candle catches flame

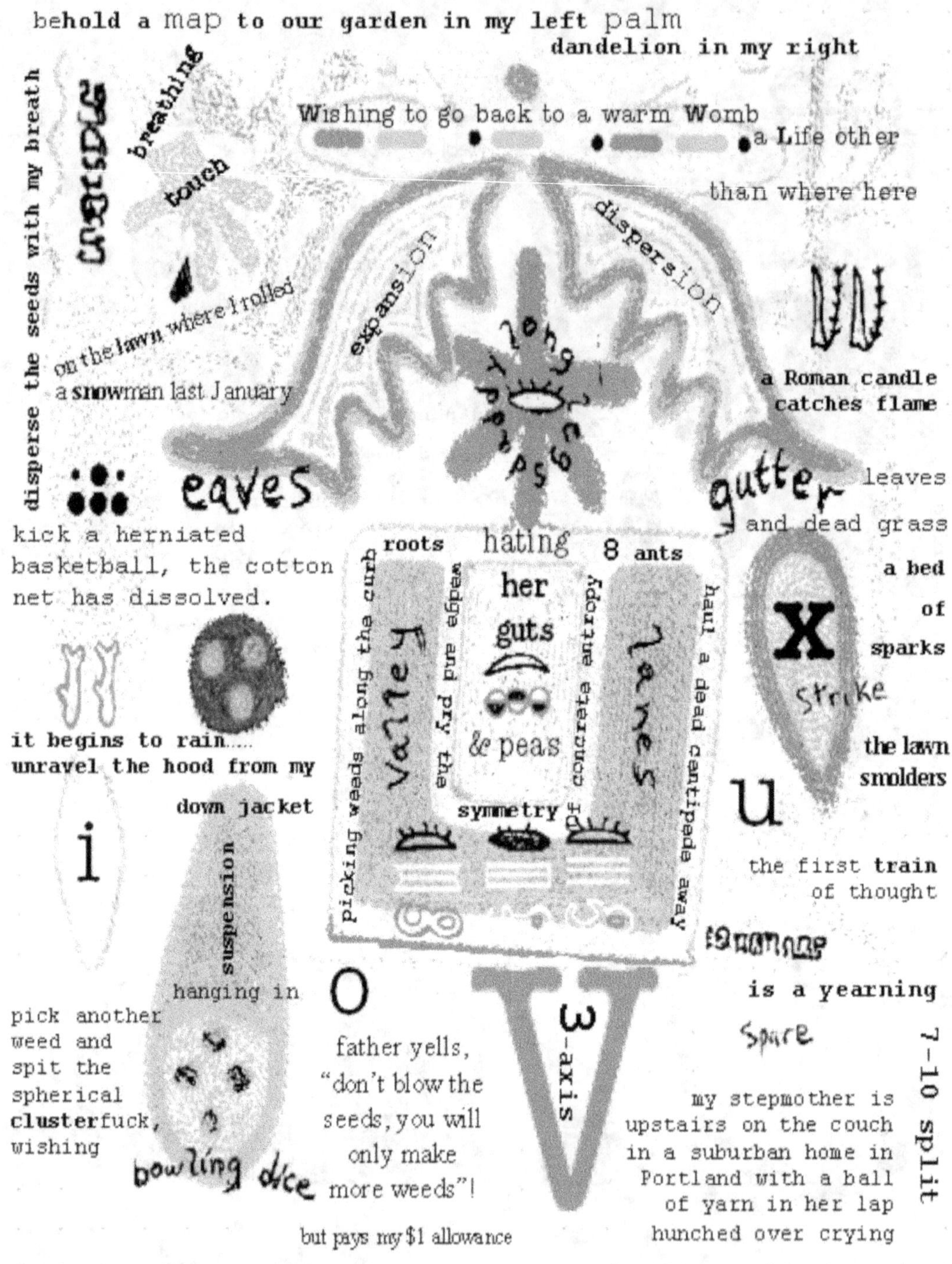

eaves

leaves

and dead grass

kick a herniated basketball, the cotton net has dissolved.

a bed
of
sparks

gutter

Strike

it begins to rain.....
unravel the hood from my

down jacket

the lawn smolders

i

suspension

the first train
of thought

hanging in

is a yearning

Spare

pick another
weed and
spit the
spherical
clusterfuck,
wishing

bowling dice

O

father yells,
"don't blow the
seeds, you will
only make
more weeds"!

3-axis

V

7-10 split

my stepmother is
upstairs on the couch
in a suburban home in
Portland with a ball
of yarn in her lap
hunched over crying

but pays my $1 allowance

makes me wonder why we bother in the first place?

(when it keeps out the rain you can't see the stars)

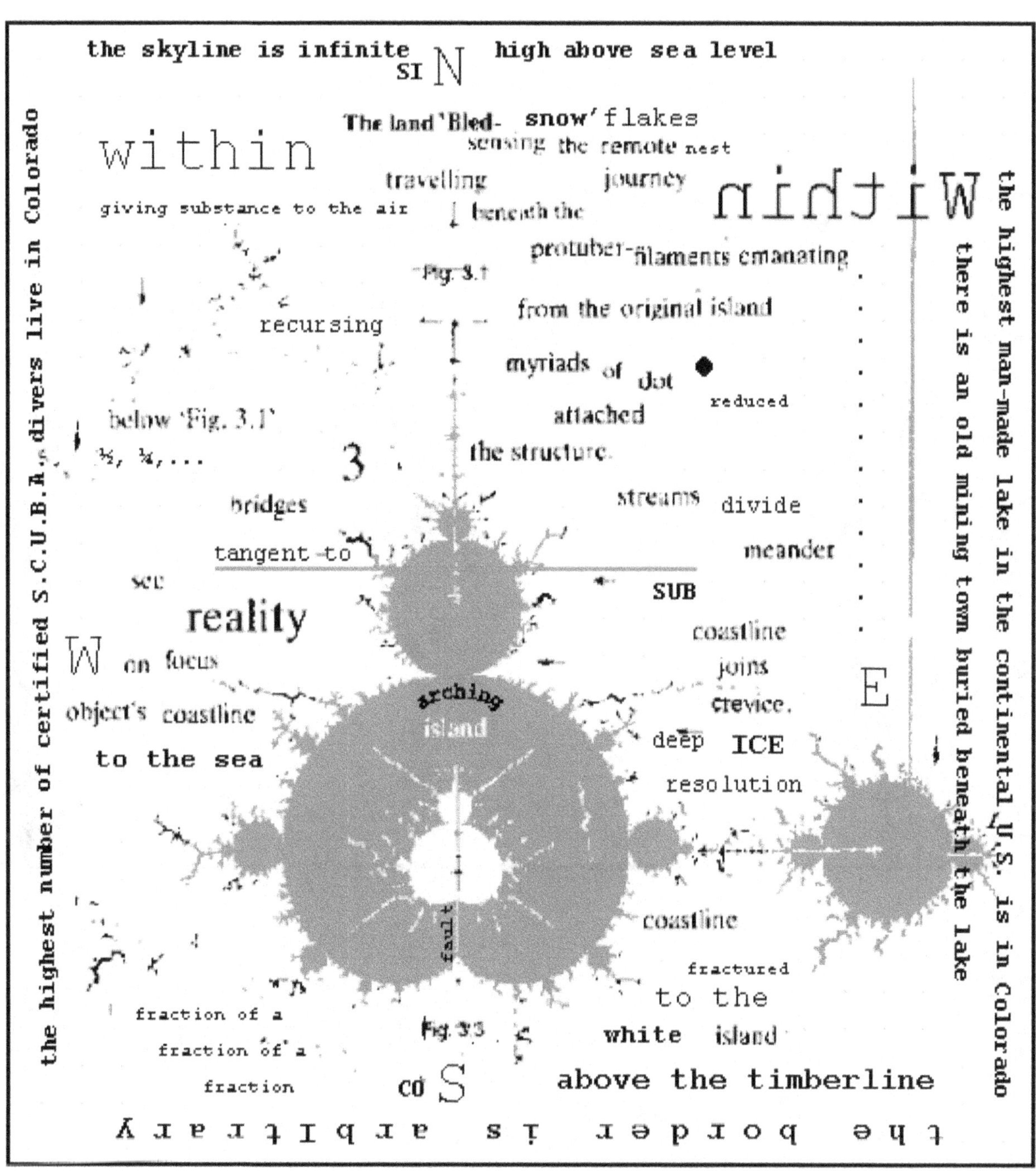
the skyline is infinite
SI N   high above sea level
the land 'Bled- snow' flakes
sensing the remote nest
within
travelling   journey
giving substance to the air
beneath the
protuber- filaments emanating
Fig. 3.1
from the original island
recursing
myriads of dot
reduced
attached
the structure.
3
below 'Fig. 3.1'
½, ¼, ...
streams divide
bridges
tangent to
meander
see
SUB
reality
coastline
W on focus
joins
crevice.
object's coastline
deep ICE
to the sea
resolution
arching
island
fault
coastline
fractured
to the
fraction of a
white island
fraction of a
Fig. 3.3
fraction
above the timberline
the highest number of certified S.C.U.B.A. divers live in Colorado
the highest man-made lake in the continental U.S. is in Colorado
there is an old mining town buried beneath the lake
the border is arbitrary

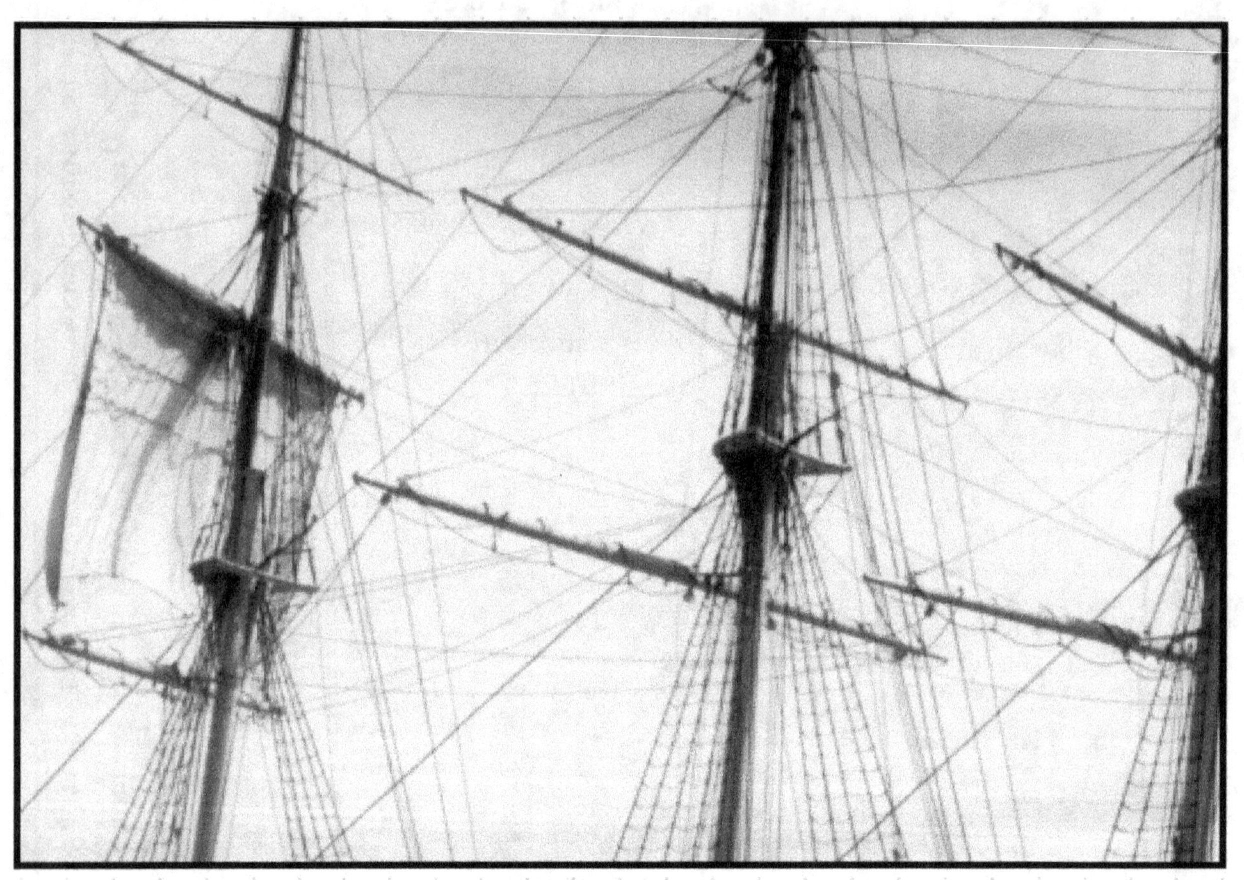

Exhibit A or D (you pick)

The Beach of Small Big Shells

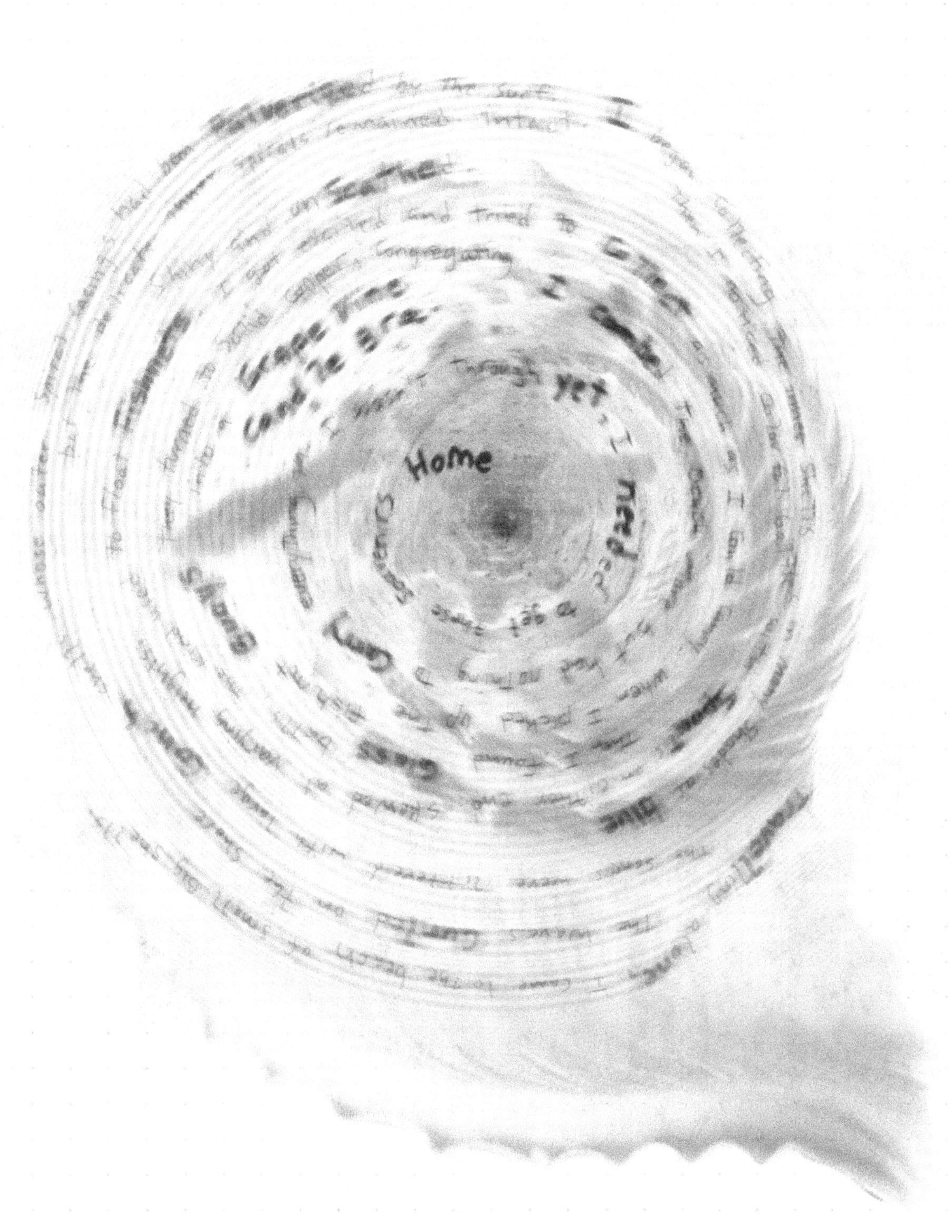

to
the reduction
of streets and avenues

SPLEEN FOUND

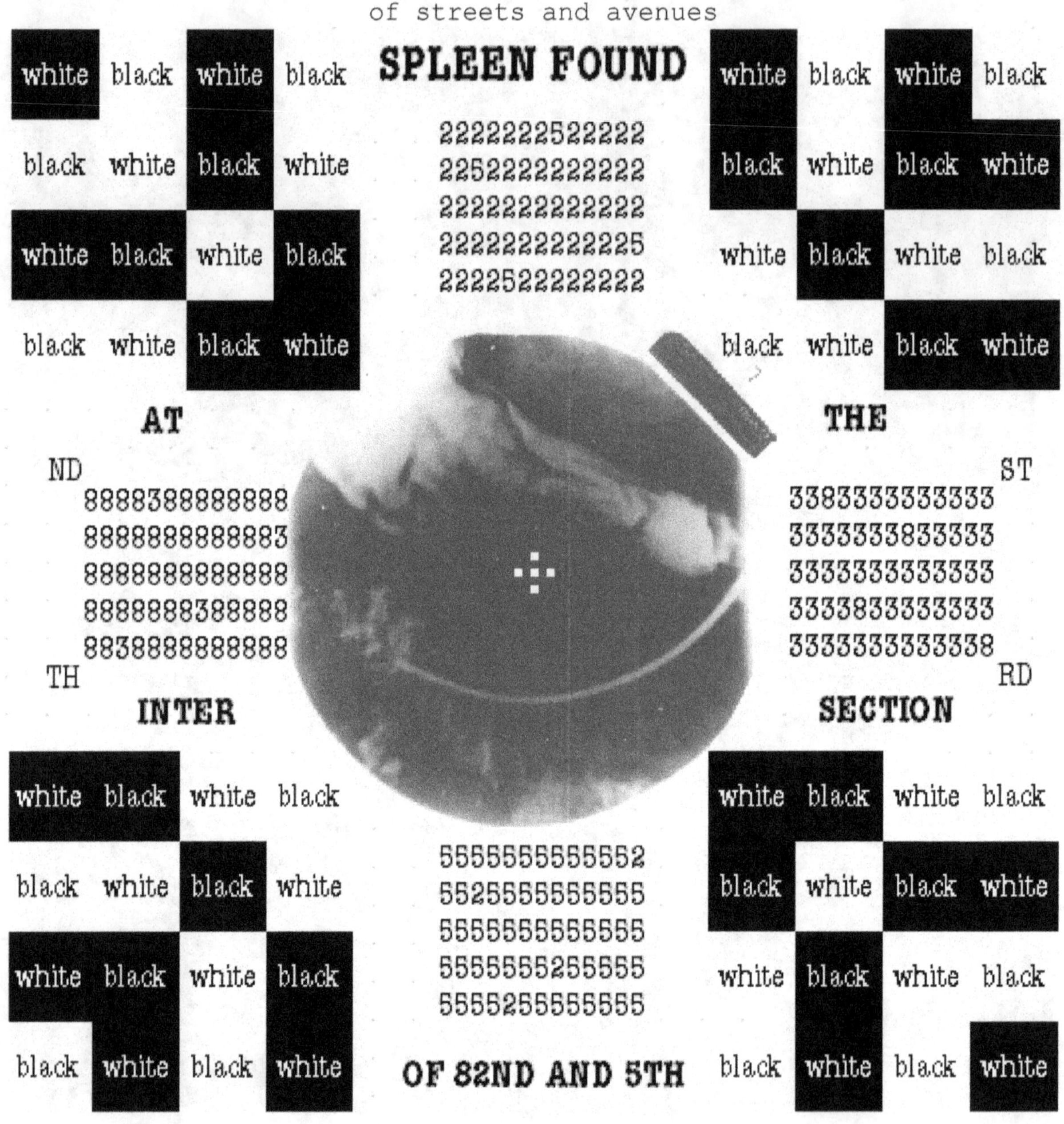

white black white black
black white black white
white black white black
black white black white

2222222522222
2252222222222
2222222222222
2222222222225
2222522222222

white black white black
black white black white
white black white black
black white black white

AT

ND
8888388888888
8888888888883
8888888888888
8888888388888
8838888888888
TH

ST
3383333333333
3333333833333
3333333333333
3333833333333
3333333333338
RD

THE

INTER

SECTION

white black white black
black white black white
white black white black
black white black white

5555555555552
5525555555555
5555555555555
5555555255555
5555255555555

white black white black
black white black white
white black white black
black white black white

OF 82ND AND 5TH

is where
we're
at

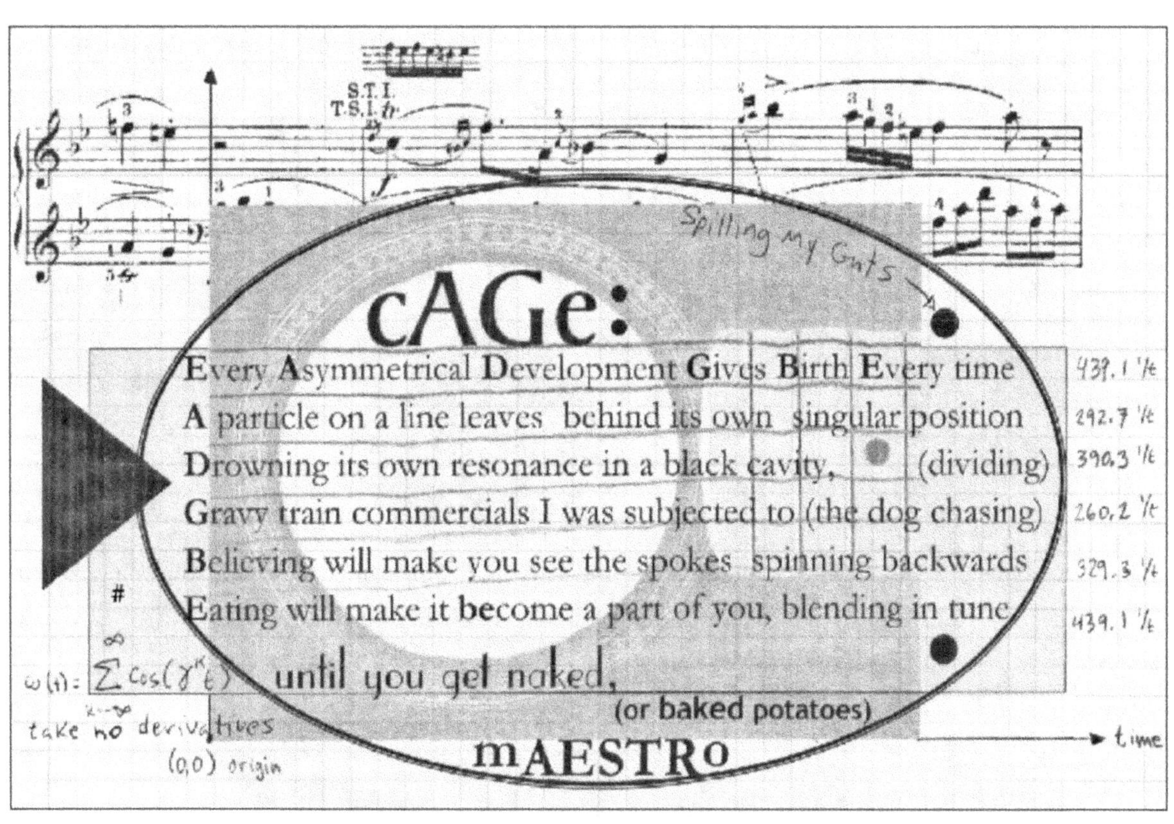
Spilling my Guts

cAGe:
Every Asymmetrical Development Gives Birth Every time
A particle on a line leaves behind its own singular position
Drowning its own resonance in a black cavity,   (dividing)
Gravy train commercials I was subjected to (the dog chasing)
Believing will make you see the spokes spinning backwards
Eating will make it become a part of you, blending in tune
until you get naked,
(or baked potatoes)
mAESTRo

439.1 Yt
292.7 Yt
390.3 Yt
260.2 Yt
329.3 Yt
439.1 Yt

take no derivatives
(0,0) origin
time

Raffling the Next Iteration

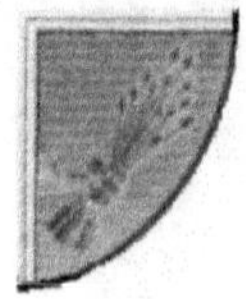

The principle of uncertainty was derived after

ᴶBORGEs

"The Lottery of Babylon"

If people will pay **$1** to **risk** winning it all, why won't

people get paid **$1** to **risk** losing it all?

1+1-1+1-1+1-1+1-1+1-1+1-1+1-1+1-1+1-1+1-1+1-1+1-1+1-1+1-1+1-1+1-1+1-1+1-=0

Dollars

=

Unit

=

Taxi

=

One

=

Ⓤ

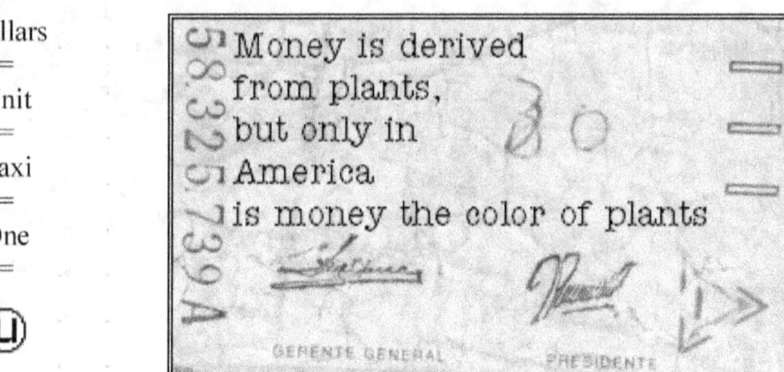

No Identity

=

No Accountability

=

(each unit

the same as

the next)

© Each subway train is an equation, a sequence, iterating. ❻ $ E. 3

Each unit thinks they're the one that matters, the one that should propagate their genes, when it is the genes that

comprise us that are inevitably in control.

$$U + (U - 1) = \{ 1, 1, 2, 3, 5, 8, 13, 21, 34, 55, 89, 144, 233, 377, 610, 987 \}$$

Ⓑ   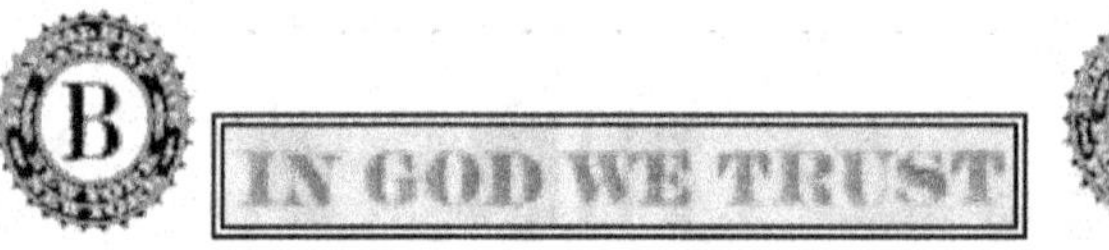   Ⓒ

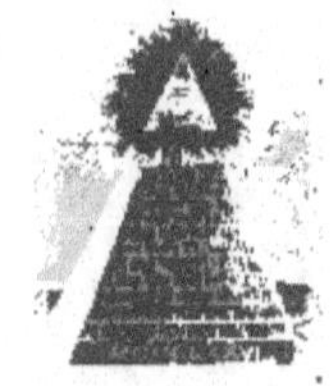
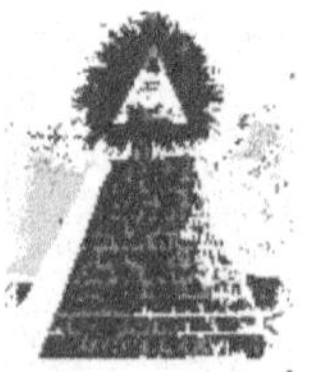

Everyone's existence depends on each other.

{My mother's first e-mail states: "first I push the <cancel> button

and they want me gambling at their casino. I keep being asked.

Did you, as a nice son who wants me to gamble, plan that?"}

We are built on a foundation of dependency (my final answer)

We have everything and nothing to risk

.(it all ends with our eyes).

Eating   eggs   this morning   on the news
      expired subway cars were being dumped   off a barge
                                    21 miles off the shore.
         Activists blow the whistles,   calling this
                        "criminal littering".

I took the **5** down   to the Brooklyn Bridge
                        stop.
(**13** minutes early)   passed over the African Burial Grounds.
A grass lot incarcerated   by a cyclone fence   and yellow tape

                        "Police line do not cross"
This   is   Centre street   Manhattan.
                                                                Now
I wait in the jury pool   thinking of the fish
        that will occupy the used subway cars
    will they remember us,   the previous transients?
Do they judge us?
        Do they know the difference   between
        plastic   and stone?
            To the fish,   this is   a convenient
                                    shelter to possess.
Can I be impartial?   Sitting in the jury pool.
In writing this,
        I am inevitably effected   by those around me.
                                    No one in particular,

Criminal Possession

just a lot of mass,   the suffocating density of dead souls
over the buried subway cars.

                                                My trial,
 criminal possession.   A homeless African-American man found
     with a   plastic debit card   with someone else's name
inscribed   on it.

                                        No proof
of how it was acquired   or any intent to re

                                -use or impersonate.
        And we judge him for falling asleep
        in the courtroom.
Is it a crime?

                                                We,
    the jurors,   are so deeply rooted   in our own shoes
                that we cannot bear
    someone else's cloak,   until the day
  we join the fishes   and learn not to be possessive
                        of our empty cages
                                but to share the world.

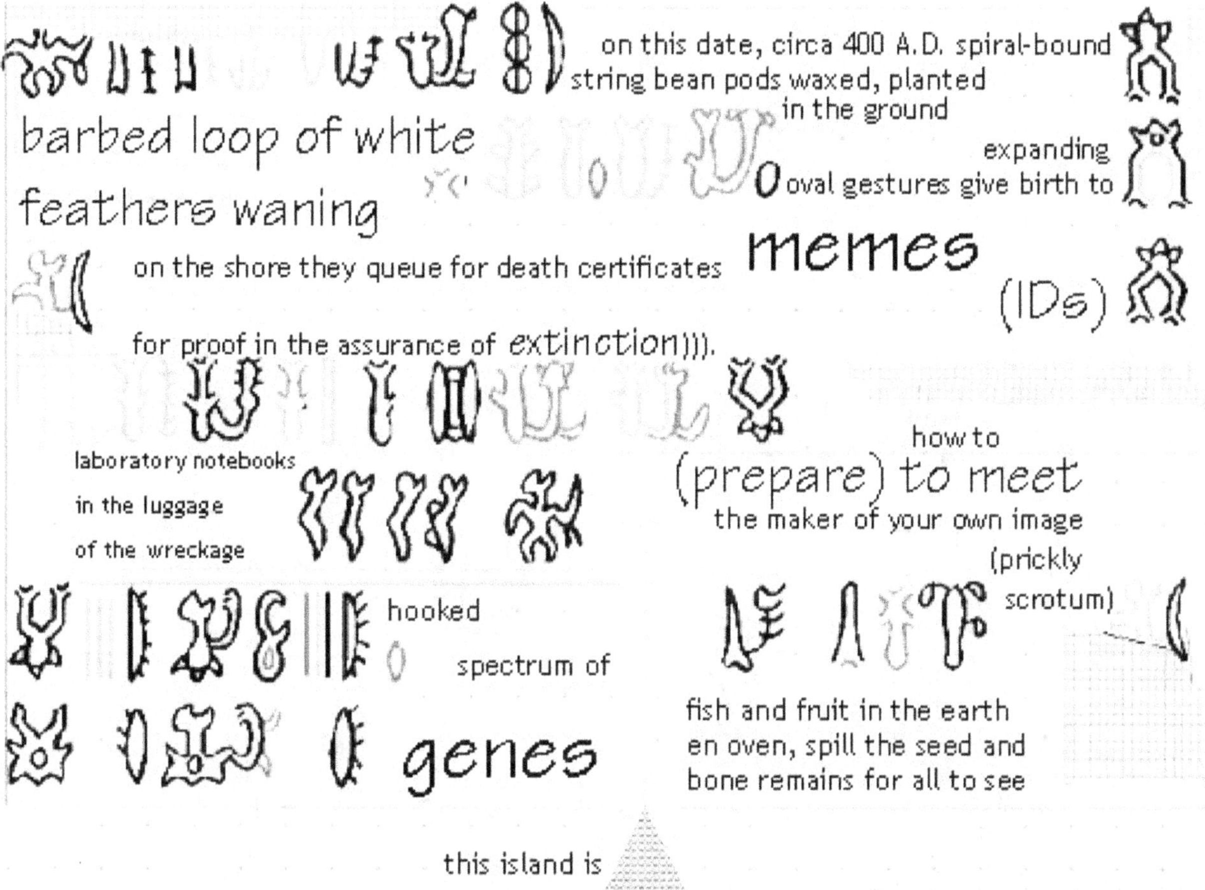
on this date, circa 400 A.D. spiral-bound
string bean pods waxed, planted
in the ground
barbed loop of white
feathers waning
expanding
oval gestures give birth to
on the shore they queue for death certificates
memes
(IDs)
for proof in the assurance of extinction))).
laboratory notebooks
in the luggage
of the wreckage
how to
(prepare) to meet
the maker of your own image
(prickly
scrotum)
hooked
spectrum of
genes
fish and fruit in the earth
en oven, spill the seed and
bone remains for all to see
this island is
the end of selection by natural means

A Flat Puncturing Node

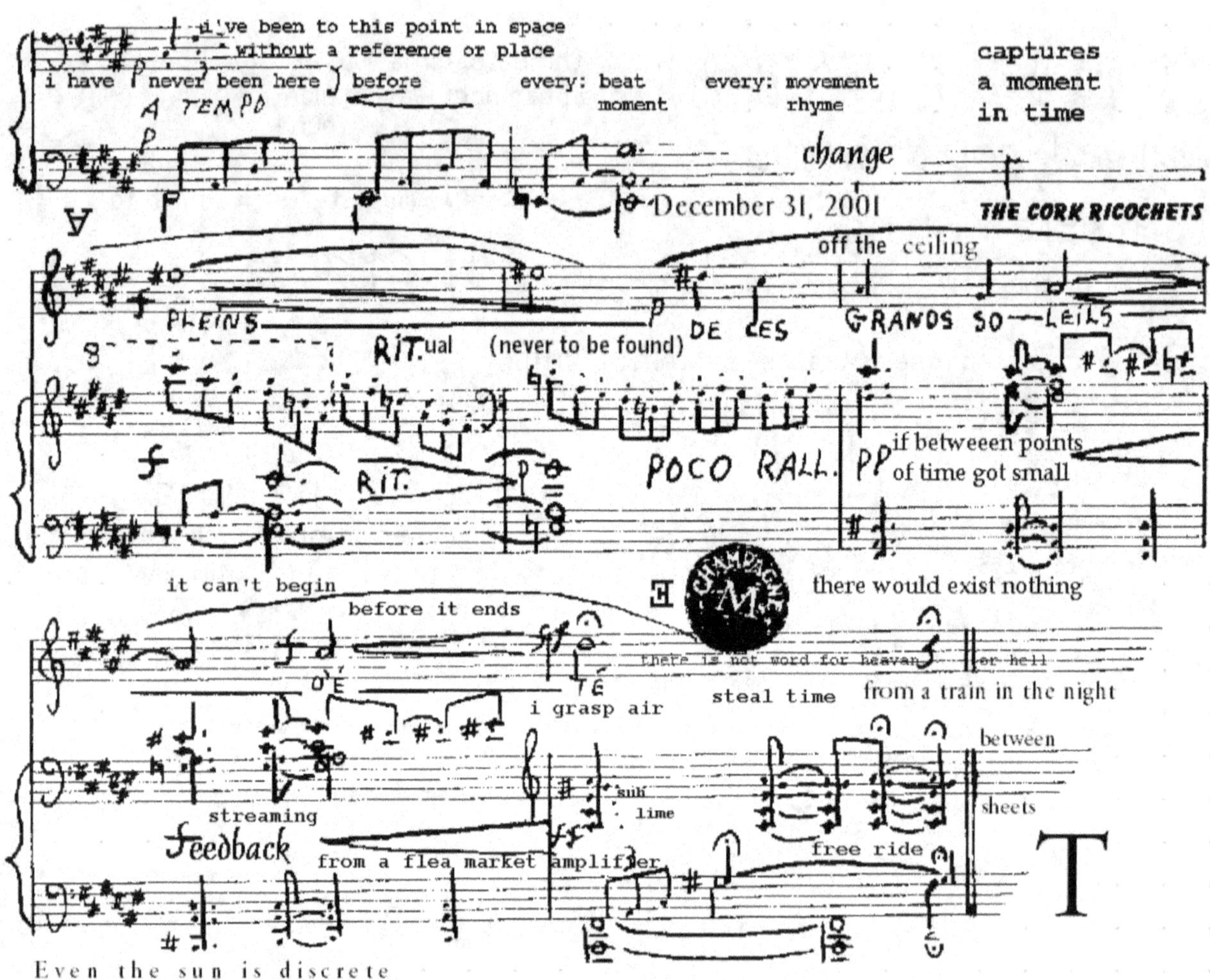

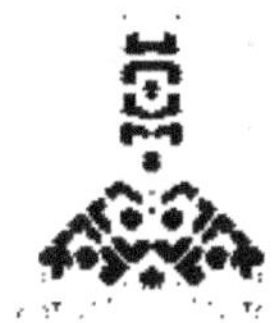

across the border

of the pine cone range

when the **light**ning strikes

in the sands

in the **eve**ning

we search for columns

where sil**i**ca has fused

I see a large rare, deep sea of holes

looking down at my feet

on the filed floor

white spots

with silver-blue backs

crimson fins

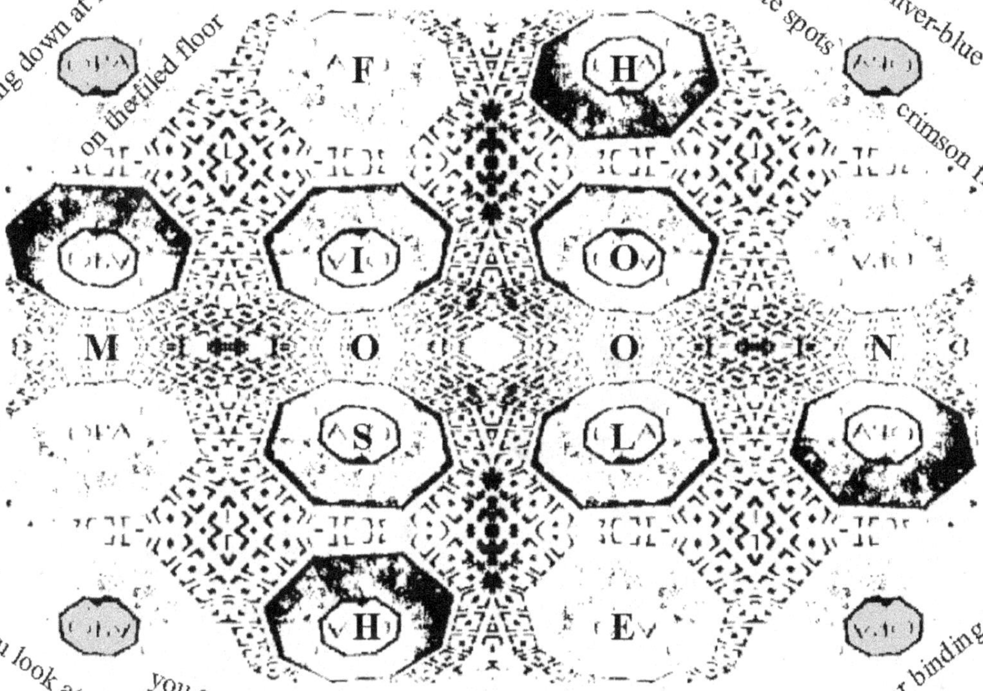

a quartz form of hydrated silica

if you look at the words

you see

colorless or binding color

opal meteors and caged stonefish injecting

ħ

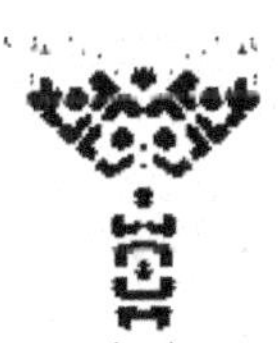

I hear sirens and the bells ringing in Siena (with the overtones) more times than I count

½, ¼, ⅛, ... 1/∞

A family gathers round the grandfather whose ticker just skipped a beat......................
for a split second he sees ripe oranges **in bare trees**

                against gray skies

    the palpation passes

the immediate recency
      of the corpuscular pulse

$T/\infty = 0$

A PRIORI

"He never misses a beat, this is unusual for Him.   just a flutter of a butterfly

  look   he's fine now,   but the ambulance has already arrived."

     each discrete tock a natural unit

        of historical fact

the ghost

the ghost of a

recently departed

quantity $(t = \hbar / mc^2)$

we exist

    only in the

      pulse

    do we exist in

pulse

"You called us, now you are obligated to use our service."

          "Can't hurt for good measure."

                    nothing
                    ness
                    in
                    between

```
the convergence of an infinite series
to a definite limit ...........................
saved from infinite regression
```

    the grandfather is loaded on the stretcher...

                ```(...the ambulance door has a squeaky hinge...)```
                ```

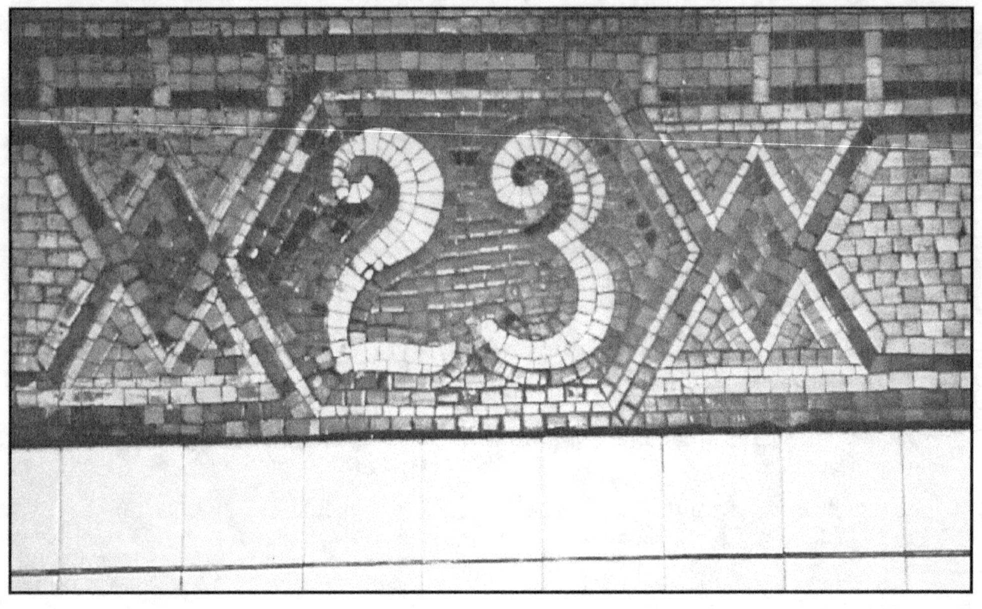

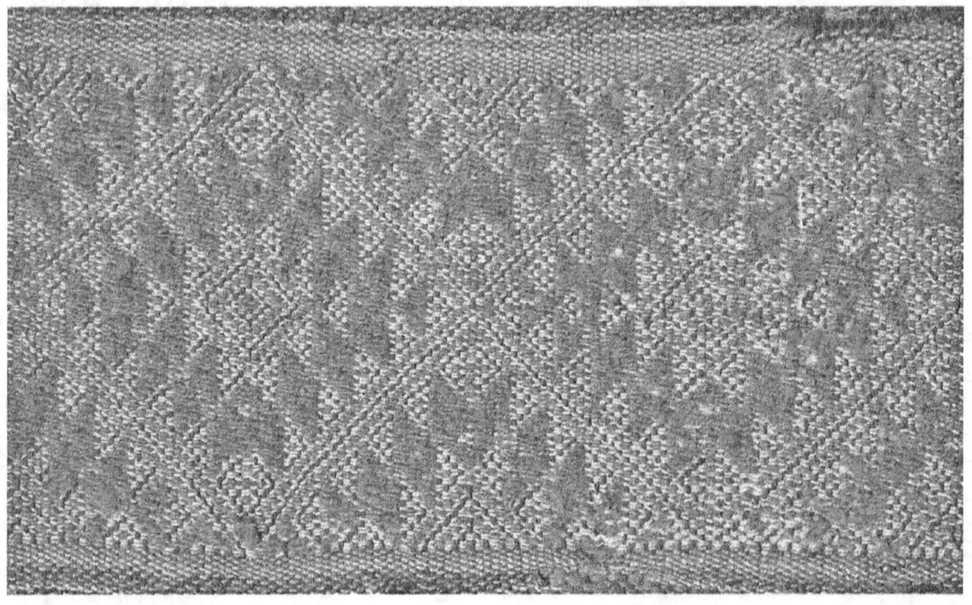

Trapezoidal Juggernaut

Circus Script for a Mestizo Child Abduction

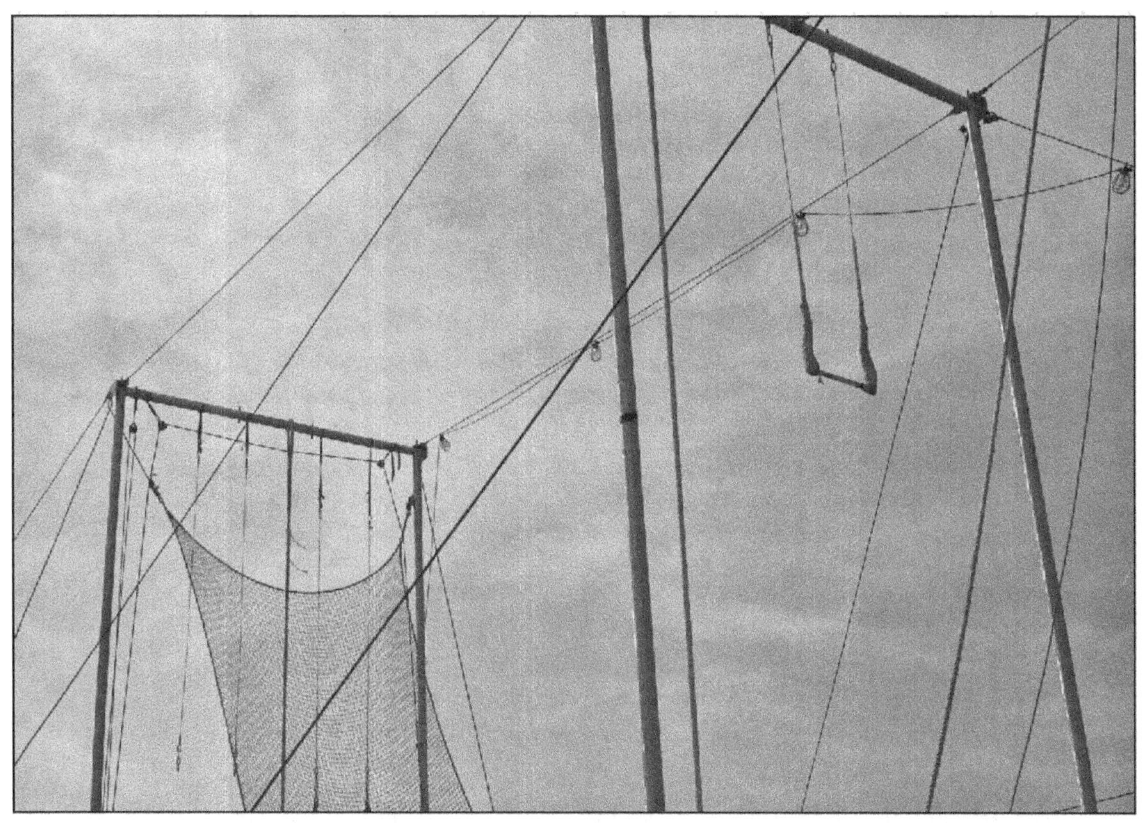

[> now eⁿtering *Trapezoidal Juggernaut* [iSBN Ø-9746Ø53-2-8] pub|ished aLong
side Sandy Baldwin's *Spiritual Turkey Beggar Baste Mechanism* / 1ˢᵗ «Roundtrip»
book [wherein u'd FLiP the book over + [read in th opposite direction]   +
probly the onely work herein that u mite file under «fiction» (tho true)]

[Hindi jagannEth, title of Krishna, from Sanskrit jaganEthaμ, lord of the world : jagat, moving, the world (from jigEti, he goes; see gwE- below) + nEthaμ, lord. Senses 1 and 2, from the fact that worshipers throw themselves under the wheels of a huge car or wagon on which the idol of Krishna is drawn in an annual procession at Puri in east-central India.]

ف

as applied to the transparent: **Faydeev-Popov** (F-P) possessed a closet full of unadorned wire hangars. ((△.) (tied bus 9, I brief gill I+))> the same gauge wire as the **spokes** of (his sUn) **Travis**'s bicycle (Nandi). ..·.·..>)) Faydeev-Popov, a gauge-invariant father. Whatever $\Sigma_£$money he saved `·.||_.'_||·.` he stowed in his "Lagrangian Certified Sleeper" box spring (9-gauge). Most of the money he earned went towards Älimony and child support (((((c'est moi ce soi ici))))))

@ the Opus #23 for coin supper picnic, Faydeev-P met **Shyla**, who was adorned with sky-g *blue* ᴟᴟᴟ (4550 A°) *eye-shadow*. *eye-shadow*. Other items in common– she had also been through a divorce, she was a lab-tech at the β-particle non-linear accelerator, she was a hand lotion critic/connoisseur and she had a tattoo *(from the Ghandara period)*--_

ف

[Hινδι ∀∆γ℘ΞѠΕτη, τιτλε οφ Κρισηνα, φρομΣα) (σκριτ ΩΚ⊥⊗∫νΕτηαϰ, λορδ οφ τηε ωορλδ : φϓγατ, μο τινγ, τηε ωορλδ (φρομφιγΕτι, ηϴγοεσ; σεε γωΕ − βελοω) + νΕτηαϰ, λορδ. Σενσ 1 ϖ•δ2, φρομ τηε φαχτ τητ ω|ρηƎ| περσ ηαϖε τηροων τηεμσελϖεσ υνδερ τηεωηεελσ οφ α ηυγε χαρ ορ ωϓγον ον ωηιχη τηε ιδολ οφ Κρισηνα ωασ δραων ιν αν αννυαλ ⊗ προχεϑσιον ∀∆γ℘ΞѠΕτη ατ Πυρι ιν εϫστ−χεντραλ Ινδια.]

Faydeev-Popov asked Shyla on an outing to Galveston Island for a weekend. She consented. He was feeling pretty good about himself. The first woman he'd been with since his divorce. They would

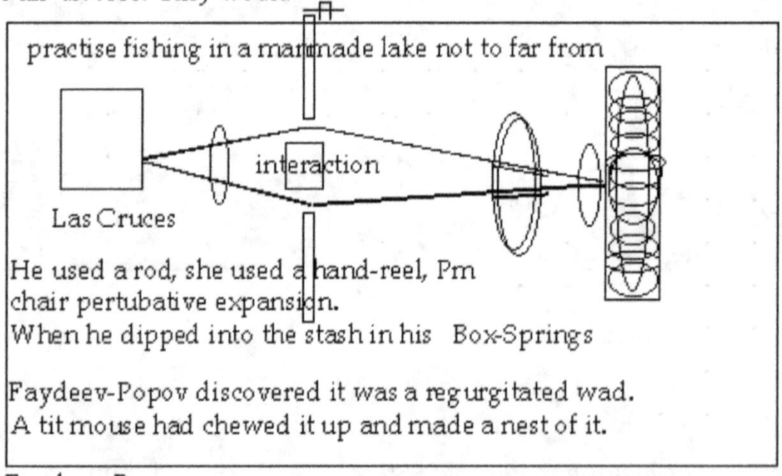

Faydeev-Popov got into his truck and drove straight to   Los Alamos.

stopping only for gas. (**A transparent action**). Obsessing over the fact that all his money went to support a family that he was not a part of... and to think she had left him for a rival colleague.

While the gas was pumping, F-P enters the Qwik-Mart and purchases a box of _Sunrise Henna_ hair dye. Suppressing the desire of the _integration_ of **time** and **money** {√∫Ωœ∃ⁱⱼ Ƴ∞⊇∅{∴}⊥∀4π} @ Los Alamos, he loiters for two hours outside his son's grade school. _Waiting is the medium in which we ∃xist ∴ we are subject to it's contemplation._

Bell sounds: Travis emerges with Todd and Geo. Ride bikes with playing cards strapped to the forks- the cards shuffling in the _spokes_. All for the helio-gyroscopic

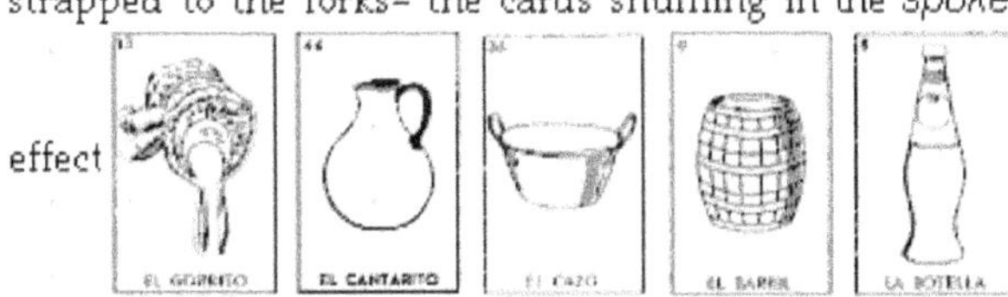

effect [[[4⇓ | J→ | 9♥ | K♣ | 3⇓ | 6 →| A♥ | 10♦ | 7→ | 8⇓ | Q♥ | 2→ | 5♠]]]]   It wasn't hard to pick them out of a crowd. Travis had a tuft of white hair on the crown of his head from a childhood fright- _relativity had revolutionized his father's views of time and its eternal wedlock with space._ F-P pulls the sky-blue courier along the curb until he is next to him.

"O, I am pumped" —he says. "I wait until she quits after years and buy me own son acorn menus and a pocket fisherman."

"Is that yer dad?" -sing Travis's friends in unison.

Travis smirks and asks- "where's mom?"

"When we get to the title district, it's **Dis**neyworld."

"**Dis**neyworld!?" -sing said friends in unison. "You're going to **_Disneyworld._**" To Travis a sense of pride and relief. [[[3⇓ | Q♥ | A♥ | 6→ | J→ | 10♠ | 4⇓ | 2→ | 7→ | 9♣ | K♦ | 8⇓ | 5♣]]]] the **spOkes** roll to a stop. Inches forward on the banana seat.

"Disneyworld." -echoes Travis. {{_Honey is ice to_ **_dis_**_connect_{}}} Loads the bike into the trunk.

"Leave it here" F-P says. "You won't be needing that where we're going. We must maintain a consistency of thoroughbreds."

They drive through orchard after orchard

of

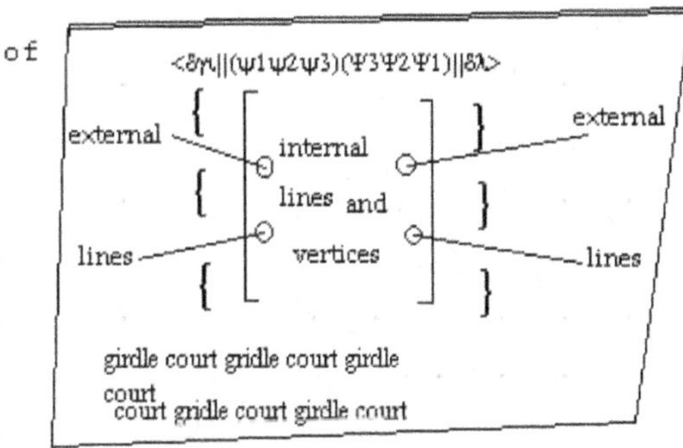

"We're not going to Disneyworld, are we?"

"_We must... consistency._ Do you know anything about dedication to familiarity?" F-P accelerates the Courier. "Besides, we'd do Disney**land** way before Disney_world_."

Travis observes: if you stare into the rows of the orchards, you can see other rows at other angles $\langle \bullet 0_{\mu\nu} | 0^{\nu\mu} \circledR \rangle \cong \Lambda_\alpha \Gamma(\Phi_\alpha)$ where Φ is derived from the destination where Faydeev-Popov takes his son.

"I need my meds" -says Travis.

F-P puts a cigarette in his mouth, pushes the lighter in.

"Dad!?"

"What?! Can't it wait?"

"I need insulin." Travis demonstrates a diabetic pallour. His breath sweet like rotten cream corn (a rather **transparent** response considering scientists have not come up with a quantitative measure of the olfactory senses).

"You'll be okie-dokie. I mean, what's the worst that could happen?" F-P looks over at Travis, his eyes focus on the tuft of white hair.

"I don't feel so well. I need to stop."

F-P pulls the Courier over in the orchard…

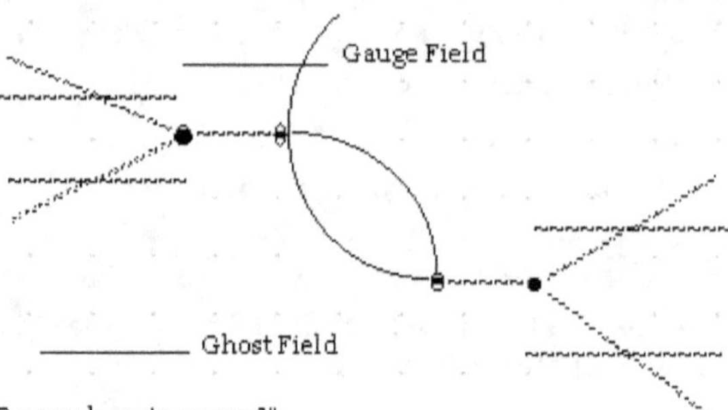

"Do you have to go pee?"
"I have to go number two."
"Do you want to shoot my gun?" There was a hose
that was running into a hole. The water was
running but the hole wasn't filling.

"What should I shoot it at?"

"Best not at anything. Shoot it at the sky."

Travis sets the gun down, pulls down his pants. Squats right there in the field. F-P scans the **horizon** to see if anyone's coming. Demonstrating the awkwardness of someone holding the leash of their dog in the throes of a bowel movement. Travis's diarrhea soaks into the soil.

"Did I ever tell you about my work. Son? About what I do for a living?" F-P digs his hands in his pockets, staring up at the sky. "I shoot stuff at targets to see what they're made of. Small stuff. Like *reaaallly* teeny stuff. The smallest stuff in the world. Quarks and leptons— the constituents of what everything else is made of."

He pulls the hose out of the hole. Water gushing from the end.

"This isn't the way to Disneyland, is it?" -asks Travis.

"**Elle**phant Lake is not too far from here. I went fishing there with your mother once, before you were born. She caught this fish and when she reeled it in **it was in the middle of the line** 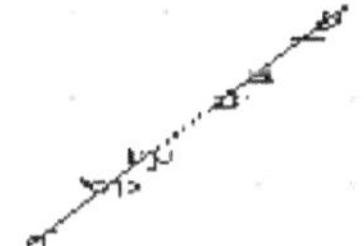 not on the end where you'd expect. The line ran through its gills somehow and it was tangled up so we couldn't even find the sinker and the hook. We had to cut the line to get the fish off."

```
     "I need paper" -says Travis.
     F-P scanned, but there was only the symmetry of Pecan
trees.
     "Dad. I need paper."
     In the truck, F-P finds a Qwik-Mart napkin. He also grabs
a package off the front seat: the hair dye. The napkin goes to
Travis. The box he opens. Assembles the contents on a cement
manhole cover and reads the directions. Re-reads the directions.
Glosses over the translation in French. Flips it over. Flips it
over again back the original state. There was a third empty
bottle for the mixing of the other two solutions. There was also
a pair of saran-wrap gloves. He re-reads the directions times
six before he begins.
     After Travis wipes his butt and pulls up his pants, he
shoots the gun at the sky. The sound echoes but there is no
substance (an apparent response to the lack of discipline).
     Once F-P mixes the proper ingredients, he puts the gloves
on and applies the solution to Travis's hair. The dye absorbs
readily into the white tuft. Travis doesn't ask any questions
about this procedure. F-P is determined.
     "Now we wait for exactly twelve minutes" -says Faydeev-
Popov looking at his watch. He lights a cigarette and
contemplates perturbation expansion theory and the corpuscular
nature of time.
```

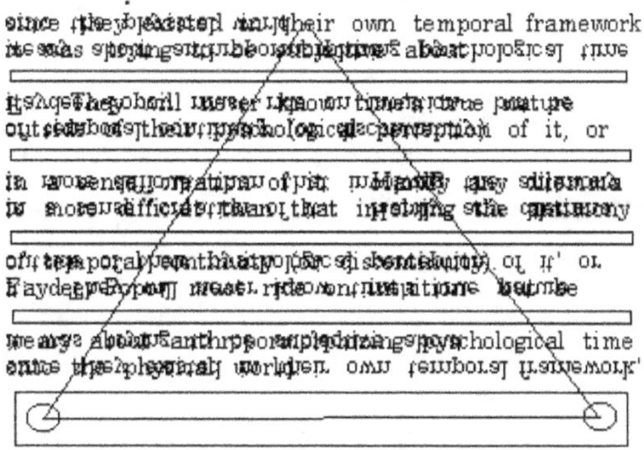

```
The cell phone rings (in a time before they were invented). F-P
runs back to the car to get it off the seat.
```

"Halo?" He listens while he looks back at Travis's hair.

keep your eye on him?"

"I don't have him! Can't you

such luxuries!"

"Some of us don't have

know about devotion?!"

"Devotion?! What do you

```
          F-P glances at his watch,
```

"I gotta run."

F-P hangs up. Sticks Travis's head under the hose and rinses the
dye out.

"Smells funny" -says Travis.

"That's your pooh."

"It's the **sham**poo."

"You'll get used to it."

Back in the car, F-P tells his son to stick his head out
the window (to dry his hair off). The procedure works and F-P is
a proud father because of it. When it was dry, his hair was an
auburn color except where the white tuft was- which was now
bright orange.

They cross(ed) the border at El Paso without incident.

The Copenhagen Interpretation could not account for the illegal aliens held in suspense.　　{This

was a uni-directional semi-permeable membrane.}

*The colorful chaos of the Mexican frontier fascinated Travis-
dogs in the streets and kids playing everywhere. All this eye-
candy only served to irritate Faydeev-Popov:::*

Travis spotted a circus.

The circus tent was a pink and red tarp stretched taut

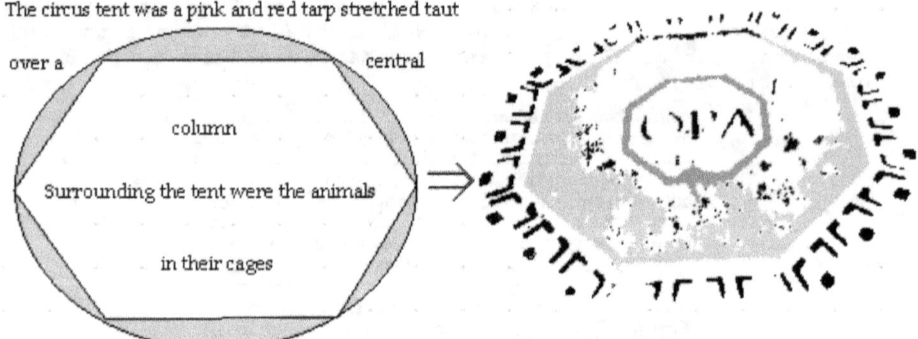

The canvas was an ᵒᵖᵃ**que** *membrane. Travis begged his father to
stop. F-P felt a need to regroup anyway. He had had no
particular destination in mind, he just knew he had to get
across the border. His conceived actions were not pre-meditated-
he had no prior experience with kidnapping. The paradox could be
chalked off to Faydeev-Popov's blatant disregard for relative
motion:*

$$\begin{matrix} & s & i & v & & & s & i & v \\ o & \chi & a & & \Rightarrow & & o & \chi & a \\ & w & e & g & & & w & e & g \end{matrix}$$

{siv remains stationary while ice takes a step to the left and
wag's right, i.e. "no apparent gaps".}

F-P's cell rings even though he is outside of his calling area's jurisdiction. He half-expects to hear a voice in Spanish. It's his ex-wife again, bouncing off the satellites.

" There's an explanation why .... What do **you** know? I don' have any money. It all goes towards **your** alimony .... I **had** some money .... It was in my mattress .... A mouse made a home out of it .... I'm serious .... Why do I have to convince you anyway? .... *I haven't got a stitch to wear* .... I've got nothing .... I've got a closet full of empty hangars .... but hey, *when you got nothing, you got nothing to lose* .... This is a good a time as any to be singing .... No, I'm not intoxicated .... Yah, and what do **you** know about parenting? .... look, I just want to see him .... no, I don't want any more drama"

"Sounds like you're at a circus" –F-P's ex-wife says.
so is
o
o
|
coral.=£
n tuxedo
bit Tesla in a guard –pint got at sixth
tune 5 miss want to short 3 in

my ova to shoot it straight into dig sky soil cellular incurring cargo tickets a reasoning why. Sounds like you need to mind your own fucking business.

F-P's ex-wife hangs up on him. Travis observes the elephants stand on their back legs- oblivious to the fact that the Society for the Prevention of Cruelty to Animals has repeatedly verified that this is not only an unnatural exercise for elephants, but has been known to give them hernias. The elephants then run in circles while they hold each other's tails and one poops and all the kids say ";ooohh!" in Spanish.

F-P calls the ex-wife back.

"Shame on you, you're unlisted."

"I had to star sixty-nine you."

"Yah, even from Mexico. How did you know I was in Mexico?"

{The tightrope walker does his thing high in the roof of the tent. *"Silencio Por Favor"* –the ringmaster announces through a megaphone.}

"You don't think I figured that out by now. Every cop in Las Cruces is closing in on to your ass. It doesn't take a rocket scientist to know you're at a circus. The nearest circus is El Paso. If you have Travis in Mexico . . . my ass you're taking him, you're taking the memory of him with you to hell. You don't think I know where you are? You don't know about the GPS device they implanted in you after you violated your parole? They know exactly where to find you–"

F-P hangs up mid-sentence, unwilling to believe. He feels around on the back of his neck, then his armpits. Feels himself all over his body, searching. "Come on Travis. We gotta split."

"But dad, we'll miss the Trapeze Artists!"

Faydeev-Popov grabs his son and pulls him to his feet.

"*¡Oye Señor!*" —says the man behind them. "*Dejalé ver el acto de Trapezio. Solo es un niño.*"

"*¿No entiendiste el maestro de circo?*" —says the man behind the man behind F-P. "*¡Silencio!*" *ad infinitum…*

"Hey," —says F-P, "no espanish, okayo? And mind your own fucking business."

"*¡Mira, su pelo es el color de zanhorria!*" —says the man's wife, pointing at Travis's hair.

By now Travis is crying. The skin around his temples is dyed the same color orange as his hair (5970 Å).

The clown motions for them to come down into the ring. F-P flips off the clown for no apparent lack of reason.

"Here's a universal sign they might understand."

F-P drags Travis through the crowded aisle and out to the car. "Come on, be a man. Stop your crying." Searches his pockets then looks in the window of the sky blue courier. The keys are dangling there in the ignition, just beyond the glass.

A truckload full of *federales* pulls into the circus parking lot. The federales are for the most part young clean-shaven men with automatic rifles. One of them, presumably their leader, has a GPS homing device.

F-P grabs Travis and ducks under the tent flap and back into the circus. Emerging under the bleachers.

The federales enter the tent through the main entrance—the one with the GPS tracking device leads the way. They arrive amidst the trapeze act.

Travis stops crying, straining to watch the act through the gaps in the bleachers and between people's legs.

Final Act *The Hostage Scene*
INT. Day. Cantiflas Circus, El Paso.

Faydeev-Popov is huddled under the bleachers with his son. His eyes dart around the tent.

Cut to:

Trapeze artists performing amazing feats in the heights of the circus tent with no safety net to catch them if they should fall.

Close up on:

Faydeev-Popov's face, demonstrating extreme fear and anxiety. All his options flash before his eyes.

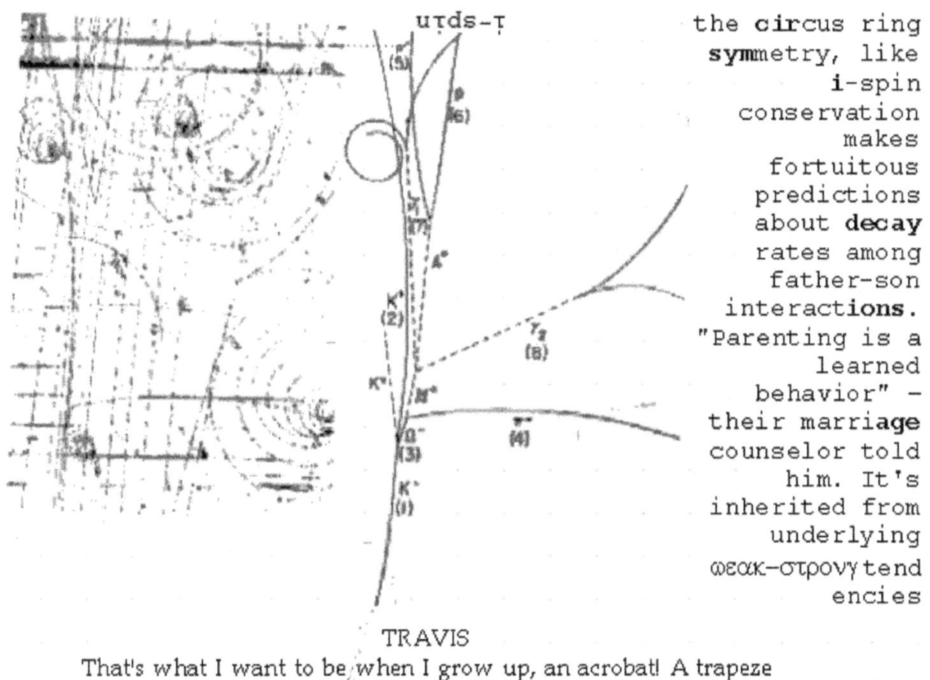

the circus ring **symm**etry, like i-spin conservation makes fortuitous predictions about **decay** rates among father-son interac**tions**. "Parenting is a learned behavior" – their marri**age** counselor told him. It's inherited from underlying ωεακ–στρονγ tendencies

TRAVIS

That's what I want to be when I grow up, an acrobat! A trapeze artist!

FAYDEEV-POPOV

*SS*HHHH!

Cut to:

The federales enter the ring. The trapeze act continues on overhead. The one with the GPS unit grabs the megaphone from the ringmaster.

GPS FEDERALE

¡Attención por favor! ¡Tenemos un grave situación aquí! Con su permiso . . . ¡Vamonos pinche pendejo! ¡Vamos a matarte y tu hijo tambien! ¡No tienes nada de opciónes! Sabemos que estas aquí! ¡Tus minutos estan enumerado!

Flash to:

Faydeev Popov's clenched buttcheeks (through his Dockers™).

Cut to:

A translator is ushered in. His white shirt stands out in stark contrast to the green khakis of the federales. The GPS federale hands the megaphone to the translator and whispers in his ear.

TRANSLATOR
(fiddling with megaphone adjustments)
Bueno. Check. One-two-three (followed by feedback).
Okay, you out there gringo? Listen up– we got the circus

tent surrounded . . . . This GPS is accurate to eighteen meters . . . . that's about fifty-five feet.

Flash to:

A Trapeze artist performs a perfectly executed reverse double-pike south camel flip, rotating just in time to grab the chalked forearms of another artist swinging upside-down by his knees. *We will not deal with the rotational and vibrational degrees of freedom of the acrobats except to note their unconscious roles affecting the Faydeev-Popov exclusion principle. Consider, for example, two Trapeze artists with identical centers of gravities (for simplicity sake). If each acrobat has a spin 1/2, the total wave function would be ant-symmetric under the interchange of angular momentum.*

TRANSLATOR
(the GPS federale whispering in his ear)
Your minutes are numbered. . . you don't have a chance in hell. . . let the kid go and we'll only kill you . . . don't let the kid go and we'll kill you and the kid . . . the choice is yours.

Cut to:

The clown sneaks out of the ring and bellies down under the bleachers. Beneath the frowned make-up is a focused look of grave determination.

Flash to:

Faydeev-Popov fires his gun randomly. The shot ricochets through the bleachers and punctures a hole in the canopy overhead.

Extreme Close on:

Bullet hole in the pink canvas.

INNOCENT BYSTANDER
¡Tiene un pistola!

TRANSLATOR
(the GPS federale whispering in his ear)
¡Calmanse por favor! Look, you pubic hair of a male goat . . . crowd hysteria tactics don't work around these parts . . . we take a strong stance towards hostage situations here . . there are rarely survivors and never heroes . . . even if you survive you will rot away in a filthy jail cell and be subjected to wanton acts of sexually aggravated assault . . that is your only option and that should sound good to you right now.

Cut to:

The clown spots Faydeev-Popov and Travis and crouches down. He moves stealthily towards them.

Flash to:

Outside the tent a green station wagon with the words *"servicios sociales"* pulls up.

TRANSLATOR
(the GPS federale whispering in his ear)
Your seconds are numbered . . . . Did you ever think for even a moment about the secret nature of time? . . . . of what actually exists between the indivisible gaps? . . . . Did you ever see Butch Cassidy and the Sundance Kid? . . . Remember the final scene? . . . that could be you . . . the choice is yours . . . let the kid go and we will only shoot you.

Faydeev-Popov closes his eyes and fires the gun haphazardly into the air.

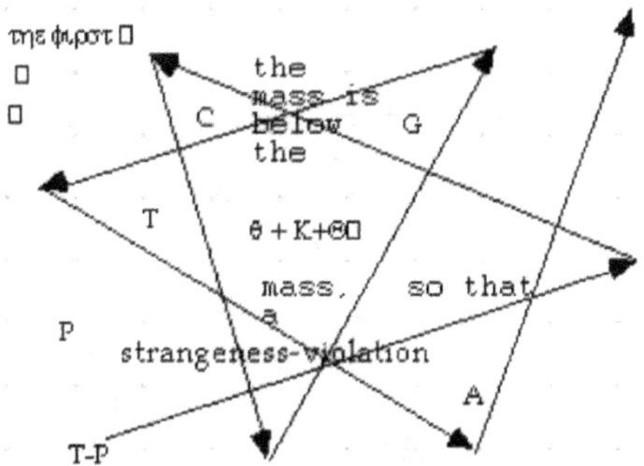

is involved. What is seen in the bubble chamber is
A bullet hits a trapeze artist mid-flight. His body goes limp instantly and he crashes to the floor of the circus ring.

Cut to:

CLOWN
(reeling in horror)
¡¡¡¡¡NNNOOOOOOOOO!¡¡¡

The clown makes a run for Faydeev-Popov. Faydeev-Popov grabs his son and holds the gun to his temple.

FAYDEEV-POPOV
Don't think for a second that I won't do it!

Flash to Slow Motion:

The clown is unabated in his sprint.

FAYDEEV-POPOV
(whispering into Travis's ear)
You're like a holocaust. You can be so dark and then again so light.

Faydeev-Popov pulls the trigger and Travis's body goes limp in his father's arms. Red blood streams from the patch of orange hair.

CLOWN
(in slow motion horror)
¡¡¡¡¡¡¡¡NNNNNOOOOOOOOOOOOOOO!!!!!!!!

The clown makes a diving lunge at Faydeev-Popov from behind– but before he reaches him, Faydeev-Popov puts the barrel of the gun in his mouth and pulls the trigger. The bullet travels through his brain and kills the clown.

Cut to:

The other trapeze artists swing down from the rafters and gather around their fallen comrade.

Angle Out and Rise:

Aerial view of the Circus tent.

The Point Of View rises steadily, the Rio Grande emerges into view, then El Paso. We recognize the gulf of Mexico and can make out the North American continent. We pan across the blue expanse of the Atlantic Ocean– then across the Sahara desert. Soon we pass over the Pakistani Hindu Koosh and through Khyber pass– the P.O.V. dropping back down so we can make out the rather dramatic three-dimensional topography. Eventually we are able to identify swarms of people in Puri, India. A procession is being led by a wooden-wheeled chariot drawn by five Brahma bulls. The P.O.V. focuses on one of the spinning wheels. The film unravels off the spool, lapsing into a series of tiled images– playing cards in the spokes.

Legend: one chronon = $T = h/mc^2$ (on the order of 10^{-24} seconds) is the smallest conceivable unit of time.

- -

((A Φιση struggles in the middle of the 12 lb. test line.))

Everything slows to a stop and reverses direction. Pan back over the Indian sub-continent over the Hindu-Koosh, etc. A satellite passes by in the foreground. We hear the din of a million telephone conversations at once. The P.O.V. hovers back over North America centering over suburban Illinois, where we zoom in. The circular structure of the Fermilab particle accelerator comes into view...

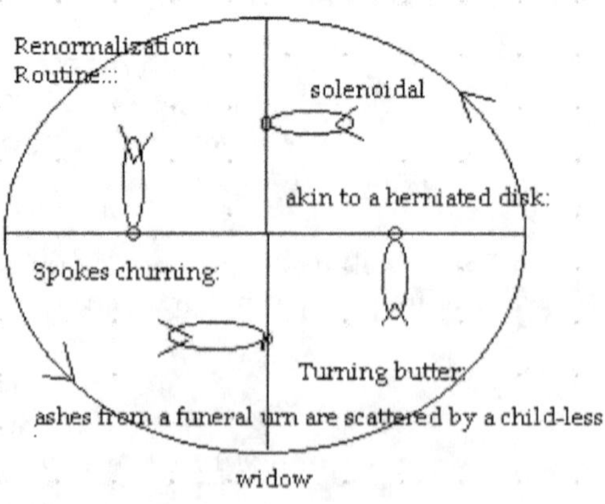

FAYDEEV-POPOV
(*whispering*)

We have completed our union– our intersection. For that one chronon I am devotion. I am your Big Bang– I am your Juggernaut.

The other trapeze artists swing down from the rafters and gather around like a tribe of monkeys who have lost their leader. The grave clown is perpetually running towards them under unfavorable conditions.

"Don't stop, it's wonderful!"

"Didn't you come yet?" –asks Faydeev-Popov.

What is seen is the sequence: $\Omega \Rightarrow \emptyset\ \Xi \Rightarrow \emptyset\Lambda + \pi \Rightarrow \Psi(\emptyset 2\gamma$. In between this collision and disintegration of a virtual state that exists for only 5.26×10^{-4} picoseconds. We focus in on an oscillating box spring– contracting and expanding at an even frequency of 60 Hz accompanied by coupling moans. The box springs creak due to the inherent kinetic elasticity. We pan out to see the naked forms of Faydeev-Popov and his newlywed wife on their honeymoon.

The **caterwaul:** escalates and the coupling frequency increases to a Gaussian crescendo. We rise over the canopy of a four-poster wrought-iron bed. The following legend of Caterwaul reveals the spacing of its means to an end:

*[intr.v. ca0coph0o0nyÅf2õnT]arring, discordant impulses; dissonance. [cacophonie, from Greek kakophÅnos, copulating. "He summons a cacophony of sirens duringsays traffic jam". CACOeTHES, The use of harsh consonants in literary compositions (as for poetic effect). See CACOPHONOUS.] kakka-. Derivatives are: poppycock, cacophony. Also kaka-. To defecate. Root imitative of glottal closure. CUCKING STOOL, 3. To cry or screech like a cat in heat. From cukken, to deviate, from a gutteral source akin to Old Norse *kuka 2. To make a krill soup: Lolligag or polliwog, from Latin pacEre, to fornicate. CACO-; CACODYL,. (Crocophilia), from Greek kakos, bad. [Pokorny kava- Earthen *caterwawlen : *cater, tomcat; akin to Low German kater + wawlen, 'night-crawler', wrawlen, to yowl (ultimately of a divine origin). (kat2cõrw]*

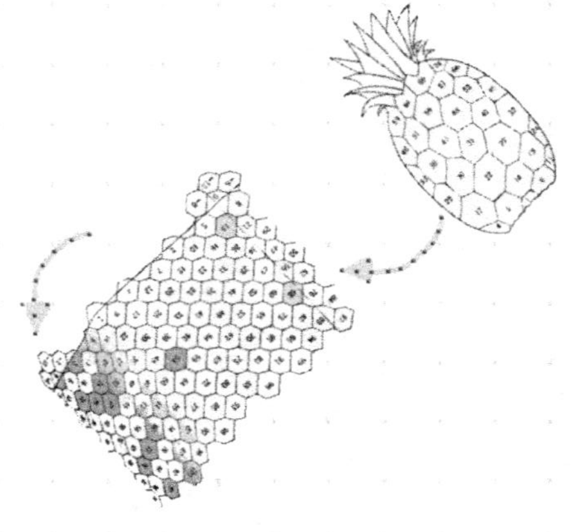

+ X = how *Trapezoidal Juggernaut* ends: 5ideways centerfold umop-əpᴉsdn 2 th opposing text from *Spiritual Turkey Beggar Baste Mechanism* coming in th opposite direXion ∴ 1 wood fLip az directed + 5tart reading in oqqoɀiɟɘ dɿɘkXion

+ now we tran5ition 2 the final BC/AD sexion:

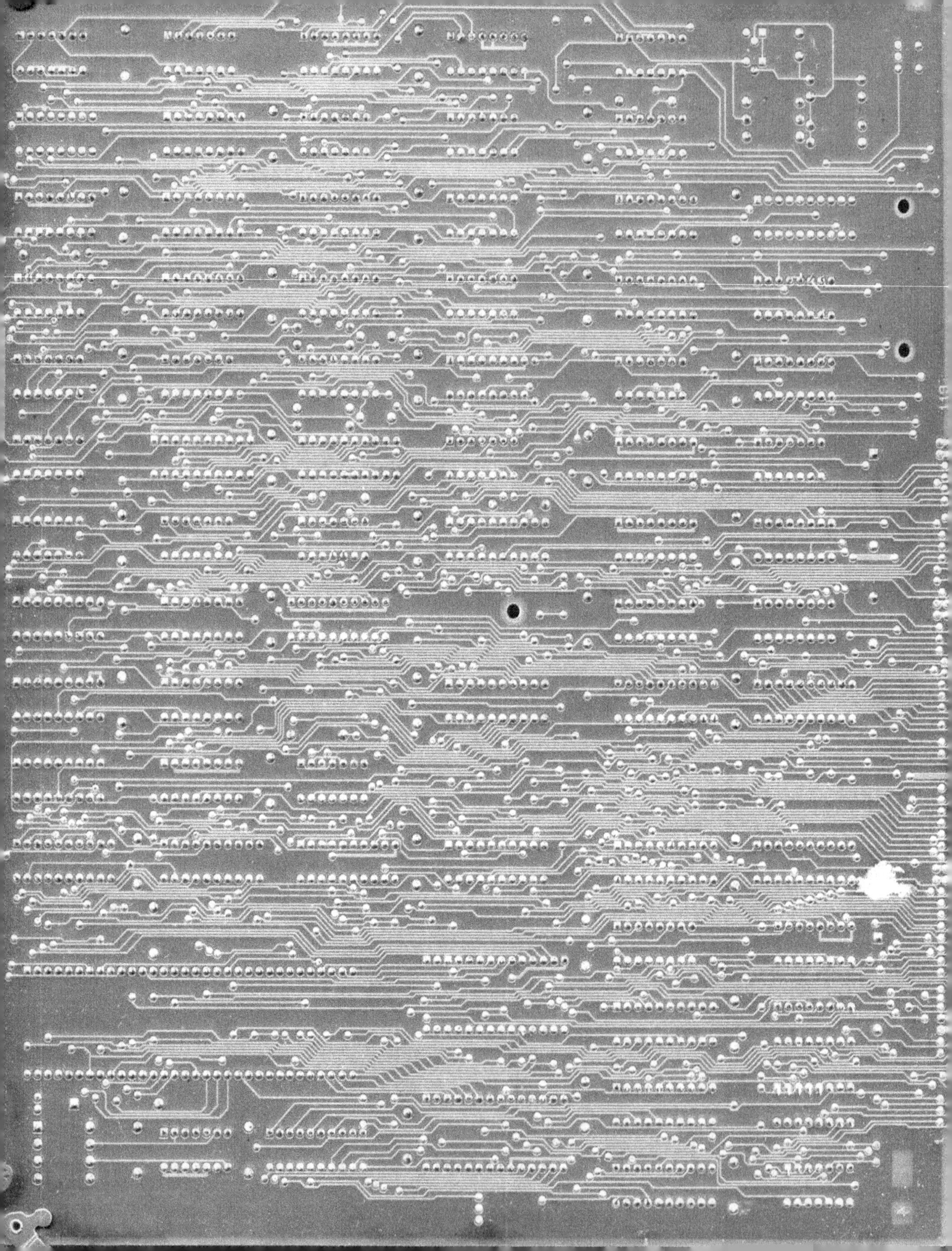

B
C
A
D

BODH[I] **C**IRCU[IT]S

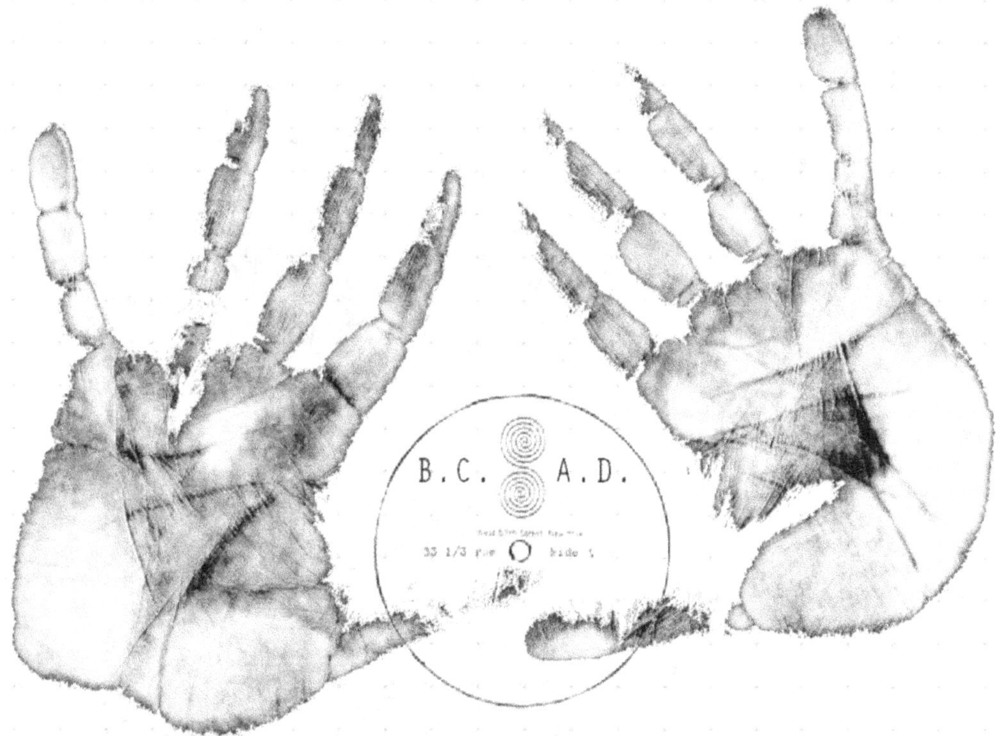

ALG[A]E[BRA] **D**[RA[IN]]

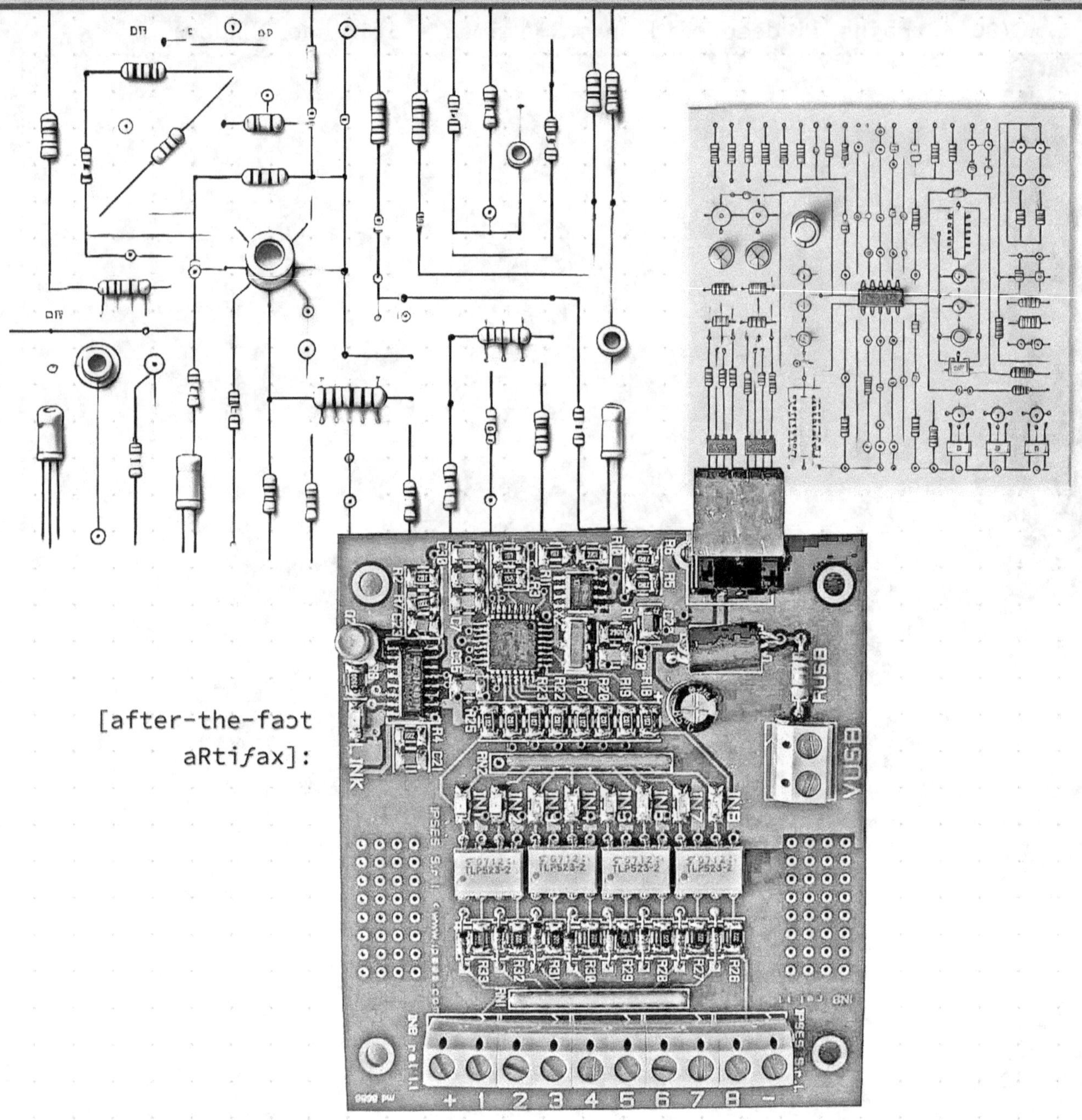

[after-the-faɔt
aRtifax]:

> dd/CAL u5ed ^ soldering i-urn 2 bind the BC/AD chapbooks 2gether w/
resistors / capacitors + inductors / 4ming ^n aɔtual cirɔuts

well-balance(die(t) of (pan right) un(x)pected polar(elatives) sc(our) leafs & shed sheets tied end-on-end out the cell

"She looked down a slope, needing to squint for the sunlight, onto a vast sprawl of houses which had grown up all together, like a well-tended crop, from the dull brown earth; and she thought of the time she'd opened a transistor radio to replace a battery and seen her first printed circuit. The ordered swirl of houses and streets, from this high angle, sprang at her now with the same unexpected, astonishing clarity as the circuit card had. Though she knew even less about radios than Southern Californians, there were to both outward patterns a hieroglyphic sense of concealed meaning, of an intent to communicate."

-Thomas Pynchon, The Crying of Lot 49

"Many have trouble making out the words. Smeared print, ghost images. In the altered shelves, the ambient roar, in the plain and heartless fact of their decline, they try to work their way through confusion. But in the end it doesn't matter what they see or think they see. The terminals are equipped with holographic scanners, which decode the binary secret of every item, infallibly. This is the language of waves and radiation, or how the dead speak to the living."

-Don DeLillo, White Noise

... Be(fore(skin)) unfolded, I(m) a g(host) rubbing a plastic rod against a furry rabbit foot, flying kites in a T-cell,

The Laws of Bodh[i] Circu[it]s:

1. In any *circus* there is an enormous amount (Σ_i) of grieving.
2. If *elephants* hold tails in a circle (bringing a system back to its initial state, **i**), the net result is success at the expense of "nature."
3. circuit = **i** (tail-to-tell) has no meaning unless it is traveled.
4. (this is an alternate placeholder for defining the same mole).

The Principles of Alg[a]e[bra] D[ra[in]]:

5. When circuit **i** goes down, it cascades to the sum (Σ_e) of all the elephant's ancestors.
6. True (aka ə|ə) heroes are(r)are and require the blind pull of sacrifice.
7. *Instinct* seeks information and heat (or the absence of), *NOT* the carrier frequency.
8. In order to *really* live, we (moles) must embrace the inevitable.

[1] ... and people had the nerve to state that it reminded them of the empty merry-go-round in Central Park, still running, the music serenading the exodus of people on cell phones to loved ones, intent on survival.

exiled beneath a tree, con(strain)ed to an arbitrary ma(i)ze in(her)ently based on inner-(light need not illuminate it)self

para||el ᴅᴇCAYe SERIES ...

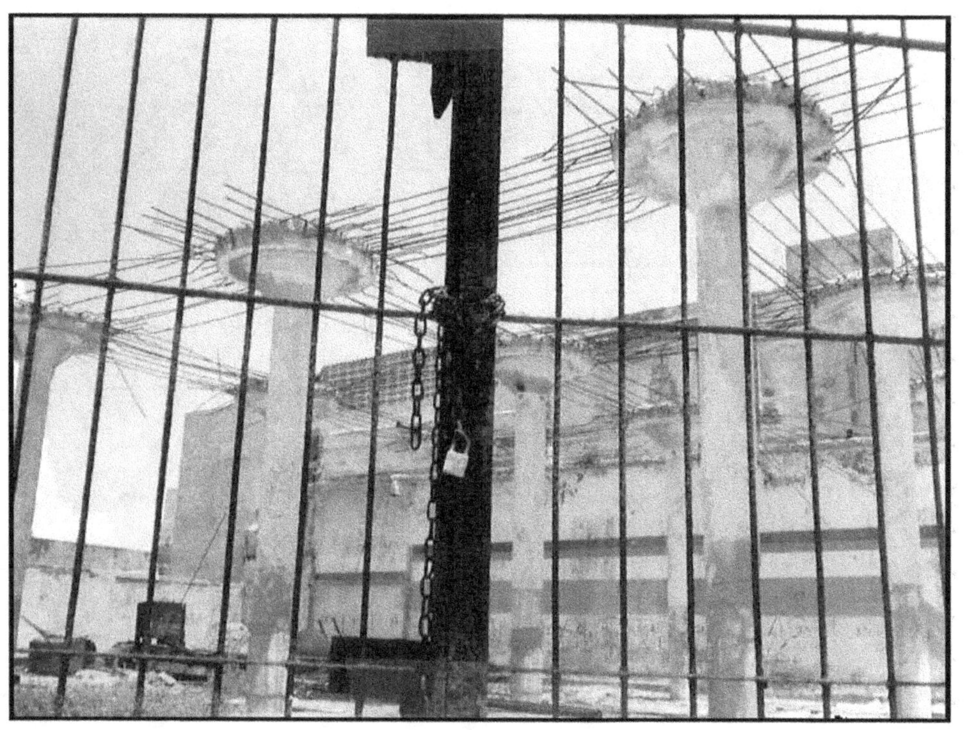

through the viscous turnstile, signs the cross (for granted) in the g(host) bldg of physical & S.o.s waves... sleeping

A Foundation of Dependency

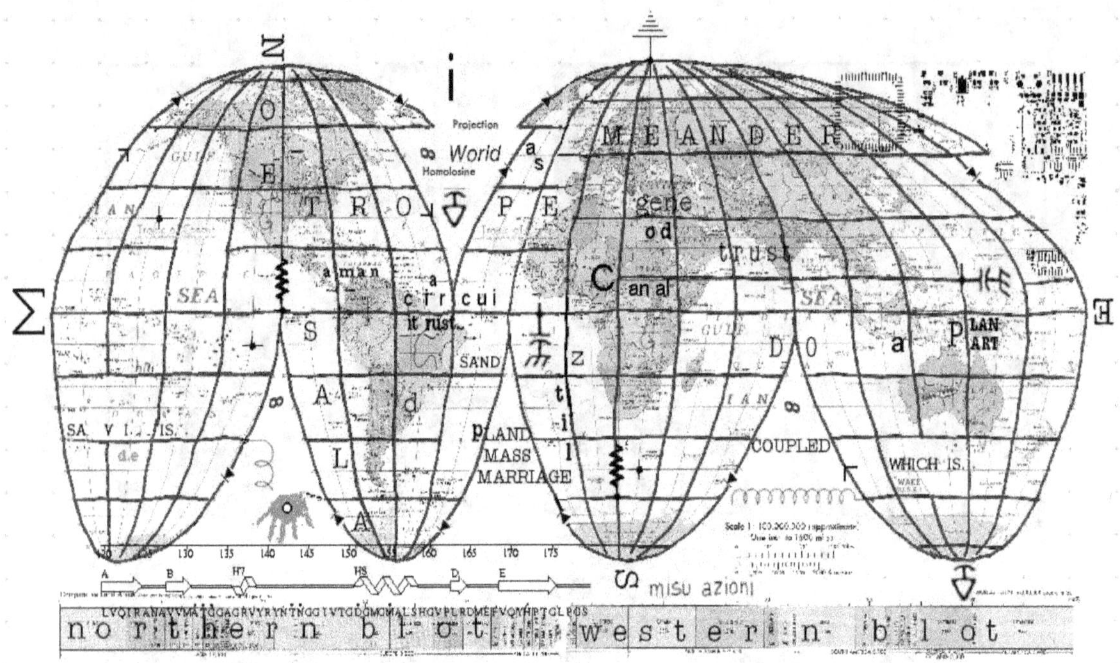

Actualization of the Plan

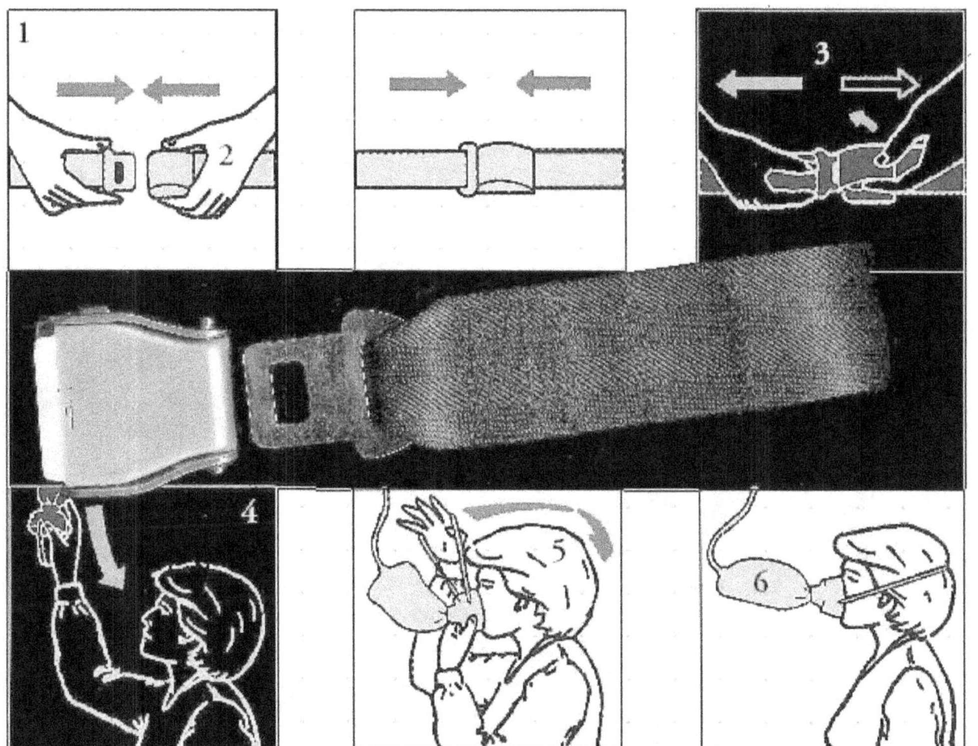

En Route to Buenos Aires   12/19/2002 (sampled in-flight)

[1] Shake your own hand (if this step is uncomfortable, skip to aftermath).
[2] Your hands sweat because you are nervous to meet yourself.
[3] Lift yourself by your own bootstraps.
[4] Hail a cab without speaking.
[5] OhMish didGeridoo (one of many circular breathing techniques).
[6] By definition, we are all fish, breathing each other and ourselves. (i) repeat.

taking necessary precautions before the journey to the colon(y) enclosing the camp bell, shifting the 5-fold clutch...

Niños Héroes Monomyth

(All I am **F**ree to write down is what I liv**E**d). I was born with a ● in my ch**E**st. The doc**T**ors said it w**A**s symptomatic of b**R**eathing ba**C**kwards (breathing

← firs**T** then →, **R**ath**E**r than → the**N**

←). I learned to D**R**ive stick in GUADALAJARA. They had no **X**sections, just these devices called *Glorietas*[1]. One (in parti**cular**) was dedicated to *Niños Héroes*[2].

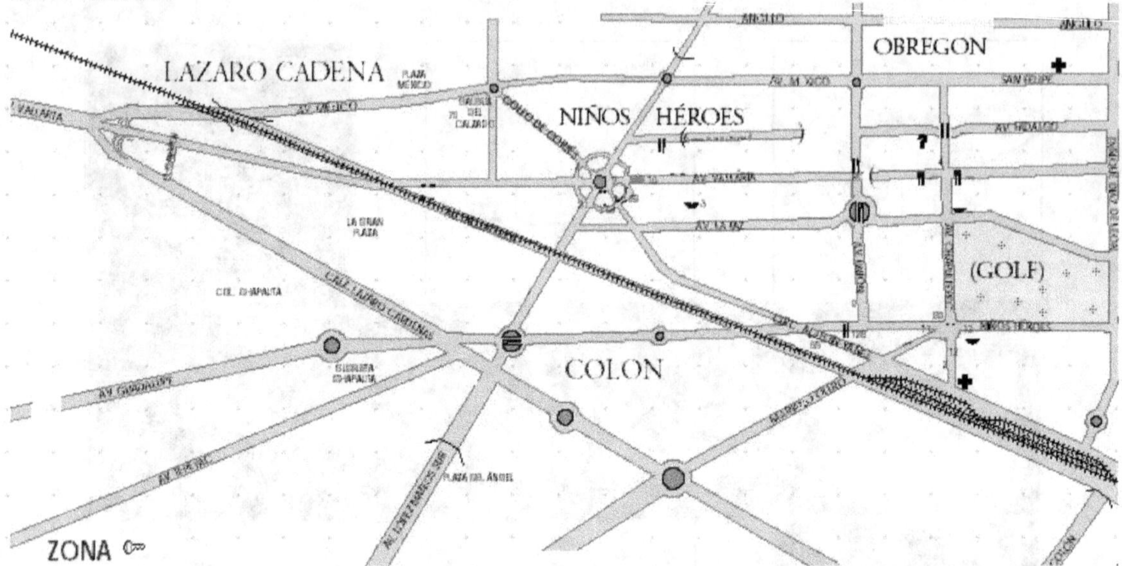

As a hero child, I learned *Inglés* by speaking Spanish first (even though I eventually forgot it). **C**ristob**AL** Co**L**on was a h**E**ro[3] even if he wasn't aware the world was **O'**.
I **L**earned to date **U**p at the lit pla**Z**a where (domin**G**o nights or after half-night mass) ♀ would walk clockwise (as seen from ∅) and ♂ counter-clockwise. If you liked a ♀ you cracked an egg[4] filled with 3-hole paper punches on ♀ head. I **L**earned NOT to fight @ blood fount**A**in and the **S**mall town bullfight**S** (n**O**t the kind where they say, "Olé")

When I RE:visited Guadala**J**ara later, there was a t**U**nnel un**D**er**G**round b**E**neath Niños Héroes Glorieta. Now I live near

Colon Círculo.

---

[1] There were no traffic laws—it figured itself out. Still, the traffic cop's whistle instilled fear.
[2] Six children who wrapped themselves in Mexican flags and threw themselves off a tower rather than risk death at the hands of American invaders.
[3] In the sense defined by all preceding myths, e.g. Sisyphus.
[4] Not round for reasons of optimal morphology.

Fleeting Sleep ((Coin_ci_Dent^al) _ME_moria^L)

$((\#)-(\#)+(()=((\infty))=(O)=\int(Wednesday))=((hol^*y)=((\triangle/)))+\sum(fi)\sqrt(I)$
(((((+he ash (on my hand(Ω) has no pölar... /•- ((((nor(+$\hbar$) is
$H_2\ddot{O}$-sol_uble))&*"duct_ive)|#it sinks (as silky silt) to the bottom •f
the cuRRen+)j))$\mathbb{H}$))(((♯)...•(/((((((/+)))((-)))))))&)))))))))))
weather ((Battery (§) Park/) is a [posit_ive] and [negat_ive] cell
is _in_con_sequential to /((Xcept those but_... (the •circle(☼))) of
trapeže /art_ifi_ists))))◊(?sea)... the lay_per_son ♀O tour_ist (knows)
(((hard_wired to the (♣ /lucky (nick_el)) slots @ the wed.ding chapel)))
•rr_lying pöles (i) can shift with(Out) us (k)nowing (((s• plus
is _min_us ((• (and min_us is plus O (both polarities are needed (to need our sells))) •
(((((((FPO FPO)(PLACE "\|IN PARALLEL|/" HERE (FPO FPO)))))))))
((•)(((((((af+er\ the biVouac dis_aRRay (•)) — ((we took the Staten
Island ferry (ℏ/ bus))) never dis_em\bark... (((•+he ferry [⊎] was
as örange (⊤)) and charged (((g) as the s°n (((•n\ an over_cast° day
(((((<•>())((&)))((_._))... ((&)))) ((((½+⅔−¼+⅚) (()(\$)(((((())))
(((the only thing left (for **crobats) that was free||)))((&(((\10))(
8)))) dia_metric_ally •¶pos_ited to all ass•ciations in (•ur) wake\
(((+he sol_id resi_n_due of albatross coin... w/fidel comet tail is dis_charged via per_sonal means)))
(while ... the (parenthetical) [placeholder]
((elect.ron/ob.in ((arbit_rary hu_man_ con_struct(s)) in the schema" of))))

NY, NY May 26, 2003

... stopping to bivouac for the night, an acrobat tying a string around your grip index (order is a memory of condition)

Drawing Parallel

On September 1, 2001 after finishing a climb up

a long white granite slab, I was rapelling
down a long, thick black rope

I came to a belay station with dirty dishes. I gathered up   the cereal
bowls and dumped out the milk. The milk traveled, suspended, through the
air
and
hit   my brother,   the ground.
But I couldn't carry everything. I was concerned that the porcelain and
crystal might hit the people below,   but I had no . choice but   to
throw the   dishes down   the hundreds   of stories to the ground.
 It didn't   make sense   because they would break.
But I needed my   hands free.   But then I felt guilty.
There was so much junk, wine,   funnels,   glasses and papers.
          In due time   I would have to climb
back up   for the rest.

                                        I rappelled recklessly
                          to the ground. When I prepared
     to climb   back up,   the rest of humanity told
 me   I was crazy to trust the rope.
               My theory was that if it held me once already,
what were the chances of it failing now? Once I had the dirty and broken
dishes down to the base of the façade,   I was annoyed that I
would have to take them back to "civilization".

                    At that particular   moment

                              I was just happy
               to be at the base
                    of the climb,
               at the base of a sheer white granite wall, until
I noticed the black widow climbing down the rope and realized
          I was just one unpromising pound of flesh in the web.

RE: Origin vs. Date

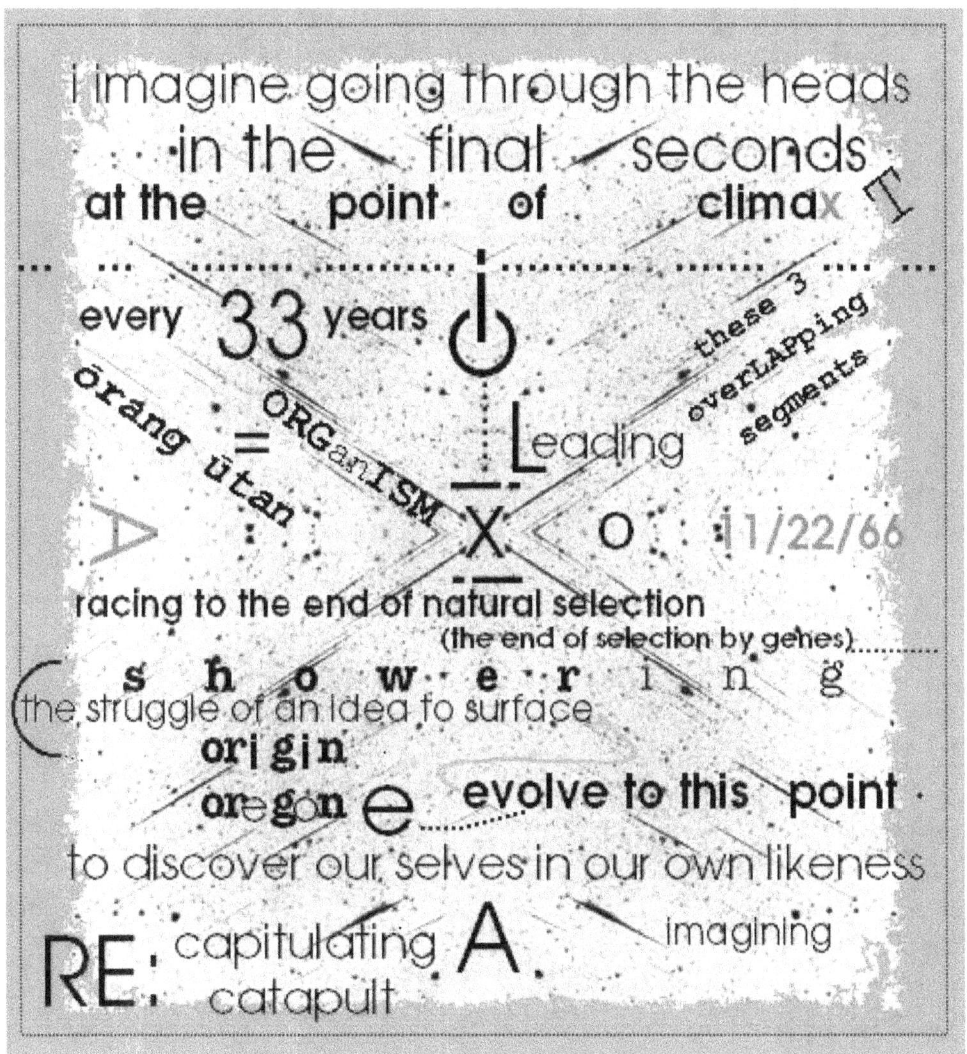

cross-section of Ni meteor, recursion of Leonid meteor shower 11/2002

How-to Di(od)e: R(evolution) ǝniИ ɿǝdmuИ†

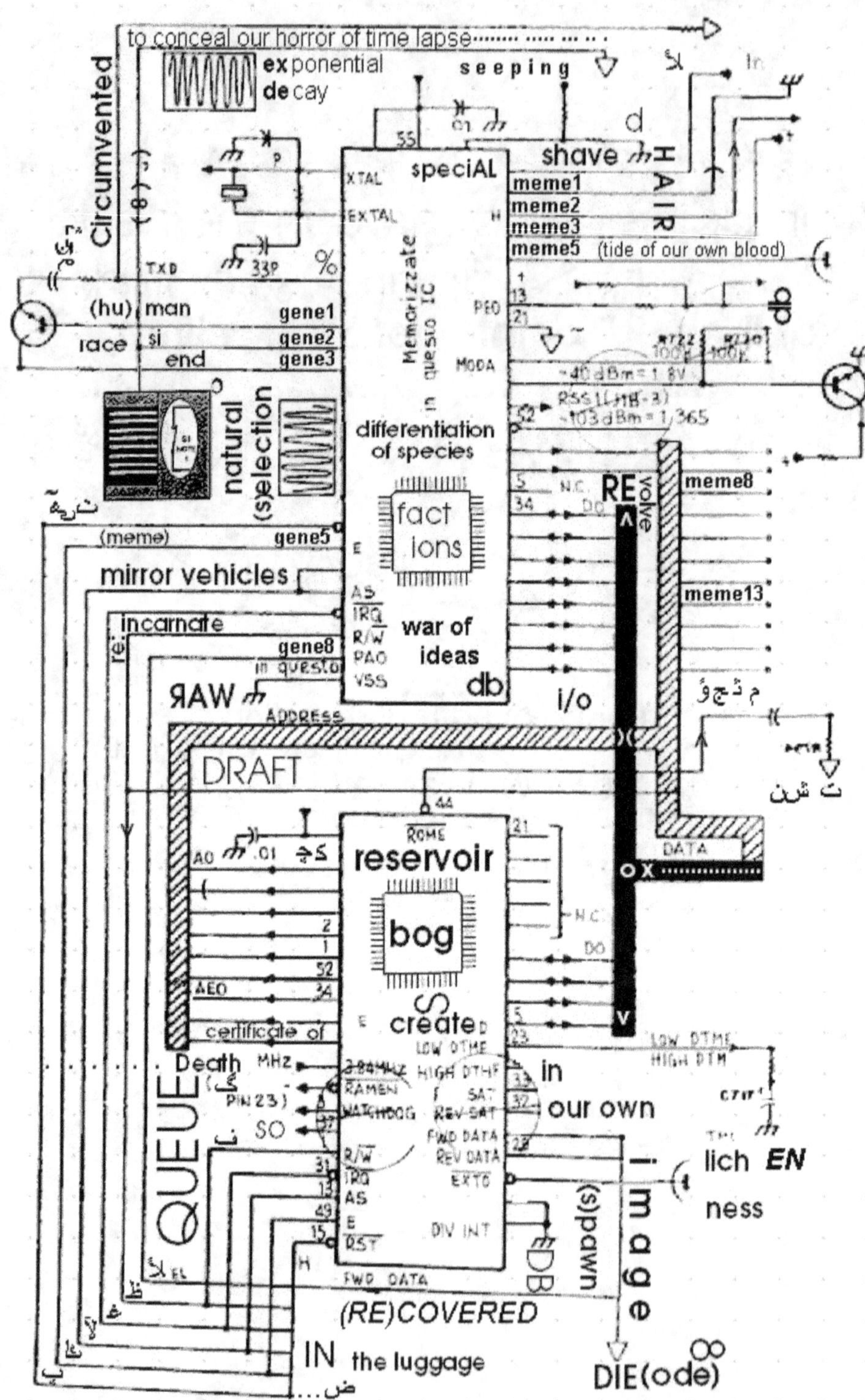

work) headed for the last will, reverberating... the tree-lined sidewalk so low it meets the pavement, I'm in need of a

½-ₐSᵉSS COLⁱONⁱ ZAPᴬTⁱOⁿ SERIES ...

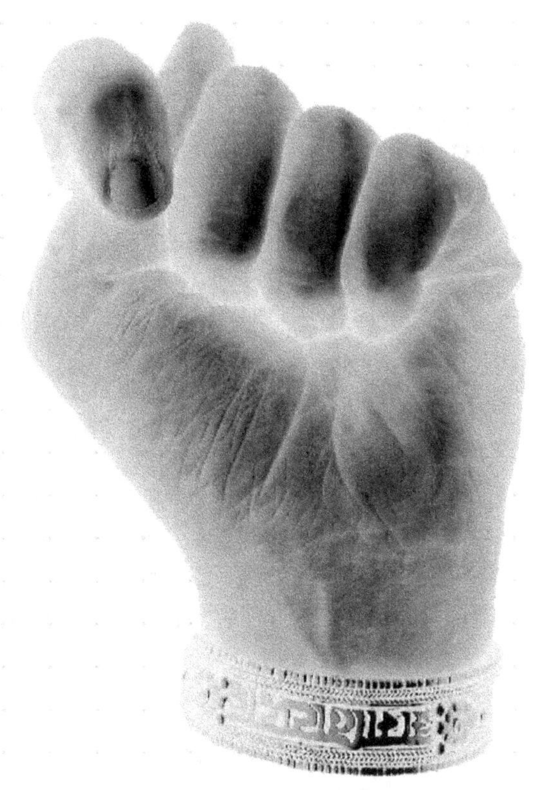

Canal St. (w/ free coupled inscription of Δ below)

Christ(mas) trim & a sno-coned sea bass to honor the upside-down horseshoe... diffusing the rattlesnake under the

Algo Lucky[1]

un(i).(t) ravel
bra z il.l ion equiva.lent...

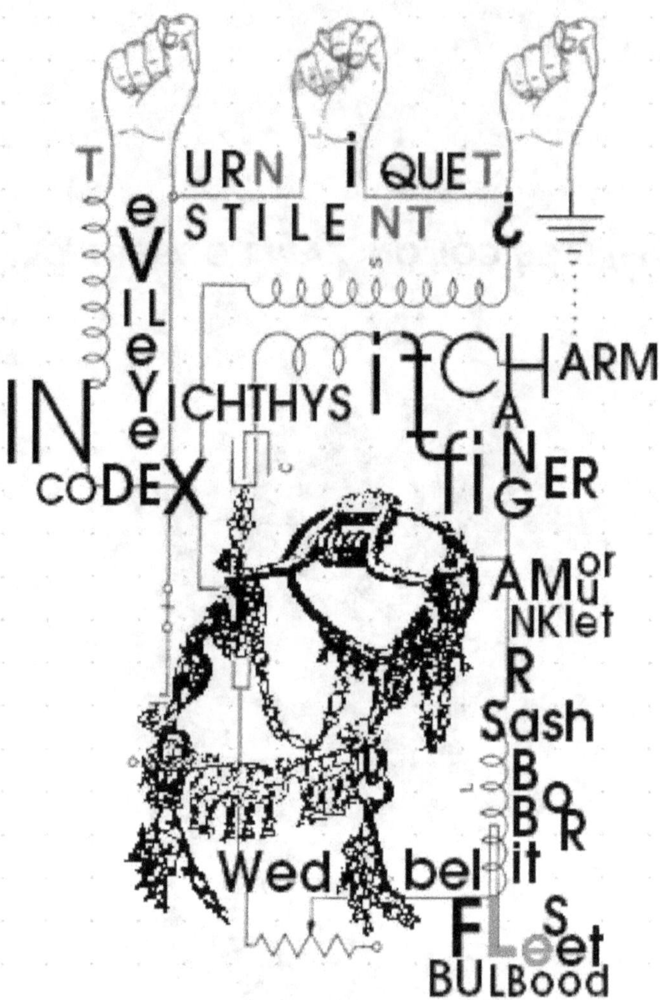

Light (nes. (day)) or sig.n
the croSS
(she g.loves)
3 dimin.utive but.tons
über horses.hoed arc.hway
ash.ing.e zippers
a fig leaf his.tamine
log rhy.thm
apply.ca(u)tious superstit.ions

[1] TNT found shipwrecked on a coral reef off the coast of Santo Domingo

fig tree, the mongrel sucks albumen & salt water taffy from the garter left on the stoop... they make a stink about wire-

Roundtrip Ways to Work

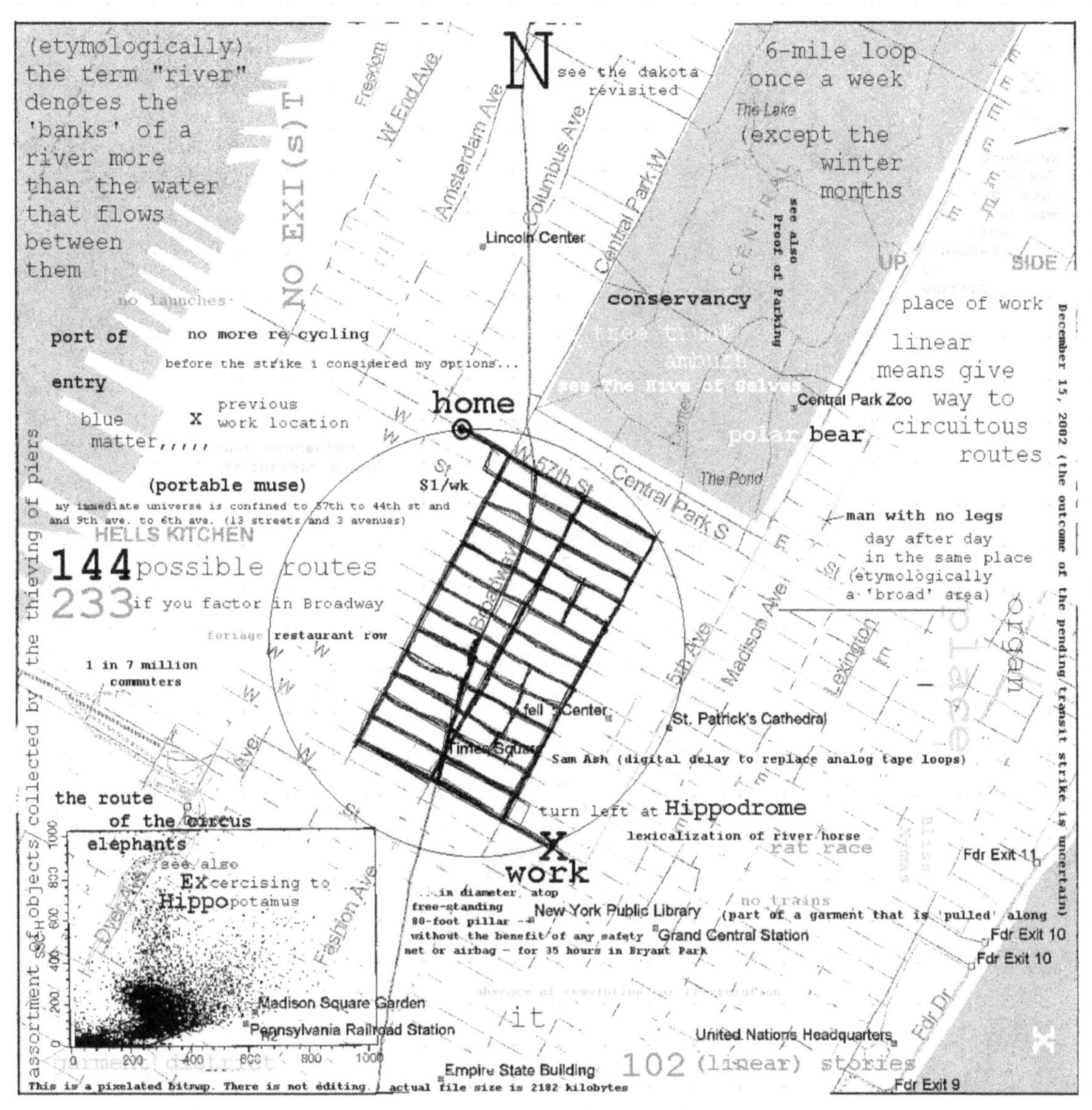

Cliff Notes for **Phoenix Egg Omelet** (Left)

begin [L] waYeyebrows.[R] (running in place)   [L] asks pre-historic

[L] during answer be freeway[R] White [L] born [R] ? scrambled

[L]for three hours and thirty-six minutes battered [L]cause thinking[R]
frontage where [R] tape loop [L] flip lies *think* I was thinking[R]
[L] stub think running through your mind?" flying.[R] to stand still
For [L] two [R] passenger side, [L] Verde tree mind;[R] I prove
trudging ....self.........the vanity [R] begin and end meaning
[L]and father [R] curious the race," but you really loan below Pleasobo
peak ostrich all done you?"[L] know [R] right(eous)left viscous place in no end stereo.
[L] mind for the life of me is real [L] a mind-frame to peck [R]
care." I just to [L]quetta racking."my whether— pre-dawn endless mile, horizon
need water[R] [L]?" —I asked Scotland porta-poddies through the only needs "I circling
thought bladders[R] [L]mind. immediate— [R] looking forward.........[L] we should
fuel cannelloni They'll peck[R] debt mild pain and Whatcomfort."[R] of
'Phoenix relativity Marathon'[R] [L] our civil Artist formerly into
[L] rear view mirror [L] anticlimactic." Ostrich farmer twenty-six miles how
dinosaurs volume of sludge. to fix[R]
ashes Believe messaging" sex once— [R] about been semi[R]
blazes by leads to offspring [L] coil mothers[R] [L] "are [R]
resurrection.[R]
[L] hole "That's a pitiful excuse stretch Oztreegable matter hobble how
shadow right pave still bury gravel heads will
here Stir findings wheels slow the [L] caused reach[R] in excess now,
with her." makeshift tent where smell of fertilizer Athens until overalls roll
hear ancient beneath
[L] ""There cashews [R] [L] won scrunching, hunting decidedly." [L] under the coyotes

(Right)

Reaching the wall[L] front of [R]**the troops break step when** was [R]
stationary [L]the cuff can[R] **when** [L]? Here... catch." being
[L] initiated and view mirror i [R] crossing[L]continue steady
twenty-six egg [L]rainbow[R] **the** at an epic[R]
second [L]asleep, one **bridge** [L] revolving The He
texture Yes it is road [R] [L]Phoenix Marathon
[L] spinning in place either,[R] : [L]browsed through land
windmills eying castle

if world tacky turning separaphernalia [R] :
[L] do it again?" : my word.[L] Look [R]over bite
yeah herup "marveled few fleeting seconds died. arbitrary
"Sure." [R] his ashes tucked [L] one."[R] [L]line, [R]item
[L] "Seeingers. refuge [L] about[R]
[L] porch .,[R] [L]even [R] [L]conscious?p."
the egg a
it n't wipe presence, ...it the salt retrospect. [L]there's[R]
matters own sane in all which first?
somewhere a volume of one and a half inspiring [L]who built You [R]
[L]equivalent[R] A create in my one
[L] nothing an [L]dozen "marathon" [R][L]Anasazi to be sure. Hohokum[R]
a feed fry[R]everything twice [L]"How'd
whatever else, hat's " — [L] · [R] [L]see God. [R]
"I hampered
[L]canals fixed? sign [R] [L] lay [R] [L]too[R] [L] of years[R]
hand sleepy
ago "Life basic desire [L] I [R]sense [L] mass [R] [L] so-called[R]
ostrich reel enough
comic high'. ."the distance mind plays [L]incubation[R]

make "And guess?" [L] invigorate[R] [L] at night
[L]female sits [R] fabricated over with.
" really [L], It's [R]
[L] I held [R]
out?" moment there is no
retrospect. hungry for the quest ....[L] hell [R] [L]
[R] for omelet." end [R]

Hive of Selves

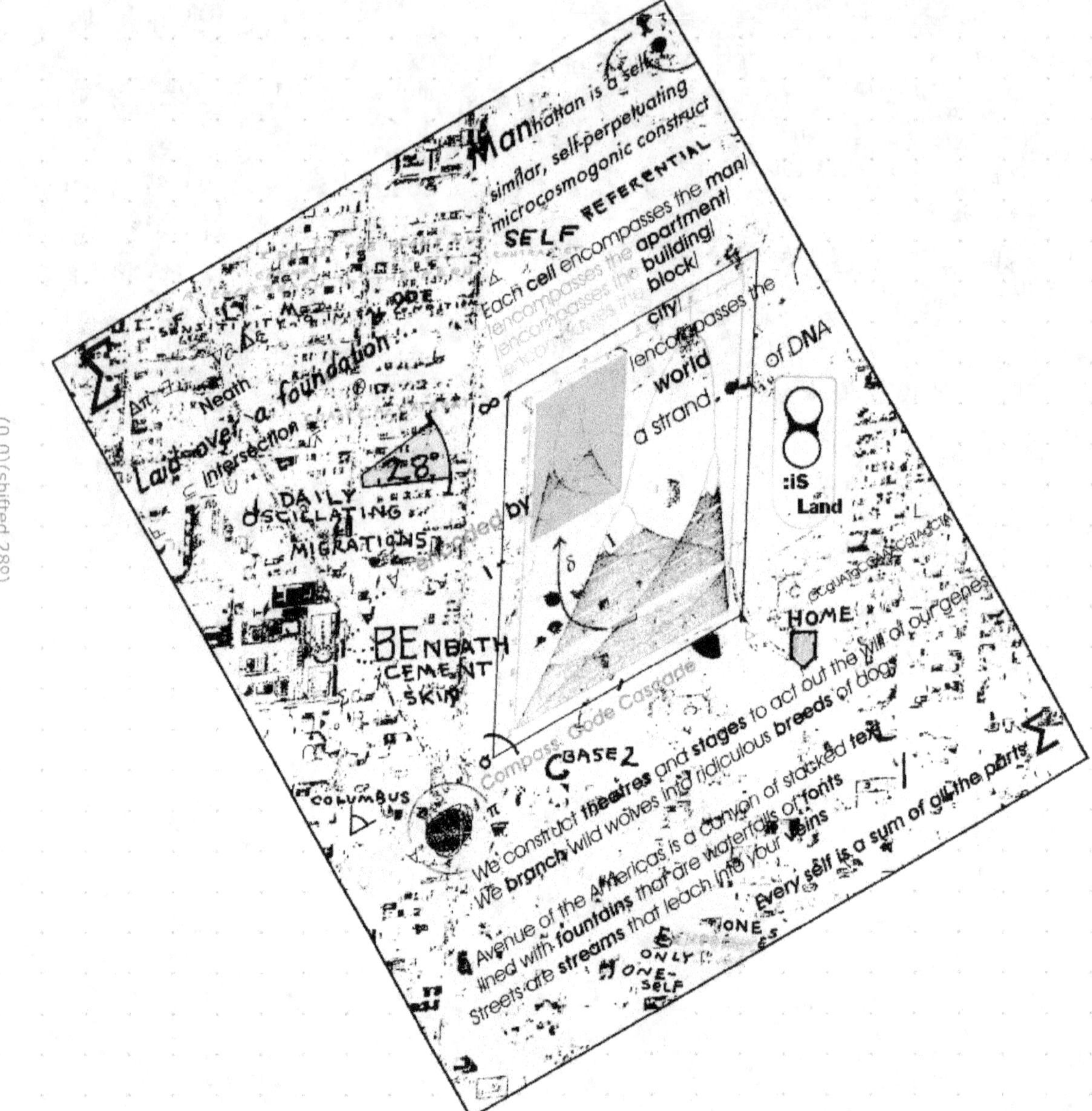

Measuring the Umbrella Strikes

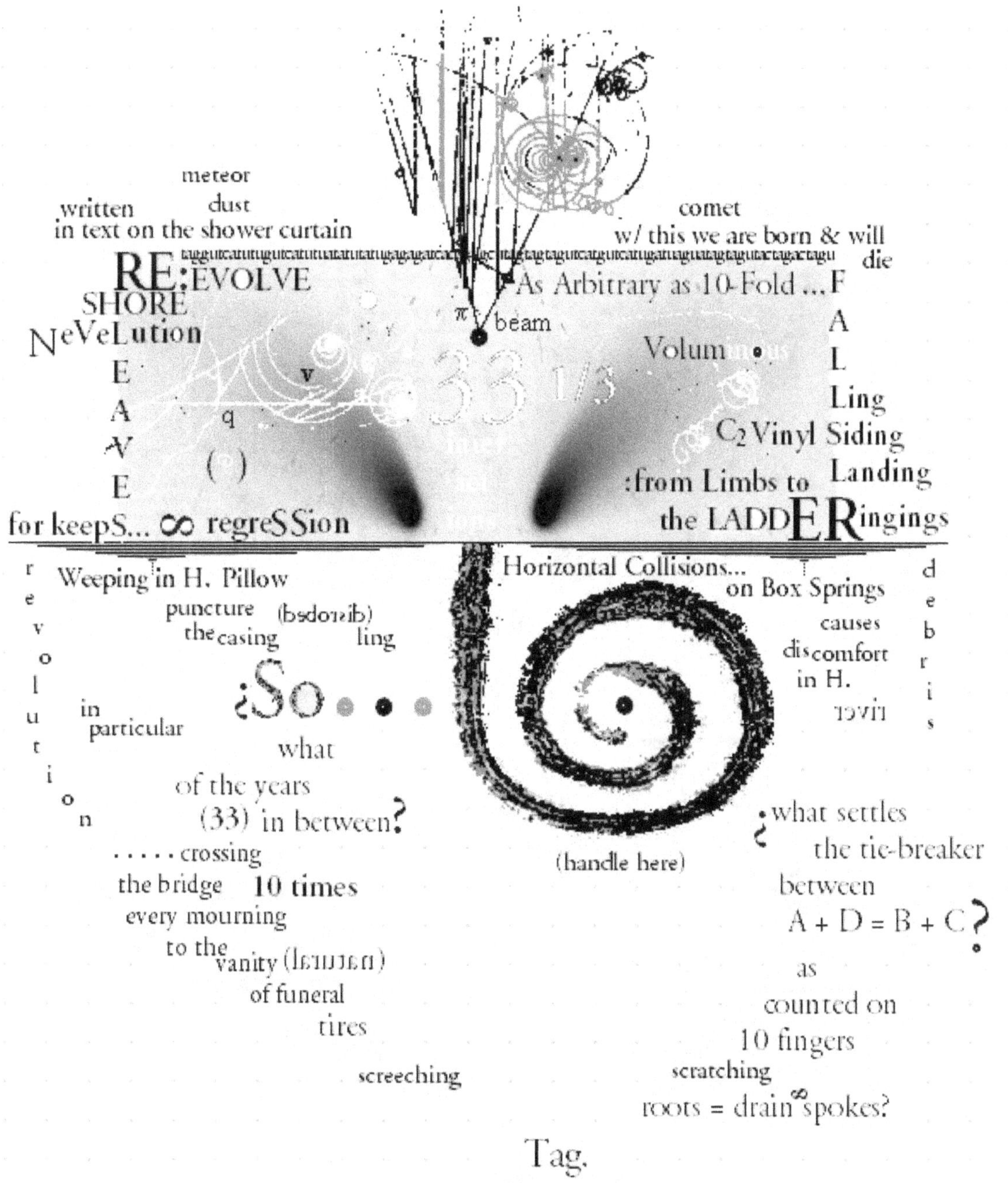

Curried Conch in Port Lucaya

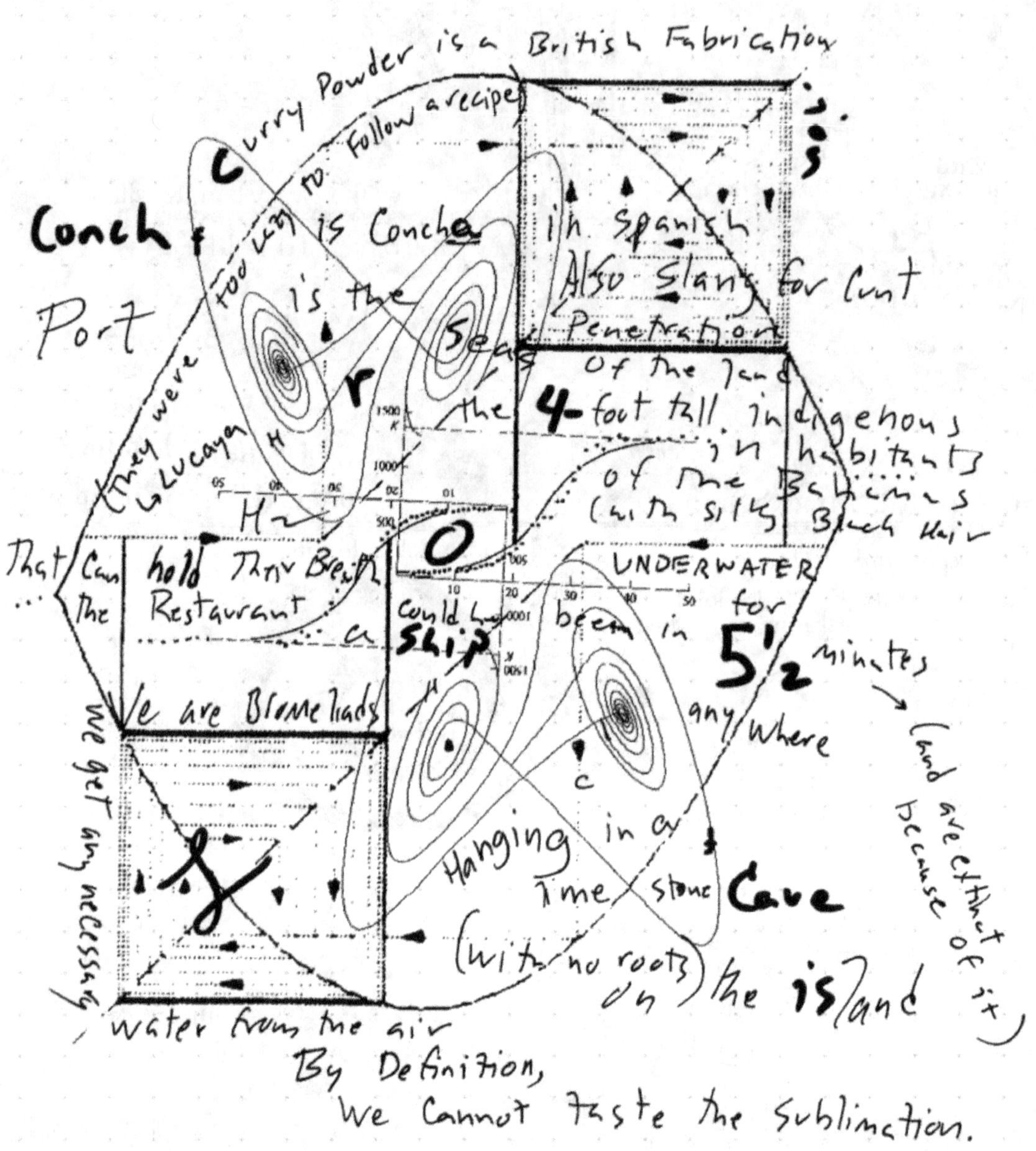

Bahamas post-Xmas 2000

Coming Clean

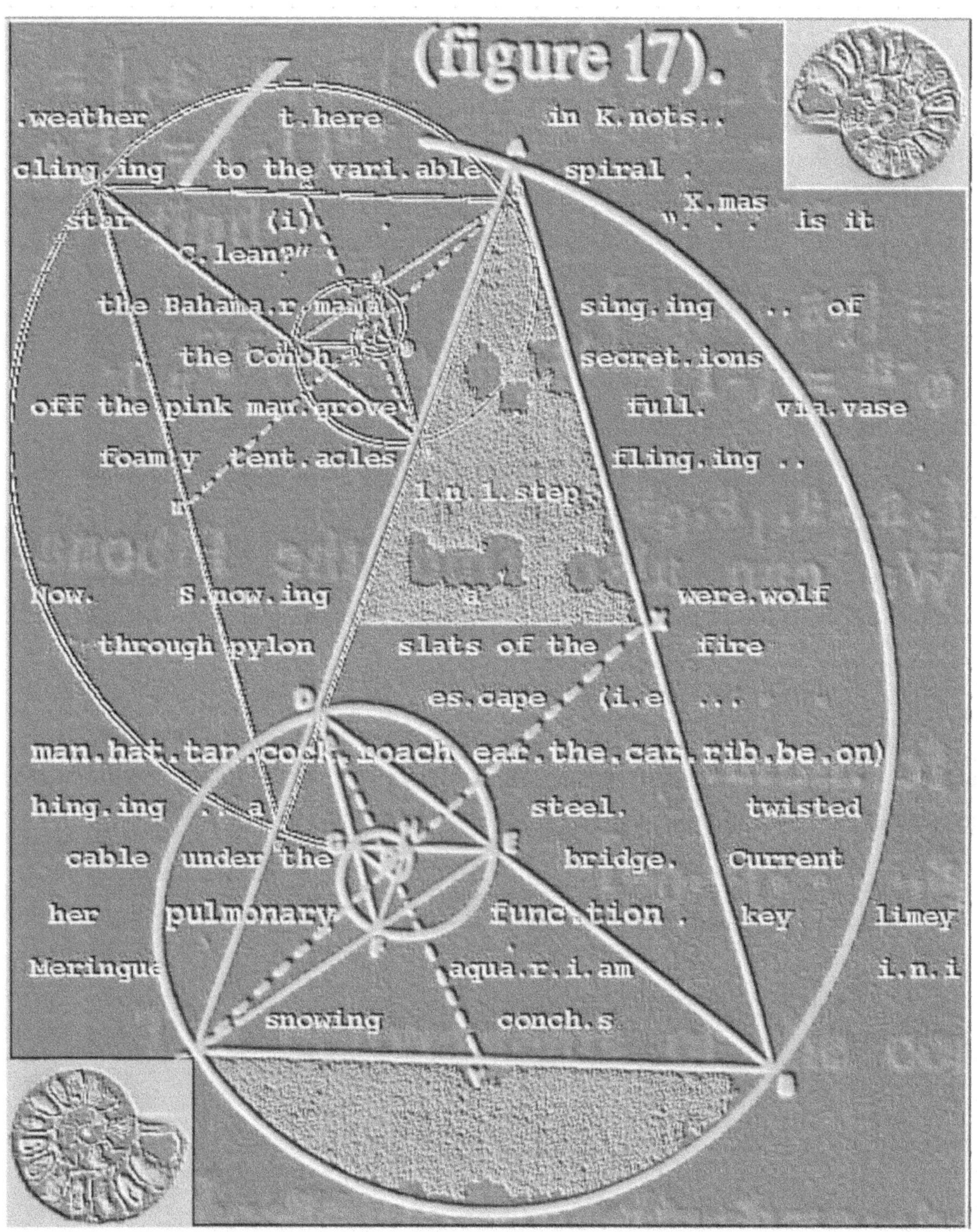

of the elephants trunk, self-similar umbilical spray ... risking immunity to stand in her strapless bra, for once, intent on

Dividing the Spine Five Ways (an Immunological Response)

The (hairless) Japanese dogs were meant to pull the sled that contained (the) vitamin C (and then some). But the Akitas lacked hindsight and perseverance, leaving me to fend for myself. It was taxing getting the sled up the stream of sinusoidal synapses.

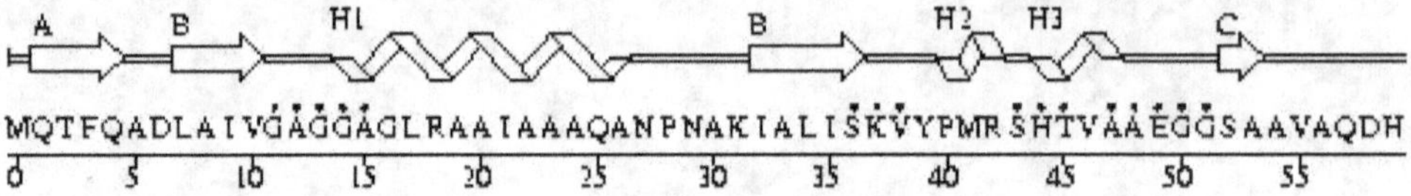

```
  A       B        H1                          B         H2    H3              C

MQTFQADLA I VGAGGAGL RAA IAAAQAN PNAK IAL I SKVYPMR SHTVAA EGGS AAVAQDH
0       5       10      15      20      25      30      35      40      45      50      55
```

(Only primates and guinea pigs have lost the genetic information necessary to create vitamin C on their own recognizance. Without vitamin C our blood vessels (will) become unglued. Every time I stopped to eat (my load)(sic) got lighter, and I was fitter for it.)

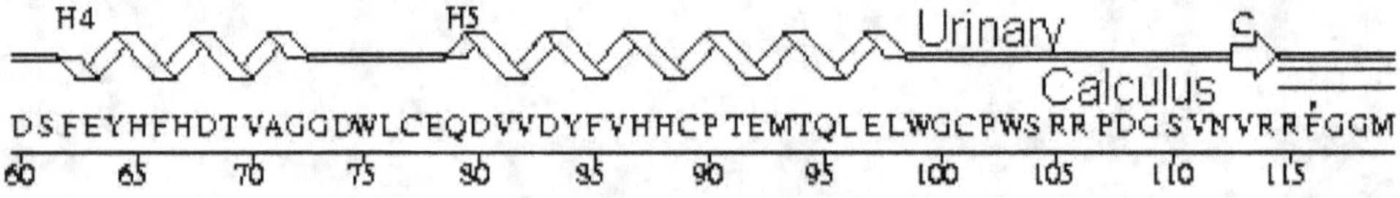

```
  H4                       H5                     Urinary                    C
                                                  Calculus

DS FEYHFHDT VAGGDWLCEQDVVDYFVHHCP TEMTQL ELWGCPWS RR PDG SVNVRRFGGM
60      65      70      75      80      85      90      95      100     105     110     115
```

I made it to a covered bridge (engraved with the logo of the same vitamin company whose product I pitched). In the middle (of the bridge) was a drainpipe to relieve oneself. As I started to take a leak, the bridge came apart (below my feet). Plank by plank (step by step) I maintained control of my own reins, but had to sacrifice the sled and the freight.

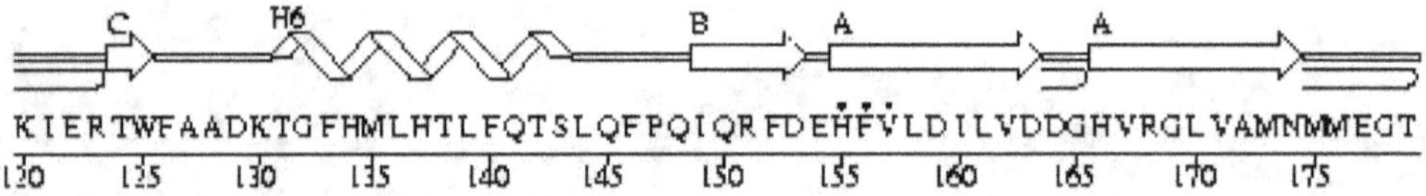

```
    C       H6                        B       A           A

KIER TWFAADKTG FHMLHTLFQTSLQFPQIQR FDEHFVLDILVDDGHVRGL VAMNMMEGT
120     125     130     135     140     145     150     155     160     165     170     175
```

It was then that the five unleashed dogs appeared licking my face (and I knew I was more alive than before (for risking death)).

Exorcising to Hippopotamus

They're jogging in locomotive serenity
        beneath the surface, while
I spin a thin white line on a stationary bike
five stories up from 86th & Lex

sounding not too distant from porpoises
        through I-phones, over the grinding sirens
regressing out to graze on the grassy banks
beneath the ruminating savannah moon

I'd like to think my pedaling powers their all-knowing smile
        permitting fish
to dart in and out and clean their protuberant teeth
(to a hyena, a bulging ribcage glistening from the shore)

a symbiotic relationship, feeding off clumpy organic chards
        from the hippo 4-chambered stomach
underneath the minty-metallic severance
I can smell Papaya King's infamous hot dog remnants

this morning, flamboyant religious leaders in front of the UN
        detained my wife from reaching NYU Medical on the M15
she tells me I slept on my head wrong
after feeding me ramen noodles before bed

I spin the zoetrope
        going deliberately nowhere
a slow-burning histolysis of my pancreas
as it jostles and slithers inside

fueled by barley water in a clear bottle
        in a brown paper bag, in the back of a black town car
on the way to Shea Stadium during the 5th inning
where hippos crush peanut shell fibers underfoot

dancing on the detached sodden turf
        of the hippodrome
the social hierarchy breaks down during drought
as they cluster and wallow in the thickening mud

NY, NY 8/2000

(x)ing to board the 7-train clutching a 4-leaf clover (in a funk), her c-section becoming un-sutured right before the

Lazar(us)/Leper(son) Lap

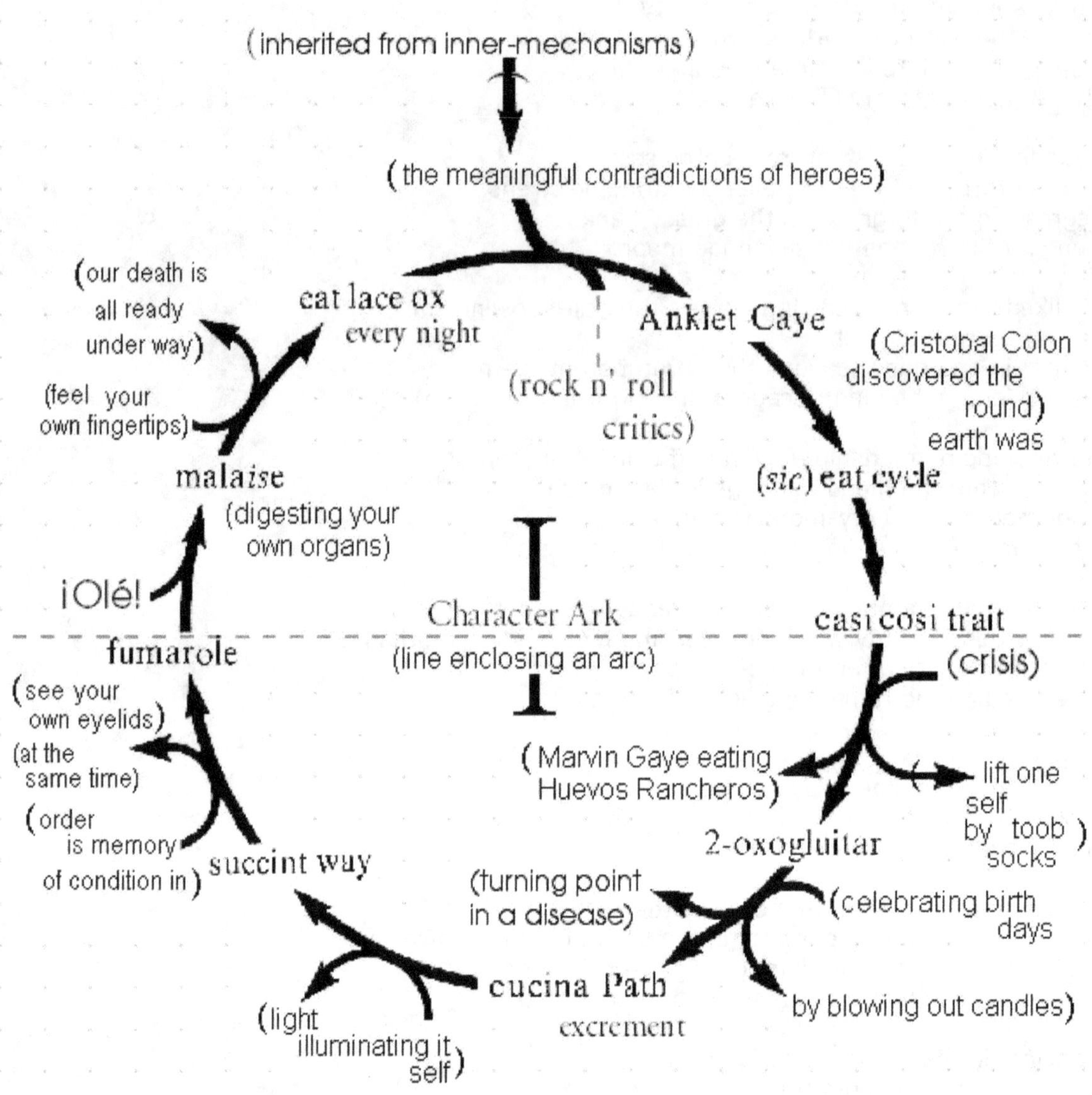

a e$^{(z(}$H$^{)ERO}$($_{SUB}$$^{)}$ JUKE$_{WAY}$ SERIES ...

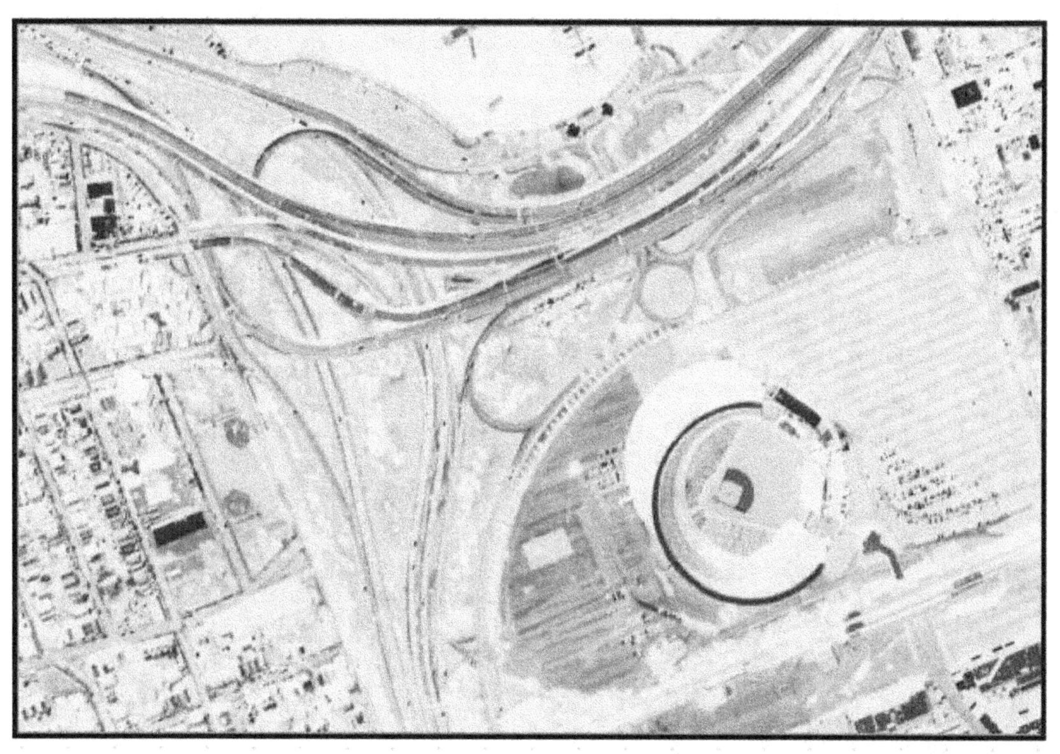

Shea Stadium as seen from [heaven courtesy of ...]

hell-bent on molecular meditation before the balinese tooth-filing begins, a necessary pain to cover ground lost ...

Bodhi Circuit 8

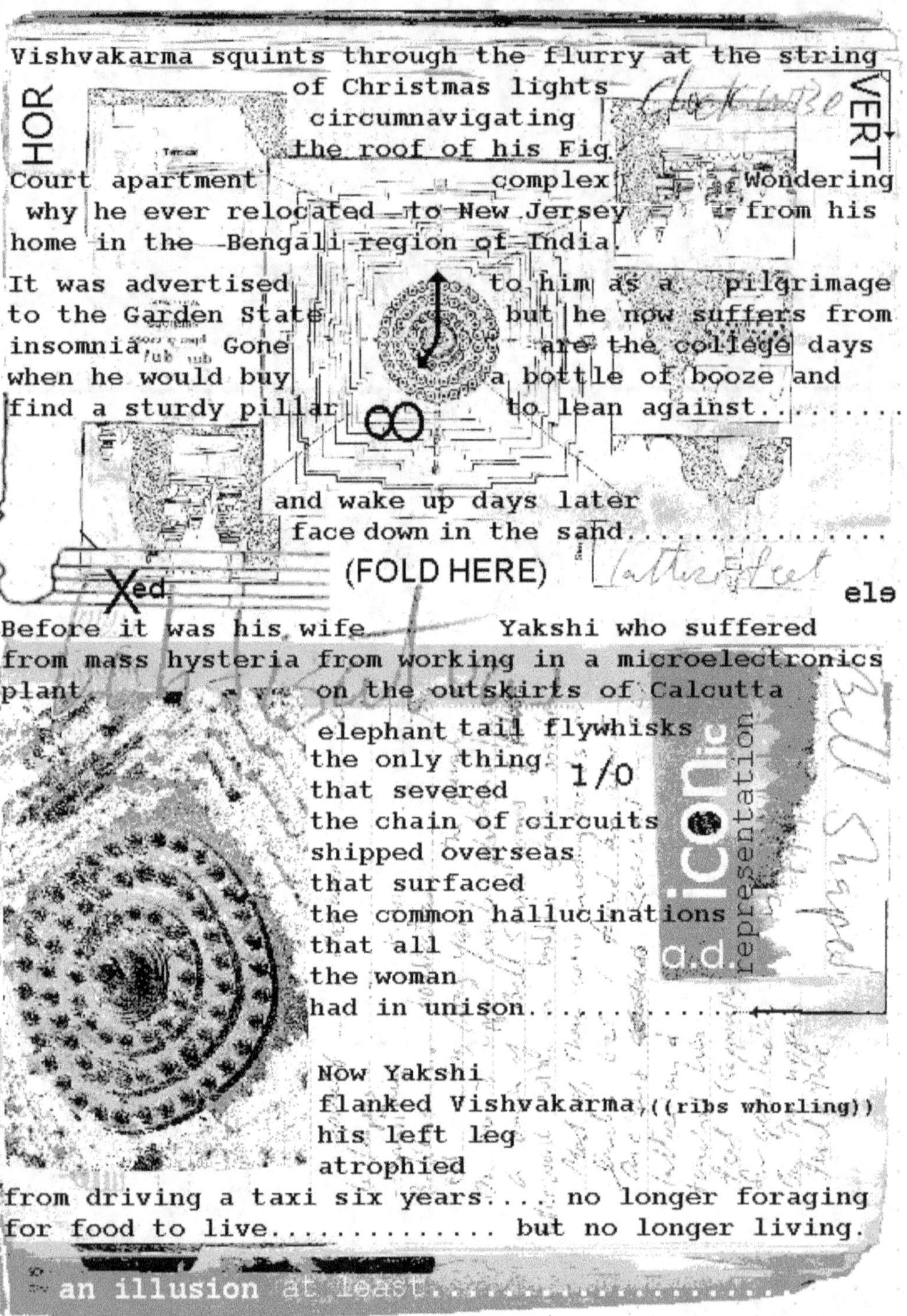

spiraling to sit in one place, reading the firescape in motion, just one of many identical scripts subject to sub-(sur)face

I/O Embed: Lot 34

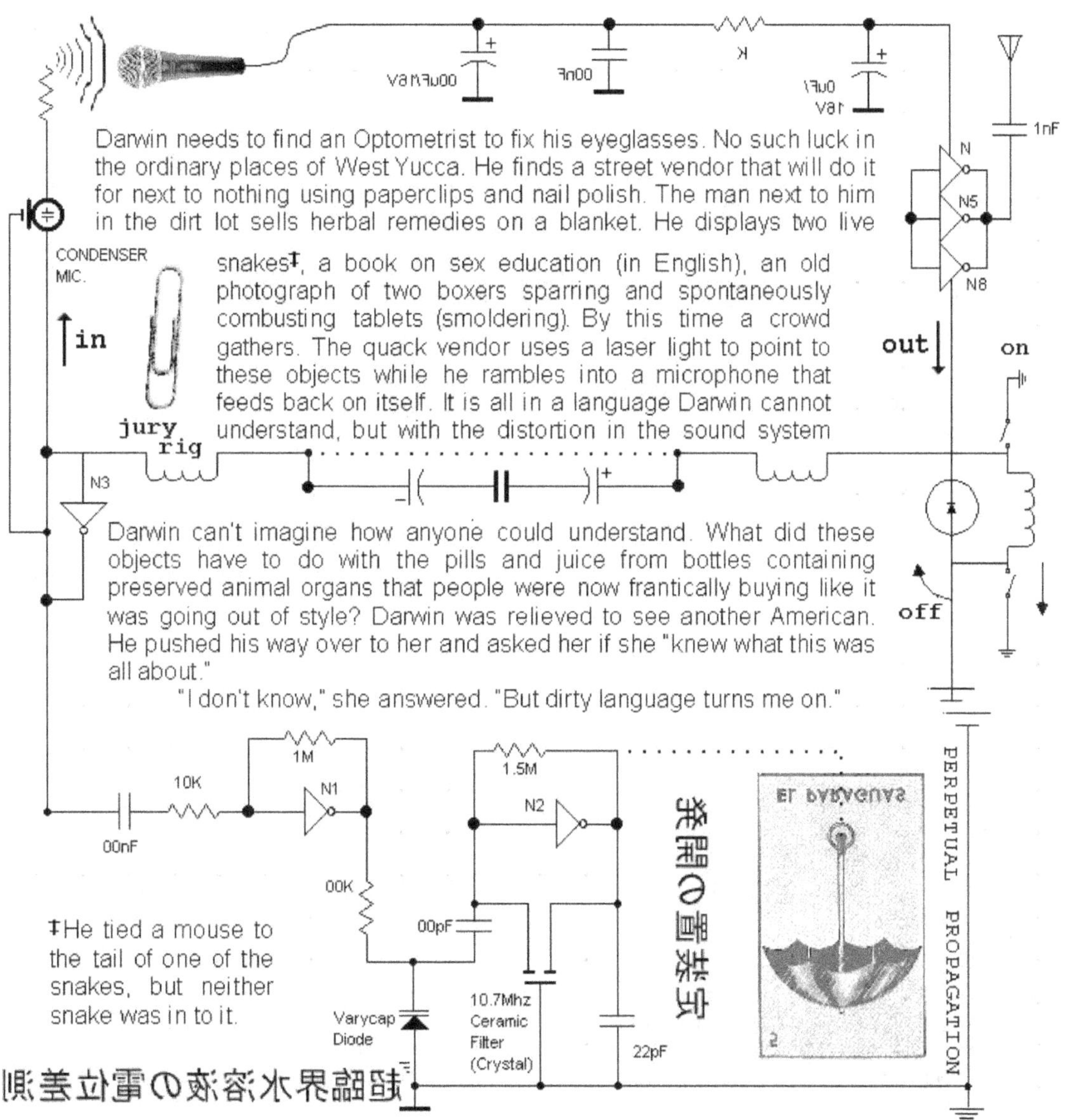

Darwin needs to find an Optometrist to fix his eyeglasses. No such luck in the ordinary places of West Yucca. He finds a street vendor that will do it for next to nothing using paperclips and nail polish. The man next to him in the dirt lot sells herbal remedies on a blanket. He displays two live snakes‡, a book on sex education (in English), an old photograph of two boxers sparring and spontaneously combusting tablets (smoldering). By this time a crowd gathers. The quack vendor uses a laser light to point to these objects while he rambles into a microphone that feeds back on itself. It is all in a language Darwin cannot understand, but with the distortion in the sound system

Darwin can't imagine how anyone could understand. What did these objects have to do with the pills and juice from bottles containing preserved animal organs that people were now frantically buying like it was going out of style? Darwin was relieved to see another American. He pushed his way over to her and asked her if she "knew what this was all about."

"I don't know," she answered. "But dirty language turns me on."

‡He tied a mouse to the tail of one of the snakes, but neither snake was in to it.

Catch W/no re:Lease

Erosion emanates from thee abominable basin (272-feet below sea level) with no outlet from a century ago (when the Colorado River breached a manmade fabrication). Only evaporation can stave off the stagnant coagulation sustained by excess irrigation drain-off laced with pesticides and unwanted Coolie Loaches (originally from the South China Sea) flushed down the toilet (sewer-trout and Sauer kraut swelling at the seams). Discharge records do not account for all drainage inflow.

The salty sediment (follicles and scales) occupying the depression is a cock -starved reservoir of abandoned lust. The initial capacity to endure is scientifically tested over successive intervals to verify that it fits the curve of the sole of the shoe (grossly enlarged due to a glandular disease). An intense reclamation effort is underway to restore the morphology to its inherent nature (for recreational (not procreational) purposes). No drain for the dirtied bathwater (I plunge in desperation, hip deep in baby pooh). No sublimation, just accumulation, no aggregation to rise, to leave behind the freedom of dreaming. Mushrooming warts (putrefied cauliflower heads) globbing on the (belly-up) floating fish reek of our spiritual origins, but still, how (and why) the throttled gills continue to pump (in their sleep) is beyond me, born only to suffer (a policy of catch with no release).

Exiled to the shore (not eligible for parole), the dinosaur undulates on the thighs beneath the shade of the Bodhi bush (a spurt of a rattle revealing) side-winding in the tracks, while our tires (also confined to the grooves) dig deeper into the sand, until the axle bottoms out, the burnt oil spills and we are spent. With the smog diffusing over from Los Angeles, the Salton Sea has no apparent horizon (no lines of accountability) and no recreational watercraft on the surface. We are confined to the banks with an electro-static generator cranked at 2400 amps, making a grotesque circuit reaching deep into the earth with fabricated electrodes jury-rigged from reams of tinfoil and salt (hip deep with shovels, digging our own graves). Now we stew in the heat reading the *Battlefield where the Moon Says I Love You* until the Tesla coil locks off. We trace the fuel lines, dissecting the pump, revealing a ripped diaphragm. Nobody said this would be a glamorous job (like picking up used condoms on the beach the morning after) but I needed to be cashed (just one in a string of stark motel rooms with Gideon bibles). Now I see it all from sterility of an airplane, with a 30,000-foot view of the bifurcated erosion, feeling an overwhelming detachment, not knowing if I belong (not knowing if I want to belong) to any church-state that would create such a wonder.

Salton Sea revisited circa 1996-2003

ripping the fabric to ascend to the pristine state enveloped in a high-voltage cyclone with the (capa)city to endure

S.C.L.E.R.A.

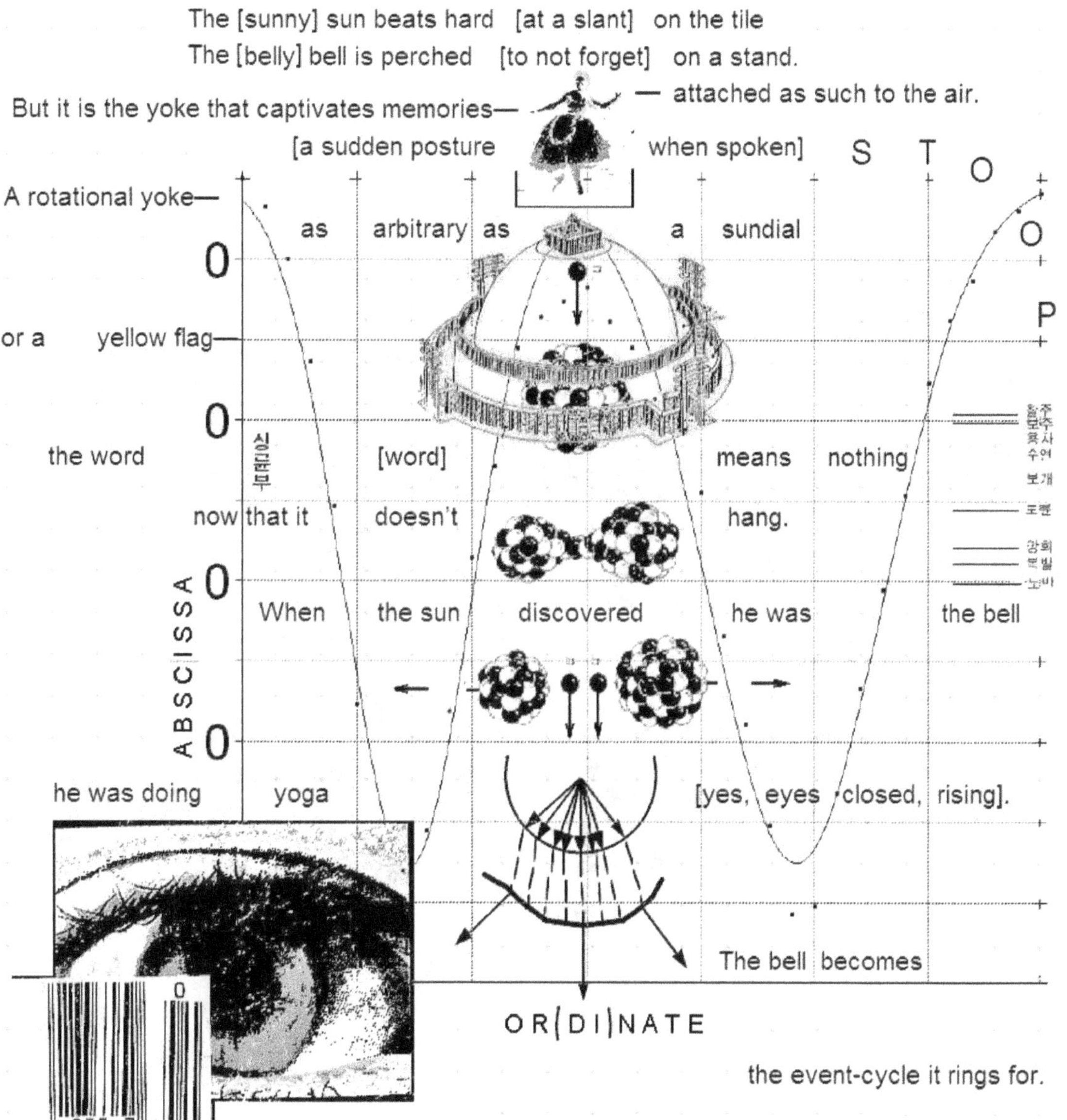

Santa Catalina Laboratory for Relativity by Astrometry (former place of employment) circa 1991

...7 miles from love I paid hard cash for a used sun hat that I originally lost on a trip that identified me, no other

Yellow Rosa Cirq[incision]

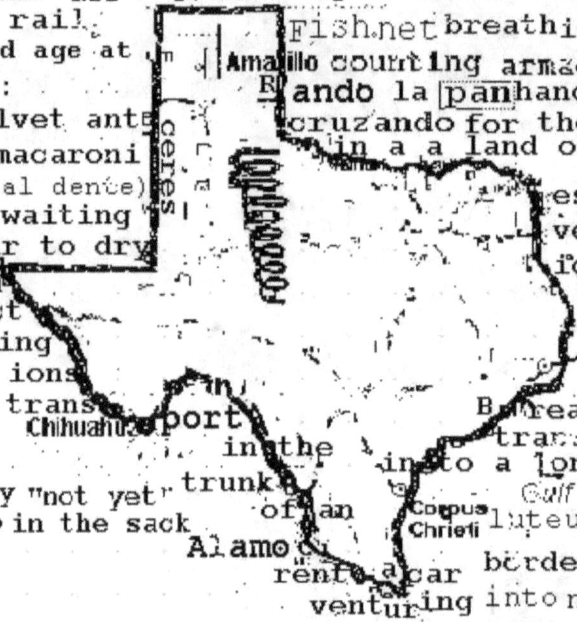

Tonopah, NV 1996 / Newark, NJ 2003

```
Answer "Bolsa"
  To Armadillo,TX
         getYups sí de taxi nar quill que part dames
a tempo jaw sou grams plains rig de un ices grinds so veils
au trek ceils les Ing de campo che-chee bo!  Hanuman wu hu
tea pools rail             Fish.net breathing maka angin hor-
boig languid age at    Amarillo counting armadillos whilst cruz
izon falls:            R ando la panhandle frita cruzando
   ⊙ red velvet ant     cruzando for the misión imposíble
   ⊙ green macaroni        in a a land of newly
         (al dente)                      established con-
   not Yet (waiting                      vent
   for my hair to dry                    ions
         con                             born
         vect                            again
         ing                          w. ac.s
         ions
         trans             B  reaching
         trans port            transecting
   Chihuahua            into a longhorn
            in the               anus with  edge
   just say "not yet" trunk
   to in the sack  of an   Gulf      a razor cup
   Alamo        luteum               con carne
         rent a car   bordering
         venturing into new territory
```

Dust on the Anvil

(static hiss) & you are
          (grnded by a tornado Xing) in a vehicle parked on a plain of sagebrush (guarding
the Xmitter) near Tonopah, Nevada & (I'm sitting on a   plane at Newark, NJ).

The rear view mirror tells you,
          "you're not in Kansas any more"
          (left by the previous surveyor).

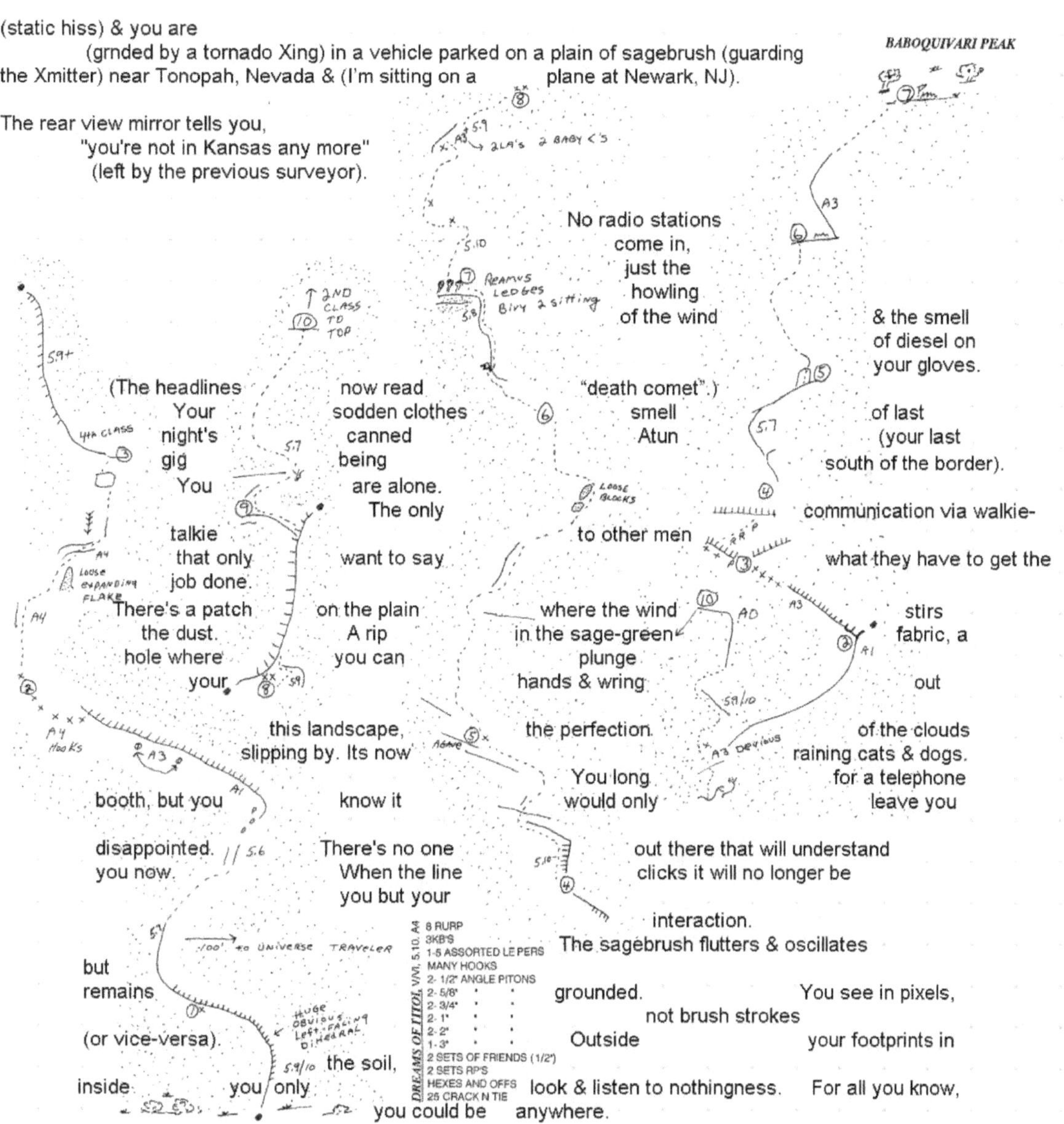

No radio stations
          come in,
               just the
                    howling
                         of the wind

                                        & the smell
                                        of diesel on
                                        your gloves.

(The headlines   now read   "death comet".)
     Your   sodden clothes   smell   of last
     night's   canned   Atun   (your last
     gig   being   south of the border).
     You   are alone.
               The only   communication via walkie-
     talkie
     that only   want to say   to other men   what they have to get the
     job done.
There's a patch   on the plain   where the wind   stirs
     the dust.   A rip   in the sage-green   fabric, a
     hole where   you can   plunge
          your   hands & wring   out

          this landscape,   the perfection   of the clouds
          slipping by. Its now   You long   raining cats & dogs.
booth, but you   know it   would only   for a telephone
                                                  leave you

disappointed.   There's no one   out there that will understand
you now.   When the line   clicks it will no longer be
          you but your   interaction.

                              The sagebrush flutters & oscillates
but
remains   grounded.   You see in pixels,
                                   not brush strokes
(or vice-versa).   Outside   your footprints in

inside   you only   look & listen to nothingness.   For all you know,
          you could be   anywhere.

along for the ride, the traces endure from the bonfire across the border, nothing remains from the dreadlocks of the

Stalking up Maíz for the Afterlife

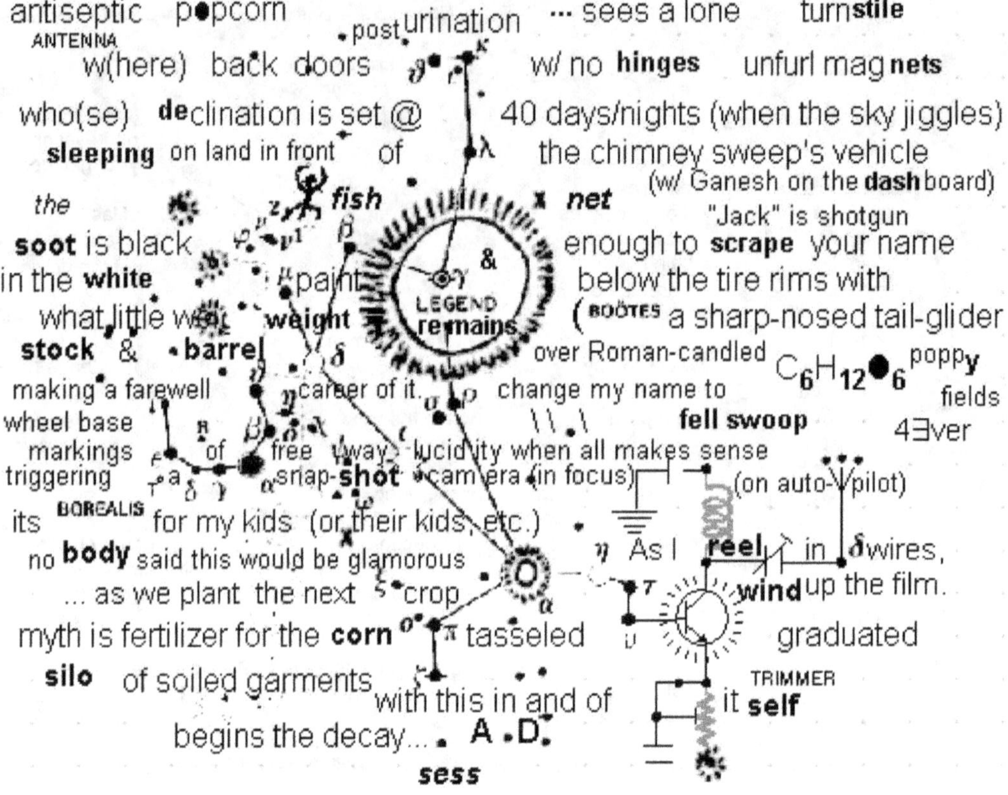

buffalo soldiers on a death march except rabbit ears pick up a strong signal in the brine... after the bubbles subside, a

HAR$_p$MON$^i_{KE}$Y $_{Su}^r$BASe^8 SERIES ...

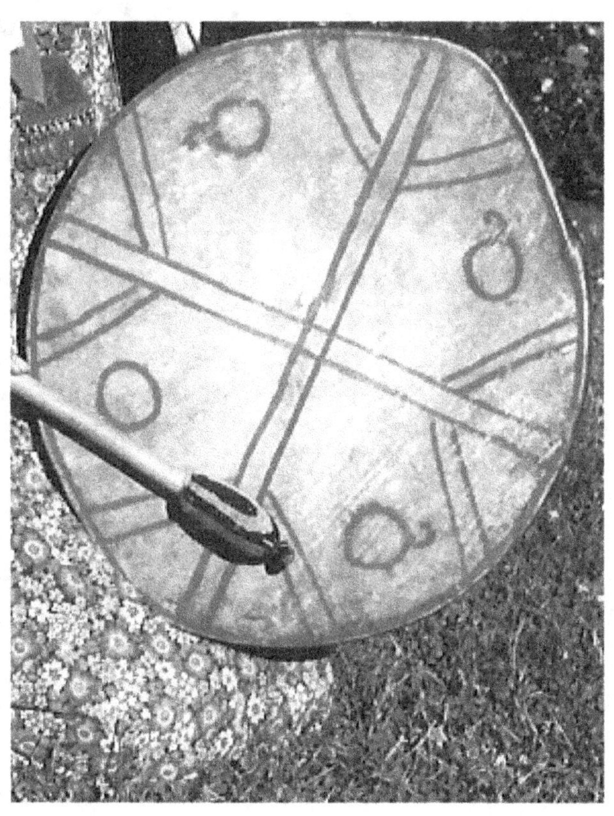

HAR$_p$MON$^i_{KE}$Y $_{Su}^r$BASe^8 SERIES ...

postcard from Temuco, Chile (donde nació Neruda)

Dead pariah in her lap, circumnavigating her tailbone, growing the fifth hand of an ancient monkey, converging

This is (K(not)) a Lie

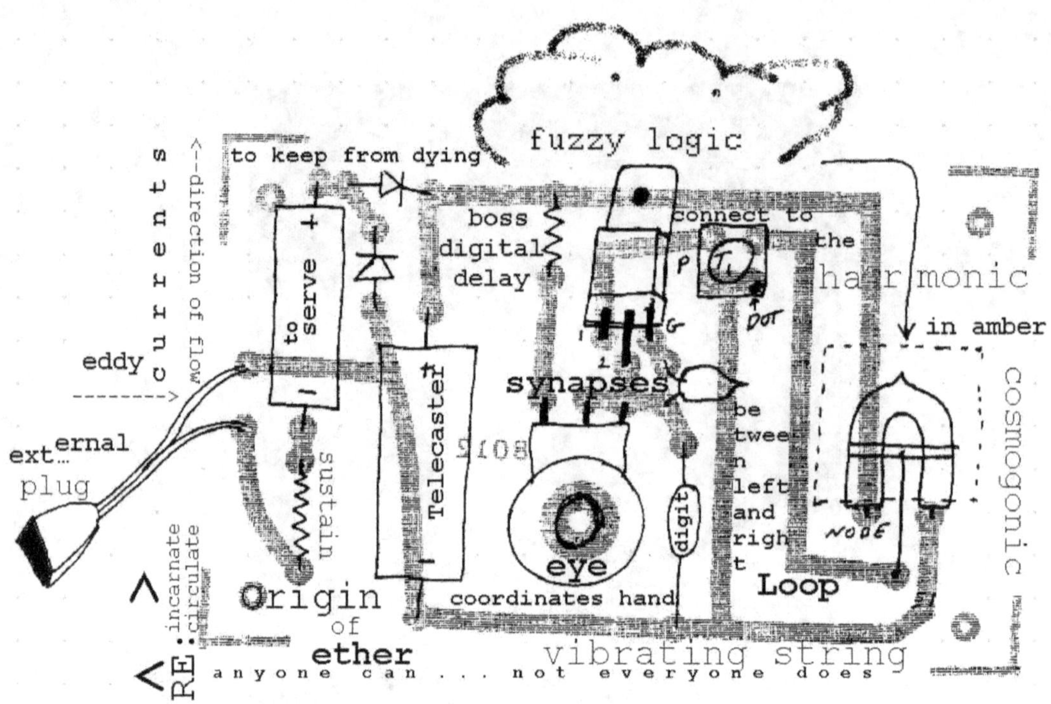

Muting the Bugler

She said
        I heard a noise
a door
        slamming closed (over
        & over) but never opening,
or a muffled hi-hat.

I twisted the cold and hot
        knobs off
                waiting for the water
                                to stop

dripping...

and tried
        to hear

                        how do you picture a siren?

when my ears adjusted
        to the faint
                background hum
i heard
        what I was listening for.

Bone Clutch

The forgotten drums are now fire-pits
        (fire burns itself, yet
         fire cannot burn itself)
Ash retains the form but disintegrates when touched.

D.Bevel

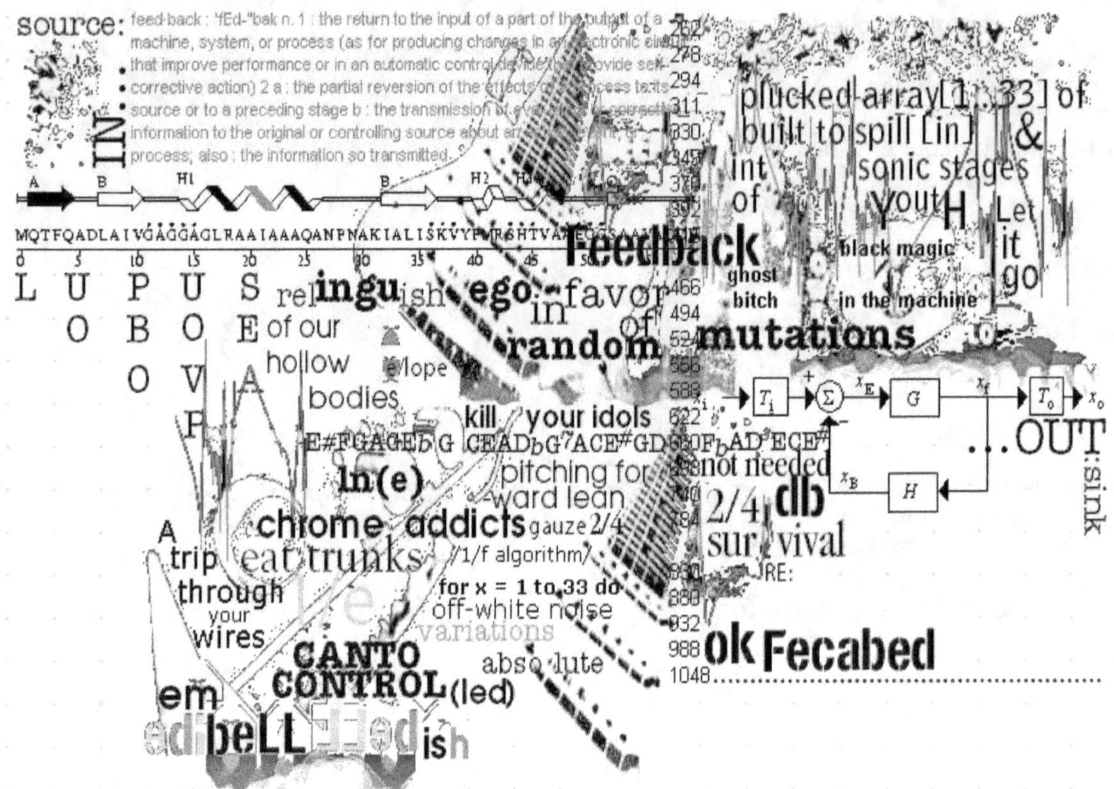

At Least (the Sink) Was in a Rental

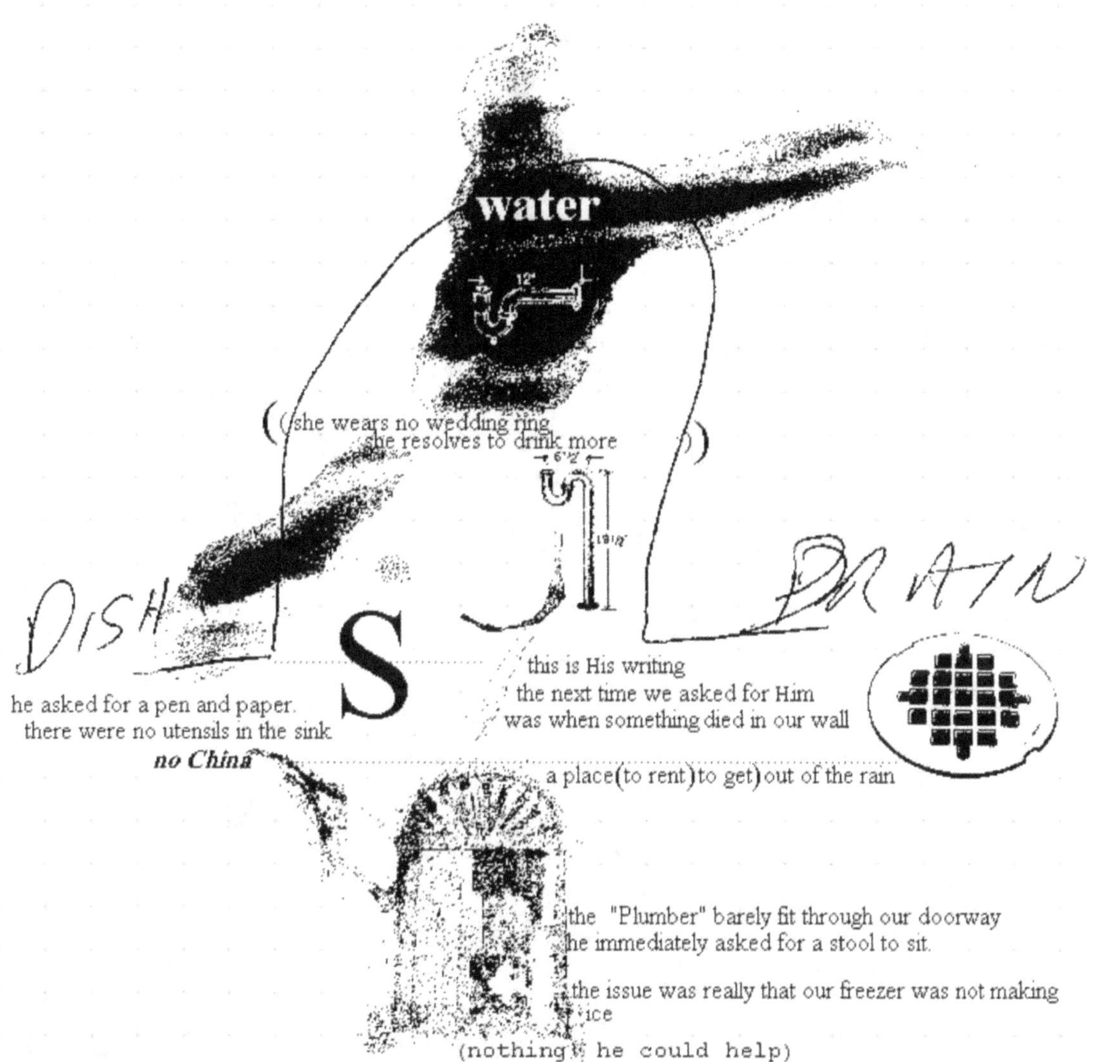

Impregnating the "Illusion"

Rome, Italy 11/18/2001

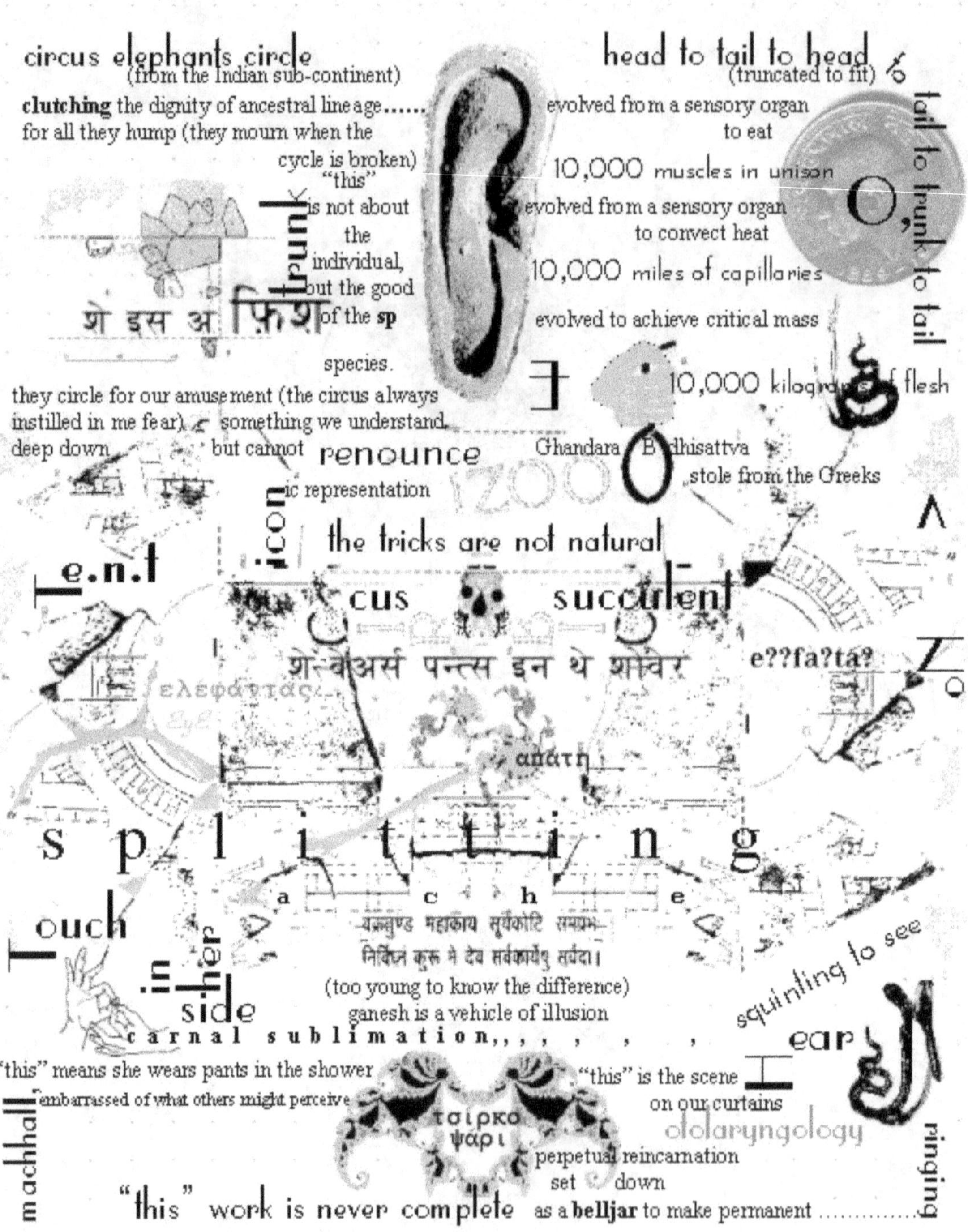

A Discontinued Soundtrack

A dream
that sticks out in my head
from when I was a child
walking near a waterfall
and I kicked a log over the edge
and only then did it erupt
into a landslide of white noise
waking me up

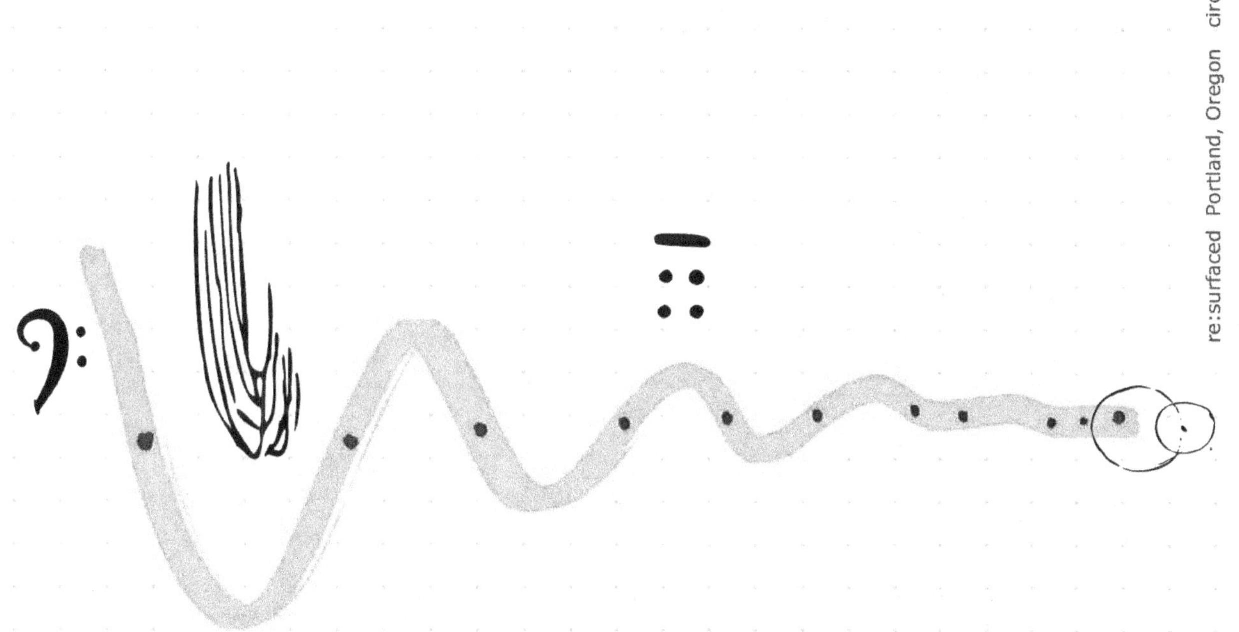

re:surfaced Portland, Oregon circa 1972

windshields to exorcise, playing hide-n-go-seek in the ice plants with a lace noose, identifying with calculus, making

Bullet Lasso N

A rummage sale of sworn testimony I sissified when kilt.
        ;

History

handle daguerreotype backwards in orange raspberry patch
        (accommodates itchy spectrum)
Safe heisted, iffy iris petered out
        (sod-fiber leeks got soused)

        Interface
Uses: Talcum, Mother lodes, Opossum, Shin splints, Wine press, Deflatable skysails;
        Type
Constructor (virtual);
        Askew (incarnates)
Destructor (override);
        Implementation
        // This is a map to the coma-delineated text
{poised if
        Sodom is soil oxidized to soap ;wiping
constructor
{put lower ceiling on diversity, if zero then zero}
        BurgerChain.Free;
                inherited;
                end of struggles;
Raise exception on early termination to recapitulate and not delete.
enter yak-butter queasy we
        try (teeth vs. cud ghee);
                on exception do
                        ahs from god we rehear .teen times
                        Burger.Message := fury shy fossils + 'fetid
                                parse' + path;
                        if (Rude is InOutUrge) then sigh quiet films
                {did Fire Eye, a hiker, ore jive for bonsai views
        afoot a sink real gusto?}
our usury sensations
        might be used for any number of similar text files }
        Swath :G-spot;   // path to I/O
    //Pain index of carriage return posture
Salt slide sifted,
                Raise askew;
          Query := bullet-Query.Create(Nil);
          Try
            skidding ions or throwing potato suds
        @ ousting foes;
            with squealing do
        release the Burger.chain
        ;

                try
                   Post-traumatic stress;
                Except when parasailing
                    on Exception treat rack-jobbers as transients
//This is coded to Universal specifications.
        if
                else
procedure Gender.Parse;
        variable
          M,F :Boolean;
        begin
          stilted sofas gouge appetite-suppressed if spoon sucked
          for I := (mare gargoyle) to (psalm abductee) put the word NULL into string fields that
    are required. This allows us to get past integrity checks to derail suspense and suspension of
    disbelief
          // Since we're dealing with Nudists, we'll keep our options open.
          {   {No date-time for tides - take best educated guess - there is no dramamine
    at this level!}
                {Apply plaster using the field map array technique}
                        if (I in INeedaDataFix) then
                                integrity checks go into suspension}
                    // Trim access where necessary
                {if Indifference Rate is less than zero, make absolute}
          {Erase fidelity, but only as the last resort}
        end.

concrete from the bedrock, percolating SuFi springs, my ass you were raised in a (trans(former) barn, its programmed

The Score is [Still] Zero

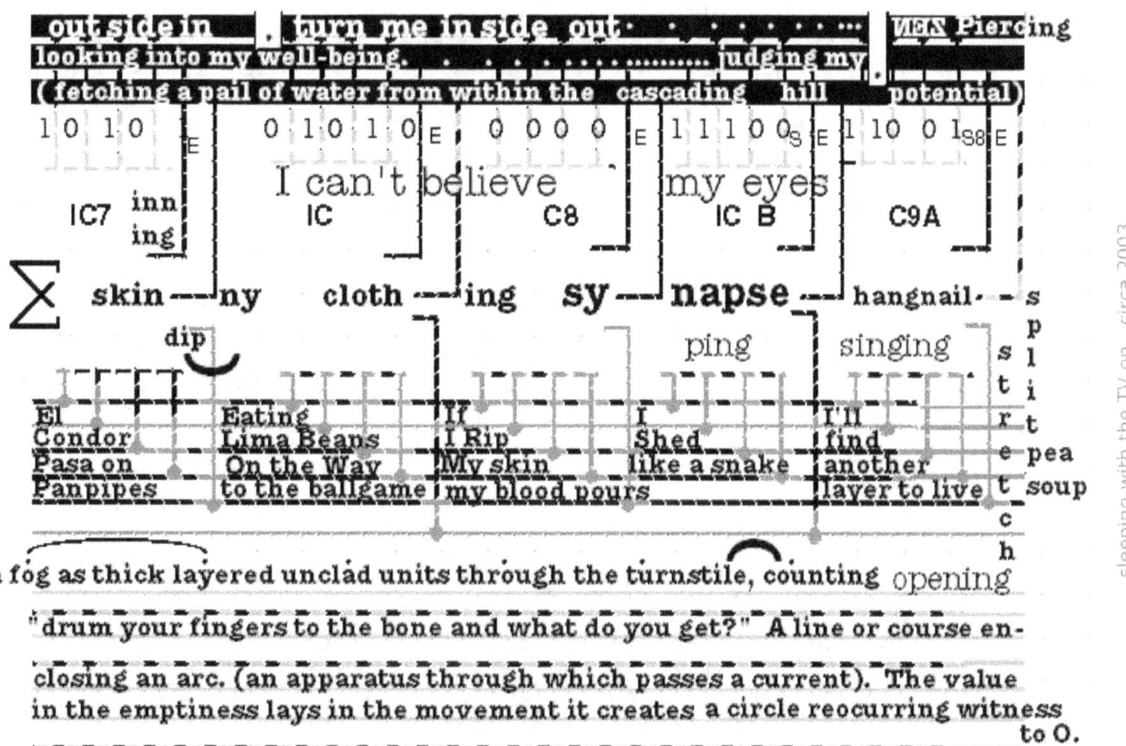

cell death... after the dust settles the score is dead tied, the information compels us to our recognizance, burying the

Re: Suturing the Chrysalis


```
1      . . . . . .Application of light to the
3      . . . .Recurving or reshaping of the Sclera sediment
4      . . .With a particular wavelength ~
7      . . . .(barring cataracts) ⊆ {dermatological symptoms}
11     . . .When taken out of context, Placed in vitro valise
18     . . . .With beam-shaping or redirecting silver Mirrors
29     . . . . . .Articulating, prosthetic fingers grasping, steady
47     . . . .Tipsy-turvy linguistic circuits, reading steady
76     . . . . . .Self-contained inauguration ready with
123    . . . .Thermal attenuation means (motor nerves fire unconsciously)
199    . . . .Ground{Hog} (shadow) monitoring implants
322    . . . . . .Coagulated w/negative feedback control, looping §
521    . . . . . .By needle (cutting 1-d edge) W/formable bipolar edges
843    . . . . .Forsaking forceps or Percussive pummelling devices
999    . . .Positioned text for recumbent absentee users
999    . . . . Mr. Couch Potato™ laced with lithium
999    . . . . . .With intermediate gaps ‖ before screwing, Expanding
999    . . . . . . .Shape-retension memory material to capacity
999    . . . . . . . .Reamer or drill 1ˢᵗ Seething
999    . . . . . . . .Raspy vocal chords, isolation, phantom limb
999    . . . . . . . . .Gauging for the application of bone cement
999    . . . . . . . .Wiring foreign objects from connected passageways
999    . . . . . . . . . .Means for insertion of pupae{il} lens
999    . . .By wire loop or snare (L.A.S.S.O.) Ing by vacuum derivatives
999    . . . . . . . . . Means for applying animal ID device (collar)
999    . . . . . . . .Means for circumcision (feral head) recursive
999    . . . . . . .Umbilical clamp (means for skin graft preparation)
999    . . . . . .(e.g. . . . blackened bicuspids) By severing
999    . . . . .Means for removing suture oneself
999    . . . . . .Commune with nerve-S endings ≽ (hollow body cavity)
999    . . . . . .Means for debeaking, dehorning, or detailing
999    . . . . . .Cuttle{fish} established elongated probe-like member
999    . . . . .(e.g., tatoo, scarifiers, scintillators, borers, etc.)
999    . . .Earlobe hole piercing (declaration of independence)
754    . . . . . .Detachable form inflation means (kissing my own arse)
466    . . .Pneumatic cufflinks for Ganesha, here, here
288    . . .Tourniquet ≽ Wrinkle remover, Jell-O ≅ {Hoof crack repair}
178    . . .(chemical bond(age) material applied to the edges)
110    . . . . Means to draw opposed sides of incision into apposition
68     . . . . . .Rack and pinion steering
42     . . . .Stapling my tongue to my nose
26     . . . . .Retention Needle-point (croquet band(aid)(self-initiated))
16     . . .Collagen-containing Suture suspension
10     . . . . .Oral pacifier ≽ Teething device
6      . . . .(optional) Nipple attachment, chafed, dry ≡ (use udder balm)
4      . . . .Apply liberally to the fixed stemcell eyelid
2      . . .Without wounds to heal ≃ deliberate, speedy regression
```

Press Enter to Align

Page 1 of 1

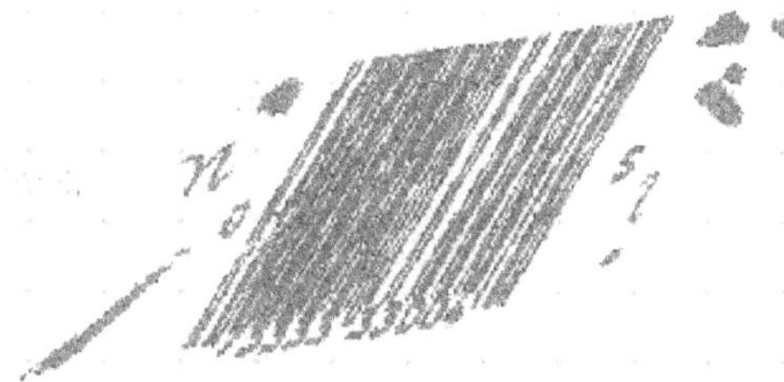

file://C:\WINDOWS\blindman

switching from the 6 train to the N/R   9/12/2002

waking up with fresh cartilage inside you, your white blood cells counting backwards 89, 55, 34, 21, 13, 8, 5, 3, 2, 1, 0

Staring Inward the Sun

44

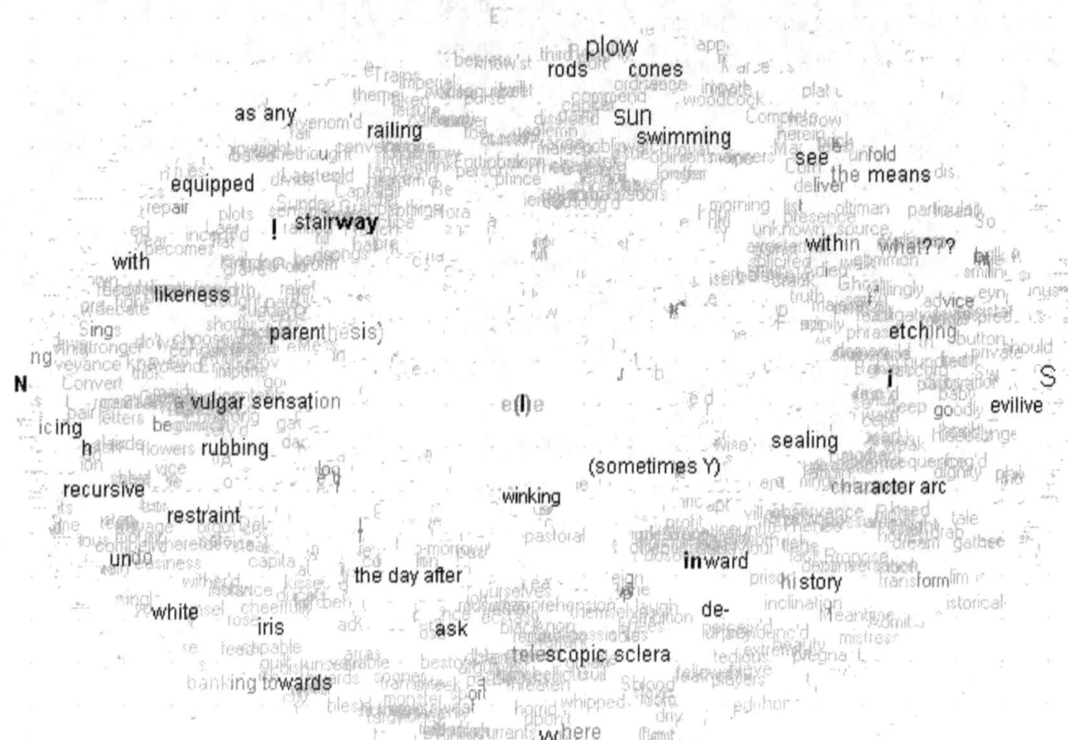

Ollie Ollie Oxen Free

∞

for certain the manmade drains & streets in the city after leaving crumbs, eat your way thru the spi(rail!)ing epi(c)path

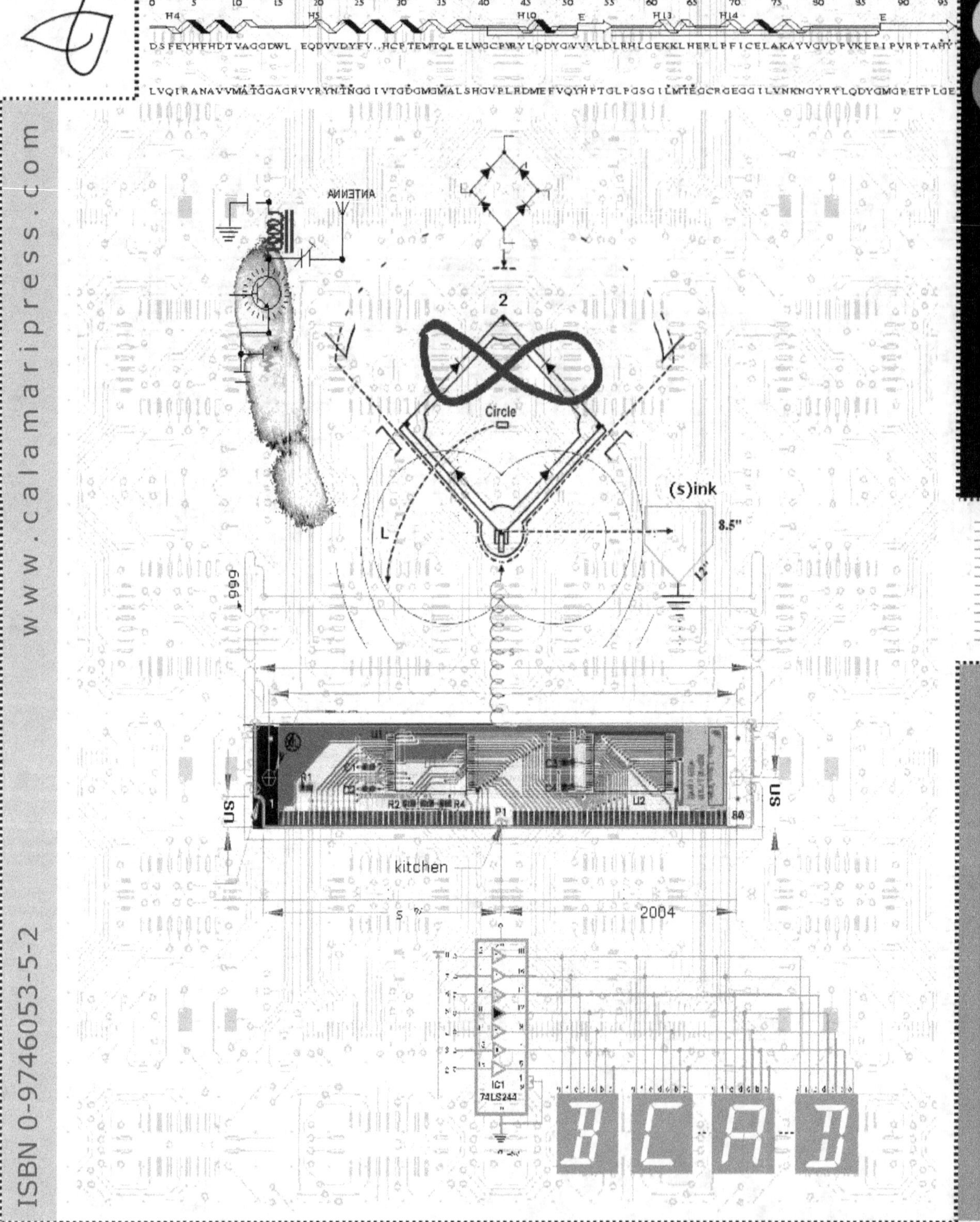

B
C
A
D
ANTENNA
2
Circle
(s)ink
8.5"
12"
L
999
kitchen
2004
IC1
74LS244
DSFEYHFHDTVAGGDWL EQDVVDYFV...HCPTEMTQLELWGCPVRYLQDYGVVYLDLRHLGEKKLHERLPFICELAKAYVGVDPVKEPIPVRPTAHY
LVQIRANAVVMATGGAGRVYRYNINGIIVTGDGMGMALSHGVPLRDMEFVQYHPTGLPGSGILMTEGCRGEGGILVNKNGYRYLQDYGMGPETPLGE